JOSEP LLUÍS SERT

JOSEP LLUÍS SERT

THE ARCHITECT OF URBAN DESIGN, 1953-1969

EDITED BY

Eric Mumford and Hashim Sarkis
with Neyran Turan

Yale University Press / New Haven and London

Harvard University Graduate School of Design / Cambridge

Designed by Matthew Monk

Set in Bulmer and Franklin Gothic by Matthew Monk

Printed in China through World Print

LIBRARY OF CONGRESS CATALOGING-IN-PUBLICATION DATA

Josep Lluís Sert : the architect of urban design, 1953–1969 /
edited by Eric Mumford and Hashim Sarkis ; with
Neyran Turan.

    p. cm.

Includes bibliographical references and index.

ISBN 978-0-300-12065-3 (hardcover : alk. paper)

1. Sert, José Luis, 1902–1983—Criticism and interpretation.
2. City planning—History—20th century. I. Mumford,
Eric Paul, 1958– II. Sarkis, Hashim. III. Turan, Neyran.

NA9085.S47J67 2008

720.92-DC22   2007029959

A catalogue record for this book is available from the
British Library.

The paper in this book meets the guidelines for permanence
and durability of the Committee on Production Guidelines
for Book Longevity of the Council on Library Resources.

10 9 8 7 6 5 4 3 2 1

Jacket Illustrations: Detail of fig. 5.2 (front), Sert portrait on
page 198 (back)

P. 198: Josep Lluís Sert, c. 1970

Contents

In 2003, the Graduate School of Design at Harvard University organized a conference and an exhibition in celebration of the fifty-year anniversary of Josep Lluís Sert's appointment as dean, a position he held for sixteen years. It also felicitously coincided with the celebration of the retirement of Eduard Sekler, the eminent historian and Harvard professor emeritus who was one of Sert's close associates. The initiative was launched by Professors Peter G. Rowe, then dean of the School of Design, and Professor Jorge Silvetti, then chairman of the Department of Architecture.

For the GSD, the events were obviously meant not only to celebrate one of the school's most formative periods but also, and most important, to reexamine the school's commitment to the urban context of architecture. The conference made clear that it was Sert who had elevated what he called urban design to the status of a central platform of inquiry at the school, laying the foundations for what is now a discipline of global importance. These events highlighted Sert's significance to the world of modern architecture and urbanism, and put a new focus on the creation of urban design, which would shape the development of the field in the United States and also the directions of specialization in the profession. This inquiry into the origins of the discipline were not meant as a return to an essence or to fictional roots but instead as an opportunity to examine with hindsight the causes of this idea and its evolution from circumstantial reactions to a full-fledged discipline and profession.

These discussions benefited from the participation of many individuals, including Xavier Costa, Kenneth Frampton, Charles Haar, Alex Krieger, Paul Krueger, Ted Liebman, Jorge Francisco Liernur, William Lindemulder, Panayiota Pyla, Josep Rovira, Patricia Schnitter Castellanos, and Richard Sommer. In addition to helping clarify Sert's role, these participants also placed urban design in a comparative perspective with other urban ideas that were brewing at the time and in the context of the design school, the design office, and urban development culture.

The celebrations also presented an occasion to bring out material from the school's archives and the Sert Collection. In an exhibition curated by Mary Daniels and Inés Zalduendo at the Special Collections of the Frances Loeb Library at Harvard's Graduate School of Design and designed by Dan Borelli, the show brought to public attention some of Sert's lesser-known projects, such as the Worcester Town Center and the South Station Development in Boston, his Harvard Planning projects, as well as sketches, drawings, and material from the archives that were exhibited for the first time. Some of this material appears in the book, and for that we would like to acknowledge the Harvard Planning and Real Estate Office, Harvard University Archives, Boston University Department of Special Collections, Boston University Physical Plant, and Spectrum Digital Imaging.

The conference also featured a walking tour with the late Huson Jackson, Sert's partner and collaborator during most of his American years, with whom he generated a formidable body of projects.

After the celebrations and conference were over, it was clear that these efforts could not stop at commemoration. A deeper, broader, and more critical inquiry into the origins of urban design in the United States was fundamental to the continuous evolution of the profession. For that, we have opted to focus this book on four main aspects of the emergence of urban design and Sert's contributions to it: the close linkages between the postwar CIAM urban focus on the "heart of the city" and Sert and Sigfried Giedion's development of them into urban design; Sert and Paul Lester Wiener's Latin American town plans of the 1940s and 1950s as a parallel platform of articulation and experimentation with CIAM principles that led to urban design, particularly in their paradigmatic Havana Plan of 1955–57; the convergence of these ideas onto the American post–World War II urban challenges in the context of Harvard and the emergence of urban design; and Sert's North American projects that most visibly embodied these ideas.

We would like to thank the book's authors for their hard work not only in making remarkable scholarly contributions but also for working with us patiently to complement each other's thoughts and enforce the general premise of the book. We are also very grateful to Neyran Turan, assistant editor of this publication, for her dedication to the project, and above all to Melissa Vaughn, director of publications at the GSD, who understood the magnitude of this undertaking from the beginning and patiently took us and the book through all its stages. At Yale University Press, Michelle Komie, Heidi Downey, Mary Mayer, John Long, and their colleagues have been exceptionally helpful and supportive throughout. We thank Matthew Monk for his elegant book design.

The preparations for this book were made possible through funding from the Josep Lluís Sert and Ramona Londas de Sert Bequest to the Graduate School of Design.

ERIC MUMFORD
HASHIM SARKIS

Introduction HASHIM SARKIS

When asked in 1969, by Robert Taylor of the *Boston Globe,* what particular elements he stressed in the training of architects and designers at the Harvard University Graduate School of Design (GSD), Josep Lluís Sert responded, "urban consciousness."[1] The interview marked his stepping down as dean of the GSD, a position Sert had held since 1953. During that time the GSD had undergone significant growth and changes in its curriculum; one of the most enduring was the introduction of urban design as a new area of study.

"The private patron is a luxury of the past," Sert went on in the *Globe* interview. "The architect will deal more and more with the total environment. More than a million acres of rural land passes into urban land in America every year. This means design of such scope as the condominiums we built in Rio in 1946, rather than individual houses. It has been argued that automation in the cities will spawn a class of drones, but I believe that people will want to improve their urban surroundings. Call it a basic faith in the improvement of man and a better life."[2]

By 1969, "urban consciousness" was being stressed in the training of most professionals, not just architects and designers. Whether through curricular changes deeply influenced by the social sciences or shifts in university politics at large, urban consciousness had come to mean an awareness of

urgent urban problems—of poverty and racial segregation—and a proactive attitude toward addressing them. The War on Poverty, launched during the Johnson era, had identified the decline of the city as one of the roots of poverty and segregation. In parallel to Johnson's Great Society program, ways to address the city's needs, beyond the highly positivist solutions applied during the immediate postwar era, were being discussed at universities, particularly in the social sciences. Although social scientists may have shared Sert's "faith in the improvement of man and better life," they were no longer willing to accept the socially disruptive transformations that the ambitious urban plans of the 1950s had brought about. In some ways they blamed that very urban consciousness, imbued by Sert and his generation on young architects and planners, for some of the urban problems they were now confronting.

Indeed, Sert's comments on urban consciousness did convey a level of optimism only a few academics would have shared in 1969, especially at Harvard after the violent showdown between students and the university that same year. This optimism could be interpreted as a sign of detachment, not atypical among designers and planners at the time, many of whom continued to operate with a professional determinism reminiscent of the immediate postwar era. This optimism could also be taken further back to the interwar period during which the Congrès Internationaux d'Architecture Moderne (CIAM), in which Sert was an active member and president from 1947 to 1956, sought to identify a set of clear directives for the modern city. Yet he would further qualify his position. When asked in the same interview with the *Boston Globe* if CIAM principles could help cure the urban ills of Boston, Sert replied, "Face the fact. The old formulas no longer apply."[3]

Sert did not predict that formulas altogether would no longer apply, and he did not discuss the ever-changing professional scope through which urban consciousness could be exercised by designers. These predicaments that would confront urban design in the decades that followed were then seen as unexplored opportunities. They were new challenges being placed at the doorstep of architects and planners, and they required not only a new and larger scale of operations but also new tools to deal with new patterns of urban growth, the complexities of inner-city renewal, and the political mechanisms and social consequences of both. Sert's faith, as elucidated in Eduard Sekler's personal account of Sert in Chapter 1, CIAM, and the GSD, lay in the ability of designers to constantly develop tools to address these challenges. The platform for such an undertaking would become known as urban design.

This book examines the emergence and development of the discipline and profession of urban design as articulated around the work and writings of Josep Lluís Sert. Through a series of accounts and scholarly studies by historians and designers, it traces the intellectual debates that helped shape this idea, especially through Sert's academic leadership at Harvard University between 1953 and 1969.

The book also traces a parallel evolution of the idea of urban design in Sert's professional career, which started in Europe before World War II and extended to Latin American and the United States during and after the war.

The chapters are organized chronologically under three thematic sections that correspond to major periods in Sert's career. The book first traces some of the key attributes of the idea of urban design back to CIAM's urban principles. It then looks at the professional experience of Sert in Latin America, and his professional collaboration with Paul Lester Wiener and Paul Schulz and with Le Corbusier, where CIAM principles were tested and confronted with such challenges as rapid urban growth, obdurate historic contexts, and implementation difficulties. It then turns to his mandate at Harvard and the parameters set for this new discipline around the Urban Design Conferences held during the 1950s and 1960s, as well as through the parallel professional career relaunched in the late 1950s in partnership with Huson Jackson to focus primarily on American campus design and inner-city development.

The chapter authors recount different origins, definitions, and roles for urban design. They also describe varied intellectual and professional networks. Despite this broad spectrum of validations, Sert insists on the singularity of the platform from which the complexities of city making and the different professions that address them could be orchestrated. That same platform would provide the common ground for a desired synthesis between architecture, landscape architecture, and planning. And yet the synthesis was not the only purpose for the new discipline. In some of the arguments here, the need to apply aesthetic considerations to the functional city prevails as one of the most pressing justifications for building this new platform. In others, urban design would come to represent a middle scale between architecture and city planning, one that would better correspond to the new scale of projects of urban renewal and redevelopment at the time, reflecting the need to provide an edifying formal articulation to the civic functions and public spaces of the functional city.

THE CIAM LEGACY

Josep Lluís Sert was born in Barcelona in 1901 to an affluent family from the lesser aristocracy. Before his graduation from architecture school in 1929, Sert encountered the ideas of Le Corbusier and the modern town planning principles that he was promoting, and he would become a key member of Le Corbusier's office. He was also the main representative of the new architecture and urbanism team from the Spanish Republic in the series of conferences and discussions that modern architects in Europe were organizing under the umbrella of CIAM. The significance of Sert's contributions to the CIAM conferences and his strong organizational role encouraged the key players in CIAM to charge him with the overdue task of compiling their city planning charter in the form of a book.[4]

Even though he was active in academic circles, the 1942 publication of *Can Our Cities Survive?* no doubt placed Sert on the academic map in the United States. Having left Spain for the United States in 1939, Sert devoted time to the book project, in part to find a job in academia. He struck a difficult balance between producing a scholarly book that

described in technical terms the challenges of modern city planning and presenting the new principles of planning to broader American audiences. The new audiences, as Jordana Mendelson notes in Chapter 3, were targeted in the language, layout, and images of the book, elements that ultimately helped to set a more populist tone for the volume and, indirectly, for the discipline.

Another important undertaking in Sert's book was establishing a continuum between the technical and aesthetic aspects of city making. The absence of aesthetic considerations in American city planning troubled Sert, and the illustrations in *Can Our Cities Survive?* frequently expose this ostensible absence. In Chapter 2 of this volume, Francesco Passanti traces the origins of this productive tension between the aesthetic aspects of city making (urban design) and its functional aspects (planning) to the early writings and work of Le Corbusier, to the Ville Radieuse, the Algiers Plan, and, importantly, to the first collaboration between Sert and Le Corbusier on the Plan Macià for Barcelona in 1932. There, the functions of the horizontal modern city contrasted against those of the old city and its geography through the vertical emphasis of skyscrapers.

THE LATIN AMERICAN EXPERIENCE

During his early years in the United States, Sert joined Town Planning Associates (TPA), a partnership with Paul Lester Wiener and Paul Schulz. Following a series of successful lectures in Latin America during World War II, TPA received a commission to design a new city in Brazil. The direct application of CIAM land use and density distribution principles to the Brazilian Motor City project, as explained by Mardges Bacon in Chapter 5, would evolve to allow for a more organic and less functionalist approach to urban planning. This approach was stressed by Lewis Mumford, an American urban historian and theorist highly regarded by Sert. Bacon examines Sert's prolific years in Latin America, from the Motor City project to the master plans for Chimbote and Lima in Peru, to Tumaco and Medellín in Colombia, and to the highly publicized collaboration with Le Corbusier on a plan for Bogotá.

In his account of Sert's unrealized master plan for Havana produced between 1951 and 1959, Timothy Hyde (Chapter 4) highlights another distinction, between the conceptual and figurative aspects of city planning, which would play a role in the articulation of the parameters of urban design.

THE PARAMETERS OF URBAN DESIGN

Sert's direct involvement with TPA and in Latin America diminished after he succeeded Joseph Hudnut as dean of the GSD in 1953. Hudnut, the first dean of the school, is credited with having hired Walter Gropius, one of the key figures of modern architecture in Europe, to lead the architecture department at Harvard, ratifying modern architecture by American academia. According to Jill Pearlman in Chapter 6, Hudnut also prepared the ground for the idea of urban design, interested as he was in both the synthesis of the different disciplines of the school and the creation of civic design, an aspect of planning that allowed for the creative engagement of public spaces and public facilities. For a while, as Sert affirmed his presence at Harvard and consolidated his ideas around a curricular program, such terms as urban design, city design, and

civic design were used interchangeably at the GSD.

Sert's assumption of this key position confirmed his important role among modernist architects. It also assured the continuity of the CIAM legacy at Harvard following the retirement of Gropius. This legacy was manifest not only in Sert's tenure at Harvard. Having established worldwide connections through CIAM, his own writings, and his professional network (particularly in Latin America), he became a catalyst for explorations of the role of architecture in shaping the modern metropolis.

At the Urban Design Conferences, chronicled by Richard Marshall in Chapter 7, several themes would be brought to the foreground, particularly concerning the civic role of urban design. The discussions would highlight a strong humanist tendency in Sert, but also the need to imbue the functional city with the more edifying attributes that Lewis Mumford, Sigfried Giedion, and the group of architects and artists who wrote the 1943 statement "Nine Points on Monumentality," Sert included, were advocating.[5]

Cammie McAtee, in Chapter 9, reminds us that some of the main experiments in urban design were being conducted through campus planning and design during the postwar period. The presence of a strong landscape architecture department at the GSD helped Sert in his endeavors. Hideo Sasaki, professor in the department of landscape architecture from 1950 to 1970, its chairman from 1958 to 1968, and a collaborator with Sert on several design projects, was interested in the collaborative process in design and in the possibility that landscape could come closer to planning, identifying himself more as a land planner than a designer.

As Eric Mumford explains in Chapter 8, during his tenure at Harvard Sert also witnessed the disintegration of CIAM as an international platform for the promotion of modern urban and architectural ideas. In response, he organized a series of conferences at Harvard aimed at identifying a new discipline to address the physical dimension of urban development in the postwar metropolis. Sert would call the discipline urban design, and while it benefited from his and others' worldwide experiences, it would be geared more specifically toward the scale and character of urban interventions in the United States. As the themes changed, and as the Urban Design Conferences moved further from the original CIAM ideas, the discipline would become more a response to the piecemeal—albeit in large pieces—transformation of the city. This approach appeared to guarantee the continuity of urban form while allowing for it to evolve to meet new working, living, and commuting standards. In addition, the urban renewal of American cities also provoked the reinterpretation of the civic role of urban centers and helped expand on the representational dimension of modern architecture.

Through design projects for American cities, particularly those cities undergoing urban renewal, Sert developed a new formal repertoire that operated between the architecture of an individual project and the urban context. Although this repertoire expanded on the urban elements of CIAM, it involved more articulated and mannered renderings. Aspects of such elements as the patio (at several nested scales), the plinth, the tower, and the pedestrian street could be traced back to the superblock configuration of CIAM and to the proposals for several Latin American cities. In Sert's work of this period, however, they became further charged with urban roles while growing more fragmented than the urban networks predicated by CIAM. As Eric Mumford observes and the account of Huson Jackson confirms, it was architecture that was reaching out to the other disciplines and orchestrating them. The work shows a range and complexity that reflects the difficulty of defining the discipline along a finite set of basic principles. Most important among these were the Harvard campus projects (Holyoke Administrative Center, the Science Center, and Peabody Terrace Married Students Housing), the Boston University Law School, and the urban renewal projects for Boston's South Station, Worcester Business District, and Roosevelt Island in New York. Some of the urban renewal projects operated as subordinates to the urban plans, others from inside out, and the projects for Harvard and other university campuses provided microcosmic models for larger urban ideas.

Sert's extended practice, as vividly illustrated here in the interview with Robert Campbell, and his influential academic career from the platform of Harvard's Graduate School of Design, propelled his ideas about urban design to many practices and academic institutions at the time. His views have been some of the most influential in shaping the skylines of the postwar United States and of international cities. Even though Sert's views would help lay the foundations of the subsequent "return to the city" movement in the United States at a time of rapid suburbanization, as Eric Mumford reminds us, these views were not the only ones. An equally strong interest in the visual aspect of city planning would launch an area of study at MIT under Kevin Lynch and Gyorgy Kepes. At other universities, such as the University of Pennsylvania and the University of California at Berkeley, new programs addressing a similar range of problems would provide different emphases to the newly forged discipline and highlight the partialities of Sert's urban design position.

Since 1969, the year Sert stepped down from Harvard, both the discipline and the profession of urban design have continued to evolve to address the ever-changing character of urban problems and to diversify the instruments and possible scopes of expertise even further. Urban theorists such as Colin Rowe, Aldo Rossi, Robert Venturi, and Denise Scott Brown, who dominated the scene in the 1970s and 1980s, persisted in their search for an architecturally edifying approach to the city but shifted the emphasis toward the historical continuity of the city and public expression. Some important aspects of urban design today bear little resemblance to the original program. For example, the links with regional planning, suburban growth, and urban renewal have weakened in favor of smaller-scale interjections such as private mixed-use development, revitalization of

historic districts, and waterfront development. Urban designers have also come to accept the absence of coordination between their interventions and the totality of the city no longer as a frustration but as an intrinsically urban characteristic. Interestingly, the new awareness in environmental and ecological issues has in recent years elevated the presence of landscape as a constitutive discipline of urban design. For example, some of the proponents of what has been recently referred to as landscape urbanism point to the architecturally biased version of urban design by Sert and some of his contemporaries.[6]

In retrospect, Sert's main contribution to the shaping of this discipline and profession lies in his insistence on maintaining an open and evolving set of principles and formulas extracted from different fields. All of the tools needed to handle the ever-changing problems of urban development should be readily accessible from the common ground of urban design. Sert's equally strong insistence on providing a singular ground may have contributed to the amorphous and multifarious nature of the discipline, but it ultimately created a large maneuvering space for effective action in the profession.

NOTES

1. Robert Taylor, "Can Boston Survive? The Sert Solution," *Boston Globe Sunday Magazine,* August 31, 1969 (Josep Lluís Sert Collection, Frances Loeb Library, Harvard University Graduate School of Design, Folder D041).

2. Ibid.

3. Ibid.

4. For a biography of Sert, see Josep M. Rovira, *José Luis Sert, 1901–1983* (Milan: Electa, 2000).

5. See Sigfried Gideon, "In Search of a New Monumentality," *Architectural Review* 104 (September 1948): 117–128.

6. See, for example, Charles Waldheim, "Landscape as Urbanism," in Charles Waldheim, ed., *The Landscape Urbanism Reader* (New York: Princeton Architectural Press, 2006), 35–53.

Part One

THE CIAM LEGACY

Chapter 1

SERT, CIAM, AND THE GSD

A Memoir

EDUARD F. SEKLER

On October 27, 1967, when Josep Lluís Sert signed for me a monograph about his work, he wrote, "For Edward and our CIAM memories." Fourteen years later he wrote into my wife's album, "My ideas never change." These statements inspired this memoir in which, based on remembered personal experiences and observations, I recall Sert and the way he touched lives, including mine and those of people in the GSD and CIAM. CIAM played an important role in Sert's career and indirectly also in the GSD.

Although I do not focus on Sert's architecture, an important preparation for writing this essay was a visit with my wife to the Fondation Marguerite et Aimé Maeght at St. Paul de Vence, France, which Sert designed in 1959 and completed in 1964 (fig 1.1). Surrounded by pine groves, the site of the Fondation is very quiet when few visitors are around. We approached it by slowly walking up the hill on a narrow, winding road under the trees until we saw the watchman's pavilion and ticket booth, placed away from the path to the main entrance so as not to interfere with one's first view of the main building. The immediate impression is of great harmony between the landscape, the buildings, and the sculptures along the path.

According to the architect, the site and its views greatly influenced the design, with the arrangement of buildings inspired by the patterns of the small villages in that part of France. Instead of creating a single monumental building, Sert developed, in a tour de force of sophisticated space-making, a variety of volumes and spaces, with exhibition rooms clustering around courts and linked to gardens. The main building rises one floor higher than all the others and is crowned by two thin concrete shells shaped as inverted half cylinders. These identify the building from a distance and shade the flat roof terrace from which one can see the Mediterranean and the Cap d'Antibes in one direction and the Alpes Maritimes in the other.

Many artists of the Galerie Maeght became involved with the project. Joan Miró, in particular,

9

went to great pains to assure the best possible collaboration with his old friend Sert; he even made
plywood cutouts with the outlines of his sculptures
to assure the correct placement of the works (fig. 1.2).

To the side of and behind the central complex
of galleries and courtyards is another group of buildings that includes a chapel dedicated to St. Bernard.
The chapel, which had survived on the site as a
ruin, was rebuilt by Sert in a manner that convinces
through its directness and simplicity. He had a
strong inner relation to the Catholic Church.

At the GSD, Sert and his students built large-
scale models of vaults for experimentation with the
best lighting conditions for the galleries. As one
walks through the Fondation, one becomes aware
of an inspired use of light, an unerring sense of proportion and human scale, and a visual consistency
that adheres to one family of forms—all in the service
of a deep attachment to Mediterranean culture and
the plastic arts.[1] "It is clear that this was a project
on which most of Sert's personal interests were
focused," an alumnus who had worked on the project in Sert's office told me.[2]

Such a close relationship to the arts and the
Mediterranean is something Sert shared with his
mentor Le Corbusier, whose pronouncements about
the necessary interaction of painting and architecture were more than once a topic in Sert's addresses
to members of CIAM, that avant-garde organization
that was largely Le Corbusier's creation.

I learned about CIAM during my years of study
in England. Eventually I translated for an Austrian
periodical the speech Walter Gropius gave at CIAM 6
in Bridgwater, and it was at a CIAM Congress that I
met Sert. Jaqueline Tyrwhitt, an important figure

Figure 1.1 Josep Lluís Sert, main building, Fondation
Marguerite et Aimé Maeght, St. Paul de Vence, France, 1964

in postwar CIAM—who later taught at the GSD and
for a while had been my teacher at the London
School for Planning and Regional Development—
suggested that I listen to a lecture that Sigfried
Giedion was giving on historical city cores. This was
a topical subject, and in 1951 CIAM held its eighth
Congress on "The Heart of the City." Giedion illustrated his talk with panels of comparative plans of
historic urban cores, such as the Agora of Priene and
the Forum of Pompeii, and these, drawn to the same
scale, attracted my attention as much as his style
of presentation, which, despite his far-from-perfect
English, was very effective.

We had an animated discussion after his talk,
and he showed great interest in the Viennese postwar architectural scene, but without ever mentioning

that he actually had begun his academic studies at the Vienna Technical University's engineering department before he studied art history in Munich. On his suggestion I joined the CIAM group in Austria, where, at his request, I organized a CIAM Junior group in Vienna, which in the following years sent two presentations to CIAM Congresses. The CIAM Council had developed these groups to help rejuvenate CIAM.

In 1953, a quarter of a century after the founding of CIAM, I attended CIAM 9 as a member. The Congress was scheduled to deal with a Charter of the Habitat (the general and complete locus of daily life) and was held at Aix-en-Provence in July. With three other young Austrian architects traveling there in a VW beetle, I had an unforgettable trip getting away from still-occupied postwar Austria.[3] When we arrived we found a cheerful confusion that corroborated the truth of a comment Giedion later made: "We exist because we have a great disorder in organization, [but] order in spirit."

Since more people than expected had arrived, not enough hotel rooms had been reserved. We ended up sleeping in a classroom of the Ecole des Arts et Métiers, the building where the Congress met. The actual meetings of the six commissions that dealt with different aspects of the habitat took place in the shade of trees in the large garden courtyard of the school.

The procedures of the Congress were informal (fig. 1.3). In his opening address, Sert as president outlined the aim and method of the Congress simply and directly. He explained that CIAM was not interested in small aesthetic experiments but in a great experiment: to arrive at the skeleton of a Charter of

the Habitat. "Nobody has yet tried it," he exclaimed. "We will try it [Personne n'a pas encore tenté, on va le tenter]." What mattered was "la foi dans nôtre idee"—the faith in our idea of working "for the creation of a physical environment that will satisfy man's emotional and material needs and stimulate his spiritual growth."[4] It must have been this idea or set of principles that Sert had in mind when he later wrote, "My ideas never change." Sert's words may sound too general and unrealistic, but only if one overlooks their reflection in his very real oeuvre of buildings and urban designs.

Figure 1.2 Joan Miró, fountain with ceramic sculptures, Fondation Marguerite et Aimé Maeght, 1964

The work of the Congress was done in critical discussions of projects submitted by the national groups, whose presentations were mostly made according to predetermined instructions about size and organization in a color-coded grid; forty of those from twenty countries were shown. Sert presided at the sessions of the general assembly and at the tripartite Commission 1 that dealt with "urbanism." In my personal notes I found comments by Sert that had struck me as remarkable; they are typical for the way he expressed his ideas in a deceptively simple yet rhetorically convincing manner.

"The superfluous is one of the essential elements of our life," is an example.[5]

I worked in Commission 2, chaired by Giedion. It dealt with the aesthetic in the habitat. The idea was to try to "awaken in the architect and urbanist the sense of the plastic form of contemporary towns. . . ." The "sense of the plastic form" is a translation of *sens plastique* in the original French version of the Commission's statement, and *plastique* may be used to indicate anything that refers to the art of giving a form to a solid substance. Thus in French the plastic arts include sculpture, architecture, drawing, paint-

Figure 1.3 Le Corbusier (left) and Josep Lluís Sert in discussion at the CIAM meeting at Aix-en-Provence, 1953

ing, and the decorative arts. This explains why the final summary of Commission 2, after referring to the necessary "preservation of the human scale against the mechanization of our time," concludes, "Having admitted that the language of contemporary plastic art is the only valid instrument that will help us to give an architectural expression to the town, it is indispensable to engage in plastic research before facing the development of a new human habitat." As Sert put it at Aix, "Before man built huts for himself, he painted caves."[6]

Le Corbusier, an important presence at the Congress, presented his Unité d'Habitation in Marseilles and made a statement about the habitat that he introduced by simply reminding the audience: "To pose the question of the modern Habitat, that is to pose the problem of the art of living today. To live with one's body and to live with one's spirit, joie de vivre and not despair."[7]

There was no lack of joie de vivre between and around the working sessions of the Congress. Mingling freely with distinguished senior figures, such as Walter Gropius and Ernst May, were many young architects of both sexes in the crowd of more than two hundred participants plus numerous observers.[8] Even serious workers in the commissions occasionally would sneak away for a game of boule or some refreshment at a bistro.

As the crowning conclusion of the Congress, an afternoon visit to the Unité was followed by a late-evening fête on its roof terrace. To be there among the strongly *plastique* forms under a full moon, with views out to the silvery shine of the Mediterranean, was a fantastic experience. At a strategic moment, a belly dancer suddenly appeared and performed in

front of the council members of CIAM, causing Le Corbusier to exclaim: "Voilà—l'architecture!"[9] Everybody enjoyed the surprise except for one young Dutchman, who got up and in walking out shouted: "What has this to do with architecture? Everyone who feels as I do, follow me!" No one did.

When, after the Congress, our small group tried to evaluate what we had seen and heard at Aix, we agreed that it had been a very successful meeting and that some speeches had significantly broadened our understanding—for example, when Michel Ecochard and Le Corbusier raised the problem of "habitat for the greatest number of people" or Pierre-André Emery confronted us with the phenomenon of an Algerian "Bidonville," a slum of the kind still topical in many developing countries as the only habitat for an ever-growing "greatest number of people." We also had learned a great deal by studying and comparing the presentations, even if we found their architectural and urban design quality quite uneven. Certainly there was very little evidence of the rationalist rigidity characteristic of some of the prewar CIAM work.

Since neither a Charter of the Habitat was promulgated at the end of CIAM 9 nor was there a publication based on the presentations collected at the end of the Congress, it did not come as a surprise that CIAM 10 would have on its program the formulation of such a charter. This Congress met August 6–12, 1956, in a new art gallery at Lapad, a pleasant modern suburb of historic Dubrovnik, a city now on the UNESCO World Heritage List. One could hardly imagine a more beautiful and appropriate Mediterranean venue for an architects' meeting. Most participants arrived by boat from

Venice after a voyage down the Adriatic past a spectacular coastal landscape.

The Congress was organized in the usual manner, but with only three commissions. Most presentations were of high quality, and the atmosphere of the meetings was very pleasant for the many participants who, like me, were not involved in the palace intrigues that went on behind the scene regarding the future leadership and direction of CIAM. It became clear, however, that momentous changes might happen soon, when Sert, prior to his opening speech, read a letter in which Le Corbusier explained that he did not attend because he was convinced that the "metamorphosis of CIAM should be based on the new generation, those of forty years in 1956."[10] Walter Gropius also sent a letter explaining that he was so busy "it would be like suicide to leave the office" and ending, "I hope the meeting will be successful and give new vigor to the CIAM activities."[11]

There was indeed no lack of vigor in CIAM activities, but it went chiefly into destroying the organization, which was finally achieved at the eleventh Congress at Otterlo in 1959 by members of the group that, as Team 10, had been charged with preparing the tenth Congress and revitalizing CIAM. I had no personal involvement in this process, but detailed research is available about it.[12] After Otterlo, however, I sent a letter of protest to a number of participants because I felt strongly that CIAM still had a mission to fulfill by setting standards of quality, and I was happy to learn that such distinguished architects as Louis Kahn and Kenzo Tange shared my opinion.

In his concluding address at CIAM 10, Sert had pointed out how many CIAM members were active in architectural and urban design education. This, he felt, could link CIAM to an important international network for useful information and helpful contacts. He also mentioned that the Charter of the Habitat could be finished at Harvard University. Clearly here he spoke as both the dean of the GSD and retiring president of CIAM, which suggests that he had fully accommodated to the new stage in his life that began at Harvard University in the fall of 1953.

Sert had not much prior experience as a teacher in academia, and, in a talk on architectural education to the GSD Student Council, he began by saying "there are many people better qualified than myself to talk about this subject."[13] But his CIAM experience and connections turned out to be invaluable in his new position, too. Housing and urbanism had been main concerns of CIAM, just as they became important in Sert's educational program for GSD. Many of his new appointees had a CIAM background, and in connection with CIAM he had honed the capacity of guiding, managing, and motivating others, so Gropius could call him the "far-sighted organizer of CIAM who was able to keep the zealous celebrities of its membership in line for fruitful work."[14]

The education of architects was the topic of CIAM discussions more than once. From CIAM 9, the report of Commission 3, *Formation de l'Architecte*, survives. In it we find statements that have their equivalent in pronouncements that Sert made to the Student Council. For example, the report affirms: "The formation of the architect . . . occurs not only in the schools. It is throughout his life that the architect must think as a humanist, in order to work as an artist with the tools of technique. (La formation de l'architecte . . . ne se fait pas seulement dans des écoles. C'est toute sa vie l'architecte devra penser en humaniste, pour pouvoir travailler en artiste, avec des instruments techniques)." Sert by comparison: "A school of architecture can . . . only deal with one phase of the long process of education of the architect, which lasts right through life."

In Sert's own opening address at CIAM 9, moreover, one finds a passage that compares strikingly to a statement he made to the students. At Aix he spoke of the "faith in our idea" of working "for the creation of a physical environment that will satisfy man's emotional and material needs and stimulate his spiritual growth." At Harvard he stated, "It is our objective, our main objective, to create a better and more beautiful physical environment, not an abstract world of empty meaningless forms no matter how good, but a world to live in, a world that makes life more worthwhile. . . . We have to believe in a better world if we are trying to build a better world. We also must believe that the architect can contribute to this better world. Otherwise we will have no role in shaping it." He then summed up that it was necessary to be concerned with the social and humanistic side of architecture, the plastic and emotional side of architecture, and the technical side of architecture. "We not only have to think of things, design them, and dream them; we have to build them. . . . I believe . . . that a school of architecture . . . should give you . . . a balance of courses that deal with these three areas. . . . If the emphasis is too strong on one area I think the student . . . will feel that he hasn't been properly trained."[15]

Having gotten an admittedly incomplete idea of Sert's motivating principles, we now have to ask how he went about realizing his ideals at the GSD, a GSD

that in many ways was very different from today's school. To begin with, it had a much smaller enrollment and faculty, which meant that it was easier for people to communicate and get to know one another. It operated in two historic buildings, Robinson Hall and Hunt Hall, the latter of which has disappeared except for some remnants now placed around Gund Hall—from the griffons and the acroterion at the entrance to the casts of the Panathenaeic frieze from the Parthenon.

Originally Hunt Hall housed the Fogg Art Museum. It was modeled after a Roman theater, which meant that it had a horseshoe-shaped auditorium that guaranteed unexpected acoustical effects. Hunt Hall also housed studios and offices, as well as a room for faculty meetings. It was indicative of Sert's practice of acting on what he preached that one of his early administrative decisions was to have this room upgraded and redesigned by Fred Bruck, a talented young faculty member. The changes included dropping the ceiling to improve proportions and acoustics, repainting the room white, and providing large window curtains, a new table, elegant Thonet chairs, and serving facilities for refreshments.

Many other decisions, of course, were on more serious matters, such as upgrading the faculty, revising the curriculum, and, eventually, in 1964, beginning the school's first capital fund drive, which enabled the construction of Gund Hall. During Sert's first decade as dean, the number of resident assistant, associate, and full professors increased by 115 percent, and the number of visiting critics and lecturers by 200 percent. Several alumni told me how much they appreciated such exciting visitors as Louis Kahn, Paul Rudolph, Werner Moser from

Switzerland, Maxwell Fry from England, Paul Nelson from France, and Ernesto Rogers from Italy. They also liked the lectures or exhibitions of work by such important modern artists of the time as Alexander Calder, Naum Gabo, Fernand Léger, Joan Miró, and Saul Steinberg.

When in 1954 I was appointed a visiting professor, I came from Vienna with some teaching experience, but I knew little about the American academic system and its rules and traditions. The same may have been true to some degree for my dean and chairman, at least during his early years in office. Perhaps this was one reason why we worked so well together. We also shared the same architectural ideals, had similar political inclinations, and loved to get back to Europe from time to time—which meant Sert was lenient when I asked for yet another leave of absence.

As far as budget, curriculum, and morale were concerned, all needed improvement after the retirements of Gropius and Hudnut. For curricular improvements, Sert asked Giedion and me to submit plans for the reintroduction of architectural history as required coursework and the creation of an urban design seminar.

We eventually came up with four terms of history, from antiquity to the twentieth century. Because Giedion was present for only one term, and even then gave only a few lectures, I had to carry the main teaching load until James Ackerman came to Harvard and agreed to take over the Renaissance course. I enjoyed working with Giedion, but I was never his assistant. Having been trained by Rudolf Wittkower at the Warburg Institute, I came to the history of architecture with an attitude and method

different from Giedion's. Giedion, however, because of his long teaching experience, was helpful in structuring the courses so they would not degenerate into a boring sequence of names and dates. Instead, they consisted of a comparatively small, carefully chosen selection of examples that could be illustrated and discussed in great detail and with reference to the pertinent reading. In my case, alumni told me, they especially appreciated my inclination to talk about the material from the point of view of the architects who created the buildings we discussed. This was not surprising, since I then practiced architecture myself.

In keeping with Sert's emphasis, the seminar we offered was called "The Human Scale." Later the title was changed to "The Shaping of Urban Space," which I taught without Giedion (fig. 1.4). Four volumes of proceedings from this seminar were published, and projects from it were shown in an exhibition that filled the "great space" of Robinson Hall and attracted much positive attention. The beginning of the Urban Design Program at the GSD consisted of Sert's own studio, this seminar, and one offered by Jaqueline Tyrwhitt and others on planning.

Urban design was, I believe, Sert's transference of the concept of *urbanisme,* the French term used in the CIAM Congresses. Urbanism by now has been introduced into the professional English vocabulary, but then it did not exist in such standard dictionaries as *Webster's* or the *Oxford English Dictionary.* Urbanisme is a word not used before 1910, and the French dictionary definition is: "Étude systématique des méthodes permettant d'adapter l'habitat urbain aux besoins des hommes; ensemble des techniques d'application de ces méthodes" (the systematic

Figure 1.4 From left, unidentified seminar participant, Eduard Sekler, and Sigfried Giedion, Robinson Hall, fall term 1959–60, during a seminar conducted by Giedion and Sekler with the cooperation of Sert.

study of methods that permit adaptation of the urban habitat to the needs of the people; the ensemble of the techniques for the application of these methods).[16] After Sert introduced urban design as an academic discipline, many other schools quickly followed suit.

Sert became active in the university outside the GSD by motivating the administration to organize a Planning Office; he also strengthened and improved the undergraduate offerings related to design in Harvard College. They were housed in Hunt Hall and administered by a department of architectural sciences chaired by a member of the GSD faculty. A blue-ribbon committee chaired by John Nicholas Brown in 1956 had recommended the creation of a new department of design, and the construction and endowment of a design center. Dean Sert was able to convince the university that Le Corbusier would be the ideal architect to design this building by arguing, "There is no Corbusier building in this country, which is as strange as if there were no Picasso paintings in our museums." Sert also had to persuade his friend Le Corbusier to accept the commission, with Sert as the local partner. This is how the Carpenter Center for the Visual Arts, opened in 1963, came into being (fig. 1.5).[17]

Sert had persuaded me to help him with this project, first as coordinator and later as director of the center and part-time professor in what became the Department of Visual and Environmental Studies (VES). Sert assisted the new department in many ways through his intimate connection with the realm of the visual arts. He discovered Mirko Basaldella, the first absolutely wonderful director of design workshops at the Carpenter Center, and later he asked Eduardo Chillida and Tino Nivola, a friend of Le Corbusier's, among others, to become visiting artists at the center.

Under Sert's initial guidance, the policy of the VES department and the Carpenter Center became clearly centered on providing the opportunity for undergraduates from all departments of Harvard College to become visually and architecturally literate as part of their general education and to test and encourage their plastic creativity, without pretending, however, that they were in a school for future professional artists, photographers, or filmmakers. The program also enabled Harvard undergraduates to take courses that would fulfill the enrollment requirements of the GSD. In later years these basic educational charges have been largely disregarded. There is no concentration now for an undergraduate who wishes to study architecture later. The building too has suffered by various disturbing changes that altered its spaces and surroundings in the years after Sert's death and my retirement.

During the first years of his tenure as dean and chairman of the department of architecture, Sert personally taught the master class studio, in which he often assigned housing and urbanistic studies but occasionally also the design of a church or another architecturally challenging building. It is interesting to learn what Sert himself thought about the way his general ideas or principles ought to be translated into specific teachable advice for the practice of architecture and urban design, in other words, what he felt he should teach about the design process. He once put it into words in an essay,[18] and it also came across when I had the privilege of accompanying him as he gave desk critiques in his studio.

Figure 1.5 Opening of the Carpenter Center, 1963; Dean Sert, Mr. Carpenter, President Pusey, Dean Ford

Sert made it clear that you should begin the design process by informing yourself about all the givens, such as climate and orientation. He also wanted you to consider carefully the surroundings of your site so your building would relate to its neighbors in a positive manner. Having steeped yourself in the requirements of the program, you then should form a "mental vision" of the volumes and spaces and their circulation links in a "conceptual promenade." From this basis—a kind of immaterial equivalent to what the *parti* was in the Beaux-Arts method of designing, in which he had been reluctantly trained—the first sketches and rough models could be developed into a basic version of the project: something of a backbone to which one could return if one later got stuck on some detail. Sketching, moreover, had to accompany the design process to its conclusion. An alumnus recalled: "He instilled in me a fundamental understanding and respect for circulation to be the basis from which a parti could evolve. The form and volume would then logically advance both on the site and in the building."[19]

In the further elaboration of the project, Sert asked that special attention be given to matters affecting the human scale, such as what would be experienced at a pedestrian's eye level or from the distance in a lively skyline. In addition, he said, the intermediate floors should not be neglected, for they "present some of the more difficult problems in terms of the animation of the building." Often restraints imposed by unavoidable conditions could become "the source of the best inventions."[20]

Sert also stressed that one could learn from vernacular architecture—in his case Mediterranean—and from the past, which one had to "know and understand . . . in order to adapt and transform bygone processes of thought, philosophy, technology, etc., to the tenets of our times." To illustrate what he meant, he would sketch, for example, a section of the famous eighteenth-century Transparente in Toledo Cathedral[21] as an early prototype for a light trap that would bring down illumination from a vertical skylight. He employed such a light trap at the Fondation Maeght.[22]

In conclusion, let us try to learn about Sert as a teacher by listening to some of his former students, who had the firsthand experience of attending his master class, for which he admitted just fifteen or so members every year. His studio was a high-ceilinged room on the well-lit second floor of Robinson Hall, where he spent two afternoons a week, from 2 to 6 o'clock. Taking his duties as a teacher very seriously, he would occasionally come in at nine in the morning if a student needed special help. His much-trusted assistant and personal friend, who also had worked in Le Corbusier's studio, was Joseph Zalewski, "a born teacher and an extraordinary

critic," as Sert called him. Zalou, as the students referred to him, would even come in late in the evening if he was worried about a student's progress with a project.

Sert, who typically wore a well-cut gray or black suit and a bow tie, is remembered by one former student as "a very formal individual and not easy to get to know on a personal basis. He could be intimidating, especially at desk crits. A very large Indian student in my master class . . . was standing erect at his table when his turn came. . . . As Sert drew quite close, [the student] fainted dead away and dropped to the wood floor. . . . Sert immediately kneeled and took [the student's] head in his arms to comfort and revive him. Such was the awe and fright students had of Sert, not knowing his very compassionate side."[23]

Others have different recollections. "Dean Sert had a gentle but firm demeanor; his energy and enthusiasm more than compensated for his modest stature"[24] recalled one alumnus, while he was remembered as "a very polite and tolerant person"[25] by another. A third even felt that Sert "was one of the human beings who had been able to save into the grown-up world the child in himself."[26]

I observed that Sert had a keen eye for recognizing talent in students and never failed to encourage and foster it, even if the students strayed far from his precepts. Thus when one student made a linear, rather visionary project for Boston that was severely attacked by a visiting critic, Sert defended the student and encouraged him to continue in the same direction, but with more attention to practical details. In addition, he later helped him to get the kind of position he was trying to obtain.[27] In a similar vein, Sert defended another student who had presented a prefabricated inhabitable capsule that was attacked by a critic because a man would not be able to sit down in it. In defense, the student drew a sitting figure into his own drawing and explained, "You see, this is one of the ways a little man could sit down." With a smile Sert said, "I can imagine a little guy sitting down like this."[28] When he detected a bad start in a design, he would diplomatically prod the student by saying, "You can do many things!"[29]

Several alumni have testified about how effective Sert's teaching was in shaping their later approach to architecture. "At first I did not connect," a former student, later a dean, told me, "but in the second year I realized there was something to learn there and what followed was the fastest, most effective learning I ever experienced. I revised my approach to design in order to achieve human scale, and added elements solely to humanize."[30] "His teaching, instead of providing set answers, rather opened up unused avenues of thinking and perception,"[31] wrote another alumnus. Just as Sert had mentally integrated Corbusian principles into his own work, so he wanted students to understand and accept his principles, but not to imitate his forms.

"Sert offered another dimension [compared to the early Modern Movement] placing great emphasis on the creation of spaces for people—a stimulating environment for work, play and relaxation. The great richness of the potential of interplay between contrasting spaces, interior and exterior, large and small, public and private, was a theme for all of us at the GSD.... This focus on people, beautifying the man-made environment for people, outlives the stylistic periods."[32] This is what an architect, who can look back at a distinguished career, wrote, while

another equally distinguished alumnus and later teacher of people who now teach or taught at the GSD, very convincingly put it in a nutshell: "Even today, when I work on my designs, José Luis looks over my shoulder."[33] In the same spirit a Japanese alumnus and later winner of many architectural awards wrote: "I consider it the greatest fortune that has befallen me in my career as an architect that he [Sert] and I became teacher and student."[34]

Several former students who are important architects today explained that the example of Sert's own work was as important in their education as his formal teaching. The following reactions, for example, to an early work, the Barcelona Tuberculosis Dispensary, are typical: "The Barcelona building represents Sert's meticulous expression of space, form, and scale. And shockingly it is a completely felicitous placement of a modern building like a long compatible friend amidst the complex and dense surrounding historic buildings and streets ... to see modernity so alive yet living so easily with and embedded in history was the ultimate lesson for me in remembering J. L. Sert and his work."[35]

This kind of admiration was as true in regard to his first remodeled house on Long Island as for his house in Cambridge and his published urban design work. At the end of one academic year he invited me to join the graduating students for a memorable evening party at his house on Long Island. He and his beautiful wife, Moncha, were perfect hosts in a setting they had created to fit them perfectly. They had arranged for a concert by a slender Japanese master of the Koto, who played his complex, unfamiliar chords in the suddenly calm, candlelit main room, while outside moonlight cast its spell over the landscape.

The Cambridge house was too small to accommodate large parties, but there were occasions when not only faculty but also groups of students were invited in. One of them wrote: "One of the Dean's most compelling lessons for me has been not what he said, but what he did by creating his own residence in Cambridge. . . . The sensitively designed spaces with their elegant works of art illustrated principles of design difficult to describe by words alone."[36] When Josep Lluís and Moncha received guests, they and their surroundings perfectly supported and enhanced each other. As the reflected light from the high vertical light trap hit the gorgeous Spanish retablo in front of one wall and the Miró on another wall, and as one caught glimpses of the Nivola painting outside on a fence of the rear patio, there was both a joyousness and a natural dignity about this habitat and its inhabitants that I have never experienced elsewhere.

As his commitments inside and outside the university increased, Sert drastically had to decrease his personal involvement with teaching, though he still attended reviews frequently. When he was awarded the Gold Medal by the American Institute of Architects, he summed up his life's message: "If I were teaching today, I would try to bring people a little closer to what architecture in my mind really is: the shaping of spaces for human enjoyment. Indoor spaces and city spaces."[37]

In a similarly succinct manner, he made a request of me when I last saw him, the evening before his final return to Spain. With a few other friends I had helped arrange the disposal of matters in his house according to his wishes, and when he asked me to come, I expected he would still have more wishes regarding practical matters, but this was not the case. Sitting on the sofa propped up by a cushion, which was necessary because of severe pains in his back, he began to talk about our shared ideals, the positive essence of his, Le Corbusier's, and postwar CIAM's thinking on the right way for shaping urban spaces. "You are the last one left here now," he said, "to keep this spirit alive." I promised I would do my best. I hope I have not failed him.

NOTES

The author gratefully acknowledges the assistance of his wife and the numerous alumni who took the time to provide their recollections about the Sert years at the GSD. Their names are given in the notes below. Essay is copyright © Eduard Sekler.

1. Eduard F. Sekler, "Josep Lluís Sert: Measure and Light," *Josep Lluís Sert: Architect to the Arts* (Cambridge, Mass.: Carpenter Center for the Visual Arts, 1978), 4ff.

2. Constantine Michaelides, class of 1957, who later was dean of the School of Architecture at Washington University, St. Louis.

3. The architects were Carlo Bayer, Fred Freyler, and Sepp Stein.

4. Sigfried Giedion, "Reaffirmation of the Aims of CIAM," *A Decade of New Architecture* (Zurich: Girsberger, 1951), 24. The quotation is published without attribution to an author.

5. Personal note of the author, made at the Congress.

6. Ibid.

7. CIAM Austria handout, translated by the author.

8. *Architect's Journal* (August 20, 1953), 217, shows a typical scene: Walter

Gropius talking to members of the
Austrian group of CIAM on the roof of
the Unité; the author as a young man
is the member standing on the right.

9. Hubert Hoffmann, "CIAM 9," *Bauwelt*
44 (1953): 16.

10. Le Corbusier, letter dated July 23,
1956, CIAM 10 handouts, Special
Collections, Frances Loeb Library,
Harvard University Graduate School
of Design, Doc. 0022E.

11. Gropius, letter dated July 25, 1956,
ibid., Doc. 0025E.

12. Eric Mumford, *The CIAM Discourse
on Urbanism, 1928–1960* (Cambridge,
Mass.: MIT Press, 2000).

13. "On Architectural Education,"
Special Collections, Frances Loeb
Library, Harvard University Graduate
School of Design, Item D47.

14. *Macmillan Encyclopedia of
Architecture* (New York, 1982), 4: 40.

15. See "On Architectural Education."

16. *Le Petit Robert* (Paris, 1984), 2051.

17. Eduard F. Sekler and William Curtis,
*Le Corbusier at Work: The Genesis of
the Carpenter Center for the Visual
Arts,* preface by J. L. Sert (Cambridge,
Mass.: Harvard University Press, 1978).

18. J. L. Sert, "Design Process," *Process
Architecture* 34 (December 1982).

19. Letter from Malcolm Davis, class
of 1958.

20. See Sert, "Design Process."

21. G. Kubler and M. Soria, *Art and
Architecture in Spain and Portugal*
(Harmondsworth: Penguin, 1959), 40.

22. See note 2. Dean Michaelides told me
how Sert referred to the Transparente.

23. See note 19.

24. Letter from William Morgan, class
of 1958.

25. Letter from Thomas Payette, class
of 1960.

26. Letter from Dolf Schnebli, former
dean of the department of architecture,
ETH Zurich, class of 1954.

27. Letter from Carl Pruscha, class
of 1964, former rector, Academy
of Fine Arts, Vienna.

28. Letter from Bernhard Hafner, class
of 1967.

29. Communication of October 10, 2003,
from Victor Mahler, class of 1961.

30. Communication of October 7, 2003,
from Roger Montgomery, former
dean of the College of Environmental
Design, University of California,
Berkeley, class of 1957. He died
October 25, 2003.

31. Letter from Arnold Koerte, class
of 1961.

32. See note 25.

33. See note 26.

34. Fumihiko Maki, "J. L. Sert: His
Beginning Years at Harvard," *Process
Architecture* 34 (December 1982): 12ff.

35. Letter from Ben Weese, class of 1957.

36. See note 24.

37. *Boston Globe,* March 16, 1983.

Chapter 2

THE AESTHETIC DIMENSION IN
LE CORBUSIER'S URBAN PLANNING

FRANCESCO PASSANTI

Within a book broadly devoted to Josep Lluís Sert, this essay focuses on the urban planning of Le Corbusier, his lifelong interlocutor, mentor, and friend. Their interaction began in the late 1920s, when Sert brought Le Corbusier to Barcelona, worked in Le Corbusier's atelier, and collaborated with him on the Plan Macià for Barcelona. From that time to the 1950s, both were leading figures in CIAM. And it was through Sert that Le Corbusier received the 1959 commission for the Carpenter Center at Harvard, the only American building in his oeuvre. At the center of their professional interaction, for much of this time, stood their involvement with cities.[1]

Through the Plan Macià, their initial collaboration, I wish to clarify the nature of Le Corbusier's own urbanism, specifically the determinant role that aesthetic concerns played in it (fig 2.1).[2] This role was obscured by Le Corbusier's own promotion of his designs, by the internal polemics of CIAM, and by the group's propaganda, all of which overwhelmingly emphasized function. In a book devoted to

Sert, it is important to set the record straight on the nature of Le Corbusier's urbanism, a central and continuing reference for Sert.

The master plan for Barcelona, known as the Plan Macià, begun in 1932 by Sert and a local group of modernist architects, with the collaboration of Le Corbusier, marked Sert's first involvement with urban planning. As an opening salvo in their campaign for the plan, Sert and his friends had published a manifesto titled "The Functional City," proclaiming that "the areas of LIVING, PRODUCTION, REST, with CIRCULATION as the linking element, are determining factors in the forms of urban agglomeration."[3]

This conceptualization of the city in terms of four functions had been borrowed from CIAM discussions of that year, focused on the preparations of the Fourth Congress.[4] Le Corbusier himself had emphasized similar functions for ten years, setting them off as clearly distinct areas in his urban proposals, such as the Ville Contemporaine of 1922 and the Ville Radieuse of 1930. The four functions were

25

soon to be enshrined as the official planning doctrine of CIAM during the Fourth Congress, held in
Athens in 1933, devoted to "the functional city."
Ten years later, Sert and Le Corbusier were still
proclaiming the same functional categories in their
respective books, *Can Our Cities Survive?* (1942)
and *La Charte d'Athènes* (1943). Only after the war
did CIAM, now led by Sert, take a less rigid view of
urban planning; and it was Sert who, in 1956, initi-

ated a program of annual Urban Design Conferences
at Harvard—acknowledging with that word "Design"
the aesthetic dimension of planning, a concern with
both the form of the urban intervention and the context for which that intervention is designed.

But it would be wrong to conclude that function
alone drove early CIAM planning, and that aesthetics
came only after the war. At the very least such a conclusion would misread Le Corbusier's urbanism and

Figure 2.1 Josep Lluís Sert, Le Corbusier, et al. Plan Macià for Barcelona, 1932–35, perspective view

Figure 2.2 Le Corbusier, Sketch for the Plan Macià, seen from the sea

the functional typologies that he bequeathed to CIAM planning—for example, the Ville Radieuse typology of a zoned linear city with a "head" of regularly spaced prismatic skyscrapers, or the similar typology of the Plan Macià.

In the Plan Macià, the nineteenth-century grid set up for Barcelona by Ildefonso Cerdá is extended by adding industrial and residential zones along its central artery, which is continued to the north and south for 20 kilometers; the medieval section of Barcelona is essentially left intact; and two or three huge skycrapers, housing the business and administrative functions of the city, are lined up in front of the old quarter along the port, each presenting a massive front toward the sea, nearly as wide as it is tall.

Two early sketches by Le Corbusier show the city from the sea: to the left in the sketches is the hill of Montjuïc, to the right is the group of skyscrapers, and in between, dwarfed by the skyscrapers, are the traditional landmarks of Barcelona, the cathedral and the church of the Sagrada Família.[5] In one sketch the

skyscrapers are labeled "City." In the other sketch (fig. 2.2), taken from farther out on the sea and showing the wider ring of mountains as well, we find this comment: "there should be skyscrapers the same height of the Montjuïc" ("il faudrait gratteciel même hauteur que Monjuich").

The functional justification of the skyscrapers is as City, using the English word for the business district, as if one said "the City in London" or "downtown Manhattan." But Le Corbusier's comment shows him grappling with the overall visual and emotional impact of the city in the landscape. Even the wording is revealing: "il faudrait . . . ," almost as if he had said "this landscape needs" (or "my design needs") skyscrapers as tall as the mountain.

Within the oeuvre of Le Corbusier, the Plan Macià can be connected with two recent urban projects of 1929–30. On the one hand, as many pointed out, the scheme of a zoned linear city with a business-administrative "head" of skyscrapers recalls the Ville Radieuse and, behind it, the earlier

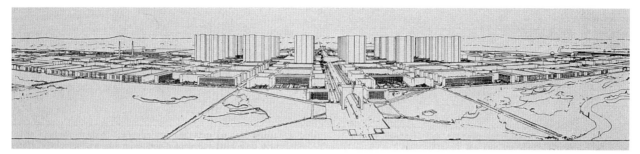

Figure 2.3 Le Corbusier, Ville Contemporaine, perspective view, 1922

Ville Contemporaine (figs. 2.3—2.5). On the other hand, the assertive presence of the skyscrapers in the landscape, their tops capped by a long horizontal that grazes the Montjuïc, recalls the viaducts in Le Corbusier's plans for Algiers and South America (fig. 2.6). I will trace these two urbanistic typologies through the earlier development of Le Corbusier as a planner; and from this review it will clearly emerge that both aspects incorporated, from the very start, artistic intentions.[6]

Le Corbusier had become involved in urban planning by writing a tract on the topic in 1910, when he was a student.[7] He began his research by reading Camillo Sitte's *Urbanism According to Artistic Principles* (1889). This book had inaugurated the aesthetic approach to city planning, arguing that there is more to planning than gridlike subdivisions, sewers, and functional considerations. Sitte put the emphasis on spatial effects, in particular on spatial containment or enclosure, an interest driven by a civic ideal of community: enclosed public spaces are where the community meets and transacts. Sitte's conceptual reference was the ancient Forum, specifically that of Pompeii, and his book focused on how

to achieve a sense of enclosure in public squares. His followers, in the meantime, had moved to an emphasis on curved streets, meant to create a sense of containment. Le Corbusier dutifully obliged by advocating enclosed squares and curved streets in his own tract.

Le Corbusier's preference soon changed, still within an aesthetic approach to planning. In the middle of boring repetitions of Sitte and his school, advocating the demise of the utilitarian American grid and the advent of curved streets, we find sudden passion in Le Corbusier's text: once the utilitarian grid is gone, he writes, "the straight street will get back its rights again, its claim to a higher beauty. The straight line, noble *par excellence* among those in Nature—but, indeed, the most rare! The majestic rigid columns of pine forests; the horizontal of the sea; the grandeur of endless plains; the grandiosity of the Alps seen from a high peak, when all the violence has merged into a vast becalmed surface." Le Corbusier is clearly thinking of the aesthetic category of the Sublime.[8] Instead of just providing agreeable settings for civic interaction, as Sitte's school had, Le Corbusier now also wants to provoke powerful emotion. Far from utilitarian, the straight

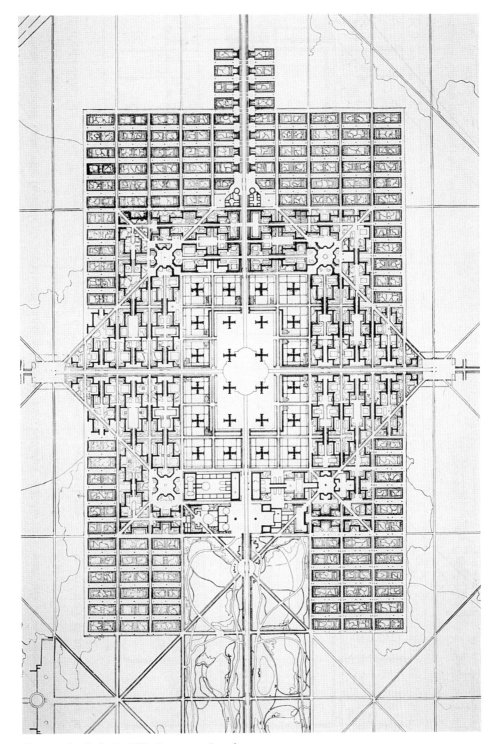

Figure 2.4 Le Corbusier, Ville Contemporaine, plan

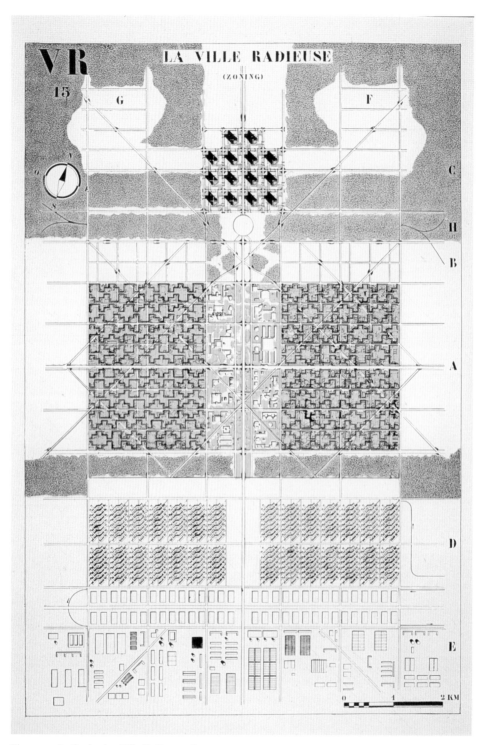

Figure 2.5 Le Corbusier, Ville Radieuse, plan, 1930

street is appreciated as iconic and transcendent.

In the same section of his manuscript, Le Corbusier also transcribed the Abbé Laugier's famous precept about urban planning: order in the detail, tumult in the ensemble. By this, Laugier intended (and Le Corbusier understood) that there must always be a guiding intention in laying out the city, and that the variety of a city must be willed, not haphazard, and made of large gestures.[9] Laugier's lesson soon colored Le Corbusier's response to Istanbul, which he visited in the following year, 1911. Le Corbusier saw Istanbul as a city laid out on three hills separated by water, and he noted the clear and uniform character of each: Istanbul proper, a sweet traditional city of mosques and wooden houses; Scutari, across the Bosphorus, a contemplative city of gardens and cemeteries; Pera, across the Golden Horn, a city of aggressive commerce, with aggressively competing buildings. He wrote: "This trinity, this grandiose unity! They are mutually necessary to each other, because their characters are profoundly different, but they complement each other."[10] Thinking ahead to Le Corbusier's urban plans— for example, his Ville Radieuse—we can anticipate

Figure 2.6 Le Corbusier, Plan for Algiers (plan A), 1933

the aesthetic appeal of clearly marking out large and uniform functional areas (skyscrapers, apartment blocks, and so forth), each area sharply characterized and then willfully juxtaposed to the others to form a larger drama.

In 1915, while Le Corbusier spent more time researching the literature of urban planning, he became influenced by a different focus of the Sitte school: an interest in the overall form of the city, which, according to Sitte's followers, should express a sense of the whole and be perceivable as a whole, not sprawl meaninglessly. The concept used in the German literature was that of "city crown," or *Stadtkrone*, which Bruno Taut would use as the title for a book published soon after World War I.[11] The paradigmatic example was the soaring medieval cathedral that provided symbolic focus and visual cohesion to the city huddled around it; but the literature was interested in a variety of visual models that might suggest a way to proceed in the present, from medieval Strasbourg to Assyrian ziggurats, Cambodian temples, the Athenian Acropolis, even the bunched skyscrapers of downtown Manhattan. While reading about this at the Bibliothèque Nationale in Paris, Le Corbusier drew the following list in his notebook: "New York and its bay, and the Acropolis in Athens, . . . and Versailles, and Cambodia."[12] In other words: the bunched-up skyscrapers of New York as a temple or monumental complex.

In 1920, Le Corbusier published his own design for skyscrapers—regularly spaced skyscrapers, cruciform, prismatic, with no cornice or spire. These are the skyscrapers that he later used in his Ville Contemporaine and Ville Radieuse. They were published in a series of three articles devoted to the notion that "architecture is the masterful, correct, and magnificent play of volumes brought together in light," and the skyscraper design was intended as an example of what that play of volumes might be. In the same article in which he published the skyscrapers, we can read that "cities must be conceived and designed, in their spatial arrangement, the way the temples of the Orient were designed, and the Versailles of Louis XIV."[13]

The Ville Contemporaine, which Le Corbusier exhibited in 1922, brings together all this homework.[14] We recognize the "sublime" infinity of straight lines in the two avenues crossing at the center; the juxtaposition of uniform functional areas, each with its own characteristic building type, to form a larger drama à la Laugier; the use of the skyscrapers as Stadtkrone, which unifies the city; the skyscrapers with their "play of volumes." As if to stress that the whole city arises from one intention, Le Corbusier even gives it the proportion of a golden rectangle, repeated three times from the center out, in a statement of artistic unity clearly intended for the arriving air traveler. The inner golden rectangle at the core of the city is a public square of sorts, defined by a continuous ribbon building, four stories high and terraced toward the center with cafés and shops, a sort of giant Place des Invalides containing gardens and rail station and airport (today we would say heliport), plus the inner eight skyscrapers. The same proportion is echoed in the overall envelope of the twenty-four skyscrapers, the composite mass that one would see if they were all wrapped together into one Christo-like sculpture. And farther out, as new rings of housing are added, the edge of the city is approximating a golden rectangle again.[15]

In the Ville Radieuse of 1930 and in the Plan Macià of 1932, Le Corbusier rearranged the functional areas linearly and changed the role of the acropolis of skyscrapers from heart to head.[16] But the typological elements are similar and incorporate the same aesthetic concerns: the "sublime" straight avenue; the Laugier-like juxtaposition of uniform characterized zones; the skyscrapers as Stadtkrone; the skyscrapers' "play of volumes."

Unlike the Ville Contemporaine or the Ville Radieuse, however, the Plan Macià is set against the background of a strong landscape, and Le Corbusier's own sketch shows him keenly aware of this: his skyscrapers should have "the same height of the Montjuïc." The architecture is not just sited in the landscape, but rather it challenges it on an equal footing, almost competitively; conversely, the landscape is not just a passive setting but is turned into an interlocutor. As we noted earlier, this attitude connects the Plan Macià to other recent urban proposals by Le Corbusier, the Plan Obus for Algiers and similar ones for South America. And if we trace this attitude back through Le Corbusier's formation we see that it too, like the typology of the Ville Contemporaine and Ville Radieuse, reflects long-standing aesthetic concerns.

In Florence, during his first trip abroad in 1907, having seen Brunelleschi's dome from far away in the surrounding hills, he noted with emotion: "Suddenly there arose, in the blue fog of the morning, this monster in stone, this hill, bigger than those around because it has order."[17] Le Corbusier might

as well have said that the Duomo is an Egyptian pyramid with bowed edges! All this came from his readings on the Sublime in architecture. In Charles Blanc's *Grammaire des arts du dessin,* an amazingly synthetic compendium of aesthetics that Le Corbusier had just read in school, the Sublime is conceptualized by referring to nature's unmeasurable and mysterious aspects, evoking infinity and the divine. Awed by nature, says Blanc, man built his first architecture as a religious monument, "a creation that must compete with nature," unconcerned with shelter but reproducing the most imposing aspects of nature, its mountains, sea, forests: the Egyptians were the great protagonists of this first stage. And architecture achieves the Sublime through a combination of large scale and the "absolute character of its geometry."[18] From Blanc, too, came Le Corbusier's tirade of 1910 about the straight line, discussed earlier.

And in Athens, a year later, the same attitude pervaded Le Corbusier's reaction to the Parthenon: "Thus came true the straightness of the temples, the savagery of the site, their impeccable structure. The force of the mind triumphs. . . . Awareness of a super-human fatality grabs you. The Parthenon, that terrible machine, broods and dominates; four hours away on land and one more on the sea, from that far, alone, it imposes the authority of its cube, against the sea. . . . The Parthenon [throws] its horizontal entablature into the distance, and holds up its stirn, like a shield, against that landscape."[19]

When, in 1929–30, Le Corbusier thought of inhabited viaducts as a new form of urban settlement for Rio de Janeiro, São Paulo, Montevideo, and Algiers, he was certainly thinking along the same lines.[20] The viaducts provided a chance to operate at large topographical scale, and their even grade provided the "absolute character" of geometry: it is not their curves but their inflexible horizontality that matters in this respect. With scale and absoluteness in hand, Le Corbusier could "compete with nature," like the Egyptians and Brunelleschi, like the maker of the Parthenon.

The skyscrapers of the Plan Macià play two roles from an aesthetic point of view. If we bear in mind the model of the Ville Radieuse, they are rhythmic verticals juxtaposed to the horizontality of the rest of the plan. If we bear in mind the model of the Parthenon and of the viaducts in South America and Algiers, they take on the landscape: they are like shields facing the sea, and they support a virtual horizontal line connecting their tops with that of the Montjuïc, the resulting "viaduct" playing against the mountainous coastline behind.[21]

A context beyond artistic intentions must be kept in mind, although limited space precludes a larger discussion in this essay. Clearly, to take the Ville Contemporaine as an example, the use of skyscrapers and airport as the iconic focus of a city (as opposed to, say, governmental or religious buildings), the naked form of the skyscrapers and their regular spacing, the use of high-speed roadways as ceremonial axes—or even as the preeminent urban form in Algiers—all these articulate what was then a new world: new technologies, new social hierarchies, new machines, and so forth. Le Corbusier's skyscrapers, for example, incorporate in their design technical developments like steel, concrete, and elevators; they incorporate American

debates about the congestion of too many skyscrapers,[22] and echoes of these debates in Germany and France; they incorporate the German discourse on *Sachlichkeit,* about the place that the new facts of modern life should be given in architecture, about industrial types and so on; all of this in addition to concerns about form. Without dealing with these other aspects it is not possible to discuss *how* aesthetic concerns interacted with them to generate Le Corbusier's urbanism, nor to assess the relative weight they held for him. My more limited intent here has been to show that the aesthetic dimension *was* present throughout the process by which Le Corbusier conceptualized his urban typologies, and it was thus embedded in the typologies themselves. But one discourse, the one on Sachlichkeit (factualness), warrants a special discussion because it, more than others, provided a mediating structure between function and aesthetics.

The discourse on Sachlichkeit had begun in the 1890s, in Germany and Vienna, as a grab bag of concerns ranging from disgust at nouveau-riche display to nostalgia for traditional German ways and admiration for English clothing. By 1910, in Germany and especially within the Werkbund association, it had developed a focus on the new urban and industrial facts of modern life, such as factories and office buildings, ships, and consumer products.[23] Because they had developed blindly through collective anonymous processes, these facts were considered representative of the society that had evolved them; hence their frank display was seen as a celebration of modern society, and the new building types, such as commercial and factory buildings, were welcomed as architectural opportunities. The architect Peter Behrens argued in 1912 that Berlin had by now become primarily a business city and that it should celebrate this new character by allowing tall commercial buildings downtown to dwarf the traditional symbols of political power, adding that the vertical masses of the new buildings would provide a visual focus and unified character for the whole city (we recognize here the Stadtkrone argument and foreshadowing of Le Corbusier's proposals). And Walter Gropius argued in 1913 that American factories and silos had a majesty and monumental power worthy of ancient Egypt because of their "large, tightly bound form."

Thanks to the synergistic relationship between function and art that he absorbed from this discourse, Le Corbusier could later conceptualize his regularly spaced and cruciform skyscrapers both as a functional solution to problems of urban density and as a "play of volumes brought together in light" at giant scale. Or he could conceptualize the highway viaduct both as a means of fast transportation and as a giant horizontal in the landscape. In short, he could produce urbanistic typologies that had, embedded in them, both a modern functional necessity and an aesthetic intent, held in productive tension.

The presence of an aesthetic intent, in tension with function, is what gives Le Corbusier's urban typologies their emotional power, and what made him such a potent presence in twentieth-century planning—no matter how we judge the merits of his contribution to this field.

Le Corbusier's concern with the aesthetics of cities grew increasingly visible in Sert's late work, in terms of both planning doctrine and design practice. On the one hand, Le Corbusier had provided a line of continuity for Camillo Sitte's belief that cities should be "designed" with aesthetic intent and not just planned, and he had embedded that belief in new urban typologies. When, in the 1950s, opposition grew against the mindless application of functional planning, Sert could react by introducing urban design into the Harvard curriculum—not as a nostalgic or resigned return to traditional typologies such as the urban square, but as a shift of emphasis within modernist planning. On the other hand, in his own late practice as urban designer, Sert drew important lessons from Le Corbusier, not only by adopting his "brutalist" use of raw concrete but also, more broadly, by understanding in his work the tension between aesthetics and function just discussed: that tension is a central factor in accounting for the mysterious and powerful presence that Sert's best late works, such as the Peabody Towers (married student housing) at Harvard University or the Charles River Campus at Boston University, assert in their urban landscape.

NOTES

1. Throughout this essay, all translations are mine unless otherwise indicated.

2. See Josep Rovira, *José Luis Sert, 1901–1983* (Milan: Electa, 2003, first published in Italian in 2000), 47–87, with extensive bibliography on p. 390; and Eric Mumford, *The CIAM Discourse on Urbanism, 1928–1960* (Cambridge, Mass.: MIT Press, 2000), 66–73. Le Corbusier published the plan in Le Corbusier and Pierre Jeanneret, *Oeuvre complète, 1929–1934* (Zurich: Girsberger, 1935; rpt. 1964), 90, and in Le Corbusier, *La ville radieuse* (Boulogne-sur-Seine: Editions de l'Architecture d'aujourd'hui, 1935; rpt. 1964), 305–309. The relative roles of Sert and Le Corbusier in the development of the plan are unclear, but the initial outline of the plan seems to be Le Corbusier's.

3. Rovira, *Sert*, 53–55.

4. Mumford, *CIAM*, 59–91; Rovira, *Sert*, 53–55.

5. Le Corbusier, Sketchbook C10, 53, 55. Published in *Le Corbusier Sketchbooks*, 4 vols. (New York: Architectural History Foundation, and Cambridge, Mass.: MIT Press, and Paris: Fondation Le Corbusier, 1981), 1: 636, 637. They are also shown in Rovira, *Sert*, 56.

6. For connected issues, see three essays of mine: Francesco Passanti, "The Skyscrapers of the Ville Contemporaine," *Assemblage* 4 (October 1987): 52–65; "The Vernacular, Modernism, and Le Corbusier," *JSAH* 56, no. 4 (December 1997): 438–451; "Architecture: Proportion, Classicism, and Other Issues," in Stanislaus von Moos and Arthur Rüegg, eds., *Le Corbusier Before Le Corbusier* (New Haven: Yale University Press, and New York: Bard Graduate Center for Studies in the Decorative Arts, Design, and Culture, 2002), 68–97, 287–294.

7. The tract was going to be called *La Construction des villes* (literal French translation of the German word for urban planning, *Städtebau*). H. Allen Brooks first called attention to this early work by Le Corbusier in 1982; more recently see his *Le Corbusier's Formative Years* (Chicago: University of Chicago Press, 1997), 200–208. A transcript of Le Corbusier's manuscript, edited by Marc E. Albert Emery, has been published as Charles-Edouard Jeanneret/Le Corbusier, *La Construction des villes* (Lausanne: l'Age d'homme, 1992), cited hereafter as Le Corbusier, *Villes.*

8. Le Corbusier, *Villes,* 98. This tirade on the straight street is directly inspired by Le Corbusier's reading of Charles Blanc, *Grammaire des arts du dessin* (Paris: Laurens, 1867; references are from the edition of 1880), a comprehensive and readable compendium of aesthetic theory. Blanc cites Pythagoras's opinion that the straight line represents infinity (p. 23), and in discussing the Sublime he mentions mountains, the flat surface of the sea, and the vertical trees in forests, as inspirations of the concept (p. 56).

9. The original sentence by Laugier reads: "Il faut de la régularité & de la bizarrerie, des rapports & des opposi-tions, des accidens qui varient le tableau, un grand ordre dans les détails, de la confusion, du fracas, du tumulte dans l'ensemble." Marc-Antoine Laugier, *Observations sur l'architecture* (The Hague, 1765), 312–313. Le Corbusier's word-by-word transcription of this passage is found in Le Corbusier, *Villes,* 97.

10. Le Corbusier, *Le Voyage d'orient* (Paris: Forces Vives, 1966), 66. The text of this section about Istanbul was written in 1911. The book has been translated into English by Ivan Zaknic in collaboration with Nicole Pertuiset: Le Corbusier, *Journey to the East* (Cambridge, Mass.: MIT Press, 1987).

11. Bruno Taut, *Die Stadtkrone* (Jena: Diederichs, 1919). Taut began writing the book in 1916 in Germany at about the same time that Le Corbusier was referring to the concept in his notes, and looking up the same examples, while researching at the Bibliothèque Nationale in Paris. Taut and Le Corbusier did not know each other, and both were feeding on a German prewar planning literature, mostly in periodicals, that is too extensive to cite here.

12. The list is among the loose notes that Le Corbusier made while reading at the Bibliothèque Nationale in Paris in summer 1915. It is kept at the Fondation Le Corbusier, Paris.

13. Le Corbusier-Saugnier, "Trois rappels à mm. les architectes. Troisième rappel: le plan," *l'Esprit nouveau* 4 (January 1921): 457–470 (skyscrapers on 465–466, quotation on 462–463).

This article was then incorporated in Le Corbusier, *Vers une architecture* (Paris: Crès, 1923). English translation by Frederick Etchells: *Towards a New Architecture* (London: Rodker, 1927).

14. The Ville Contemporaine (contemporary city) was exhibited at the Salon d'Automne in Paris, in fall 1922. Good illustrations are found in Le Corbusier and Pierre Jeanneret, *Oeuvre complète, 1910–1929* (Zurich: Girsberger, 1937; rpt. 1964), 32–39. The first edition, in German, was published in 1930. For a more detailed discussion of this project, see Passanti, "Skyscrapers of the Ville Contemporaine."

15. I have discussed elsewhere the golden proportions of the Ville Contemporaine and the broader context of Le Corbusier's use of proportions in his design. See Passanti, "Proportion, Classicism, and Other Issues," 77–81, esp. 80. Note that the "urban square" does not fit the regular grid on which the skyscrapers are laid out: to achieve a golden proportion (an irrational number), it must violate the square grid of streets, hence it must run outside the grid on two sides, and inside the grid on two other sides.

16. Le Corbusier, *La ville radieuse*, 156–173.

17. Letter to his teacher Charles L'Eplattenier, November 1, 1907, kept at the Fondation Le Corbusier, Paris.

18. Blanc, *Grammaire*, 8, 23, 26 (where Blanc discusses the Egyptian pyramids as mountains), 55–57 (architecture competing with nature), 58, 76–82 (absolute character of geometry).

19. Le Corbusier, *Voyage*, 154, 161.

20. Le Corbusier, *La ville radieuse*, 222 (São Paulo, Montevideo), 223–225 (Rio), 226–249 (Algiers, see esp. 236, 247).

21. The most direct parallel is between the "virtual viaduct" of the Plan Macià and the actual viaduct of the plan for Montevideo: in both, a horizontal line grazes the top of a mountain overlooking a port. In the plan for Montevideo, a straight viaduct, which begins far inland, reaches the city on the coast, grazes the mountain dominating the bay, continues horizontally, undeterred by the steep slope of the mountain and by the water of the bay, and ends abruptly in the center of the bay.

22. On the issue of "congestion" and the typology of regularly spaced skyscrapers, see Passanti, "Skyscrapers of the Ville Contemporaine."

23. The literal translation of the word "Sachlichkeit" is factualness; a commonly used term is objectivity. On the Werkbund, see Frederic J. Schwartz, *The Werkbund: Design Theory and Mass Culture Before the First World War* (New Haven: Yale University Press, 1996). On the notion of "modern vernacular," its role in the discourse on Sachlichkeit, and its importance for Le Corbusier, see Passanti, "Vernacular, Modernism, and Le Corbusier," with ample bibliography in the footnotes. On the specific role that Sachlichkeit played in the development of early Le Corbusier, see Passanti, "Proportion, Classicism, and Other Issues," 88–90. The seminal essay on the issue of Sachlichkeit and modern architecture remains William Jordy, "The Symbolic Essence of Modern European Architecture of the Twenties and Its Continuing Influence," *JSAH* 23 (October 1963): 177–187. On Jordy, see William H. Jordy, *"Symbolic Essence" and Other Writings on Modern Architecture and American Culture,* ed. and with an introduction by Mardges Bacon (New Haven: Yale University Press, 2005).

Chapter 3

CREATING A PUBLIC FOR MODERN ARCHITECTURE

Sert's Use of Images from GATCPAC to *The Heart of the City*

JORDANA MENDELSON

One of Josep Lluís Sert's key talents was his understanding and employment of modern media, especially photography and the press, to promote new ideas about architecture and urbanism. Sert's opportunities and frustrations with promotion were at the core of his early development and his experiences with Le Corbusier.[1] Those early lessons stayed with Sert throughout his career and were put to use in a range of activities, from individual house designs to ambitious plans to revolutionize urban planning.[2] This essay explores Sert's engagement with the graphic arts to track the architect's transition from Europe to the United States, from avant-garde print culture to international publishing.

Making effective use of mass media was no easy task for Sert (or any architect in the early twentieth century), even though he had a good model to follow in Le Corbusier. From the early stages of his career it appears that Sert was aware of photography's power to make images out of the built environment. But for Sert photography was also a diagnostic tool for leveraging a space for modern architecture and

urbanism within the public sphere, especially in three cases: with his involvement with GATCPAC (Grup d'Arquitectes i Tècnics Catalans per al Progrés de l'Arquitectura Contemporània) and the magazine *A. C. Documentos de Actividad Contemporánea* in Barcelona in the 1930s, and with two books drawn from his work with CIAM, *Can Our Cities Survive?* (1942) which he wrote, and *The Heart of the City* (1951), which he coedited. By understanding the dual role of photography in these publications—as a creative *and* promotional tool— we gain a glimpse into how Sert documented architecture's relation to its context. We also learn about Sert's awareness of the power of print culture to propel ideas about architecture—often captured through photography—and its context to new audiences.

LEARNING FROM LE CORBUSIER

Even before meeting Le Corbusier in person, Sert had encountered the architect's ideas in *Urbanisme* (1925) and in three other books by Le Corbusier that Sert had purchased on a trip to Paris. Notably, Le

Corbusier dedicated a chapter of *Urbanisme* to "press clippings" (*coupures de journaux*). Featured in the headlines, editorials, and articles that Le Corbusier reprinted were observations of, complaints about, and caricatures of the pressures that the city brings to everyday life. Sert was familiar with Le Corbusier's coverage in the press, especially those articles about the architect written by Rafael Benet for the Catalan newspaper *La Veu de Catalunya*. In 1928, Le Corbusier arrived in Barcelona with an invitation from Sert to present his ideas on urbanism to the Catalan public. Meanwhile, Sert and other young Barcelona architects formed GATCPAC and took primary responsibility for the magazine *A. C.* Sert's friend Josep Torres Clavé took on the role of magazine editor. Le Corbusier was enlisted to help the group propose an overarching urban reform plan for Barcelona. Aspects of the Plan Macià, which GATCPAC and Le Corbusier named after Francesc Macià, president of the Generalitat de Catalunya from 1932 to 1933, appeared repeatedly in *A. C.* and formed the basis for public exhibitions.

In the correspondence exchanged by the architects in GATCPAC and with the Madrid members of the national group, which adopted the name GATEPAC (Grupo de Arquitectos y Técnicos Españoles para el Progreso de la Arquitectura Contemporánea) in 1931, and especially between Torres Clavé and both Fernando García Mercadal and José Manuel Aizpurúa, one appreciates the challenges that the group faced in bringing out a top-quality, widely distributed, and profitable magazine. Photographs were exchanged between the offices of *A. C.* and architects worldwide. Within Spain, *A. C.* became a reference point for new maga-

Figure 3.1 Josep Sala, photographs of Sert's apartment building on the calle Muntaner, Barcelona, in "Arquitectura Moderna," *D'Ací i d'Allà* (Spring 1932)

zines, such as *Gaceta de Arte,* whose editor, Eduardo Westerdahl, requested articles and photographs from the group. Advertisements had to be solicited, subscribers had to be kept track of, and editorial policy had to be set, all while the architects made of *A. C.* both a reference guide and manifesto for modern Spanish architecture. In many respects, *A. C.* was where Sert and others learned about the politics (and possibilities) of publishing. Writing to García Mercadal to explain the delay in the publication of the first issue of *A. C.,* Torres Clavé was quick to admit: "Our inexperience has of course been the first and primary reason for this delay; but you shouldn't doubt our will and enthusiasm."[3]

Members of GATCPAC saw the power of photography to transmit a carefully composed vision of modern architecture. In addition to writing articles on photography in *A. C.* and being avid readers of illustrated journals from across Europe and the United States, Sert and other GATCPAC architects hired Catalan photographer Josep Sala to document their newly constructed buildings in and around Barcelona. Many of Sala's photographs appeared in early issues of *A. C.*[4] In spring 1932, Sala became the artistic director for *D'Ací i d'Allà,* one of the city's most popular illustrated magazines, and transformed it into a sign of conspicuous cosmopolitanism, complete with a large format, a spiral binding, and full-page photographs and publicity. In the first issue under Sala's direction, his photographs of Sert's apartment building on the calle Muntaner accompanied an article about "Arquitectura Moderna" (fig.

3.1). The clean-lined images communicated a dynamic vision of the young architect's residential building. Sala, who had an active practice as a commercial photographer and graphic designer, understood the power of images to sell modernity as an idea to readers of *D'Ací i d'Allà* and *A.C.*

In about 1933, a young Austrian photographer in exile from Germany named Margaret Michaelis became a leading photographer for *A. C.* and for GATCPAC's many architectural and exhibition projects.[5] Unlike Sala, she did not have an established practice in Barcelona, nor was she fluent in Spanish (or Catalan) at the time of her first commissions. Michaelis, who had trained and worked in Berlin and Vienna, arrived in Barcelona with a modern pedigree that matched the architects' vision for their

Figure 3.2 Margaret Michaelis, photographs of G. Rodríguez Arias's apartment house, Barcelona, in *A. C.* (1934)

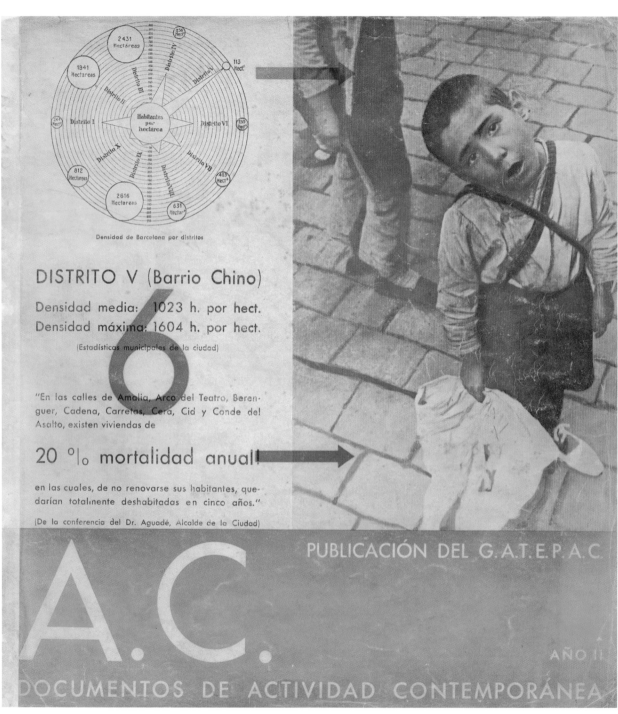

Figure 3.3 *A. C.* (1932), cover. Photograph by Margaret Michaelis.

magazine. Her photographs of Sert's house in Garraf, and of the work of several other GATCPAC architects, including Germán Rodríguez Arias, created an iconic image of modern architecture that became widely identified with GATCPAC in magazines and books both within and outside of Catalonia (fig. 3.2).

At the same time that GATCPAC, and Sert in particular, were promoting modern architecture, the group also was tackling the problems of urbanism and the functional city. In the proposals to reform Barcelona that GATCPAC published and exhibited, it was Michaelis's photographs of the city's fifth district, the so-called Barrio Chino, that most effectively communicated GATCPAC's aims to clean up, modernize, and rationalize the city by demolishing Barcelona's slum district.[6] During a brief visit to Barcelona around 1932, Michaelis took photographs in the district and continued to do so throughout her time in Barcelona. The sixth, ninth, and twenty-fifth issues of *A. C.* featured Michaelis's photographs of children, street urchins, and the towering image of a port-side laborer who inhabited the Barrio, along with the prostitute, the anarchist, and children whose vital statistics formed an integral part of the GATCPAC's research and reports (fig. 3.3). Her photographs continued to appear in *A. C.* and other Spanish publications even after she had left the country during the Spanish Civil War. At that time Sert, too, was absent from Barcelona. He maintained contact with Torres Clavé, who edited *A. C.* through its last issue, in 1937.[7]

PUBLISHING FOR A NEW AUDIENCE

Sert's work with GATCPAC, and especially *A. C.*, formed the foundation for his efforts in the United States. In his "Biographical Notes" from this period he highlighted his roles in both the group and the magazine.[8] When his book *Can Our Cities Survive? An ABC of Urban Problems, Their Analysis, Their Solutions* was published in 1942, it included images from GATCPAC's projects, including Michaelis's photographs (figs. 3.4 and 3.5). The documentation from GATCPAC and CIAM was combined with material that Sert had gathered from libraries, archives, and mass media to make his manuscript relevant to the American experience. He paired photographs with graphs and lightened up both by including cartoons from the daily press. While recognizing the

Figure 3.4 Margaret Michaelis, photograph in montage, Barcelona, in "Insalubritat," *A. C.* (June 1937)

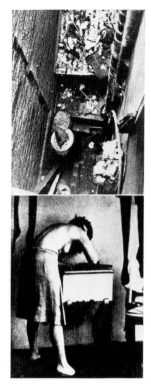

OVERCROWDING. *Nine persons in one bedroom!* A miner's family in Jemappes (Belgium). The entire floor space is covered by mattresses, the entire mattress area by human bodies. This is an extreme case of overcrowding, but there are millions of other cases only slightly better. Overcrowded homes with three and four per room are common in many big cities. To the right are other typical views of slum homes (above, looking down into a "ventilation and lighting" court; below, the family's "bathroom"). Compare the plan below of a black slave cargo ready for a voyage with the view of the bedroom above.

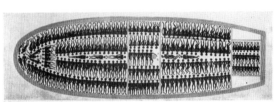

Plan of a slave cargo

25

Figure 3.5 From Josep Lluís Sert, *Can Our Cities Survive?*

need to address a new community of readers, Sert relied on his contacts from Europe to ensure that his ideas would be communicated through the language of modern design.

One of the precedents for Sert's book was Sigfried Giedion's *Space, Time and Architecture* (1941).[9] The book's many illustrations, large format, and cover (by Bauhaus-trained artist and fellow émigré Herbert Bayer) ensured its immediate success (fig. 3.6). Bayer, who worked on exhibition designs for the Museum of Modern Art in New York (*Bauhaus: 1919–1938*, 1938; *Road to Victory*, 1942; *Airways to Peace*, 1943), was also building a reputation as one of the most advanced graphic designers in the United States; his articles on typography and layout appeared in the leading advertising maga-

zine *P. M.* in 1939–40. Although letters between Joseph Hudnut, dean of Harvard's GSD, and Dumas Malone, director of Harvard University Press, indicate that Bayer's prices were higher than the norm for academic presses, Hudnut agreed to allow Bayer to design the jacket for Sert's book, arguing that the book's presentation would greatly affect its success (fig. 3.7).[10]

Sert wanted the book to make an impression. Its reception was important, he felt, not only for spreading CIAM's ideas but also for helping him secure an academic post in the United States.[11] Throughout the editorial process Sert maintained regular correspondence with the Press, especially in relation to the permissions required to reproduce extensive graphic material. Sert also was involved

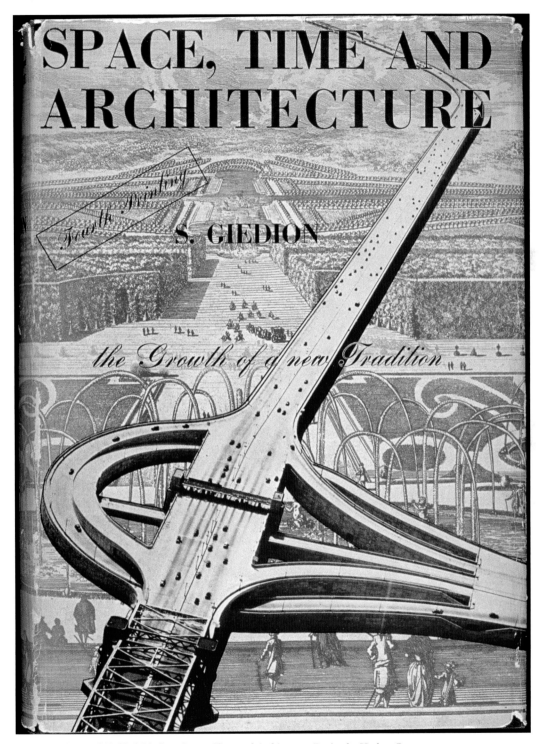

Figure 3.6 Cover of Sigfried Giedion, *Space, Time and Architecture.* Design by Herbert Bayer.

Figure 3.7 Cover of Josep Lluís Sert and CIAM, *Can Our Cities Survive?* Design by Herbert Bayer.

in the layout of the book and its promotion.[12] The editors at Harvard University Press recognized the novelty of Sert's approach, writing in a memorandum dated January 17, 1941, that his "photographic documents" and extensive use of plans and graphs would make the book appealing to both the specialist and the layman.[13]

The images garnered immediate positive response from critics. A reviewer for *Architectural Forum* wrote: "One of the most impressive features of the book is the really magnificent use of pictures. The numerous illustrations have been selected with such care that they come close to telling the story by themselves." Elizabeth Coit in *Architectural Record* went even further: "The format is striking, the short wide page lending itself admirably to the almost poster-like popular presentations of the 'chart' or manifesto or confession of faith adopted at the C.I.A.M. congresses of 1933 and 1937.... Over 300 illustrations ... help to hold even the most casual reader, and the very jerkiness of the text is effective." But the book that the *Christian Science Monitor* labeled "popular in form" was not accepted as such by everyone. Frederick Gutheim complained in the *Magazine of Art,* "A volume measuring 9 × 12 inches which costs $5 and contains more than 250 pages can hardly be considered a popular book; it does not even contain the possibilities of larger circulation through cheap reprintings." The final production cost was approximately $8,000 (up from the initial estimate of $5,300).[14] Sert's use of images and modern design paid off in terms of critical reception but no doubt taught him a great deal about the nature of publishing in the United States and about reaching a popular audience.

AN "IMPERFECT" ALBUM

In 1950, Sert began work on another book, also based on CIAM's meetings and members' projects. Titled *The Heart of the City,* and coedited with Jaqueline Tyrwhitt and Ernesto N. Rogers, it was similar to Sert's earlier book in that it relied on photos, graphs, and dynamic design elements such as colored paper to catch readers' attention (fig. 3.8). Unlike *Can Our Cities Survive?* this new book was not about making the perfect academic primer on urbanism. As Sert explained in a February 1951 letter to Serge Chermayeff: "We plan a symposium type of book, with colored illustrations, something that can be gotten up quickly and does not pretend to be perfect. I think Corbusier has the right approach on this type of book, and perfect books dealing with architecture and planning are so boring anyhow."[15]

Sert's remark is revealing but a bit deceiving. "Not perfect" did not mean careless or unintentional. Indeed, the look of spontaneity and flexibility that Sert hoped to communicate in the book was carefully planned. He asked Tyrwhitt and Rogers to send him sketches of the layout, and he encouraged them to make the book "have as much popular appeal as possible." He directed that the illustrations "show *people,* wherever possible."[16] The inclusion of people in photographs of modern architecture and urban planning had been a significant feature in both *A. C.* and *Can Our Cities Survive?* In *The Heart of the City* this element took on the role of protagonist. Humanism and history were interlaced and communicated to readers through visual evidence. Abstraction was eschewed in favor of images of the city populated. The inside front and back cover announce the book's attempt to reach a broader audience by reproducing Saul Steinberg's drawing of the Piazza San Marco. Sert returned to Steinberg's cartoonlike depictions in his own article on "Centers of Community Life" by juxtaposing the artist's rendition of the Galleria Vittorio Emanuele in Milan with photographic documents of the ebbs and flows of human movement in the Piazza del Duomo (fig. 3.9).

Unlike *Can Our Cities Survive?* in which the photographs were often fused into a full-page montage, almost posterlike in appearance, in *The Heart of the City* the individual images are carefully spaced so that the viewer connects the remarks of each architect with the contextual photographs of the area under discussion. The photographs in both books—documentary in style and purpose—emphasize content over manipulation, transparency over obfuscation. The purpose of the book is to teach through visual demonstration, and in this task photographs take center stage in translating the technical language of the urban planner into a visually coherent set of image-ideas. Repeated throughout the book, these

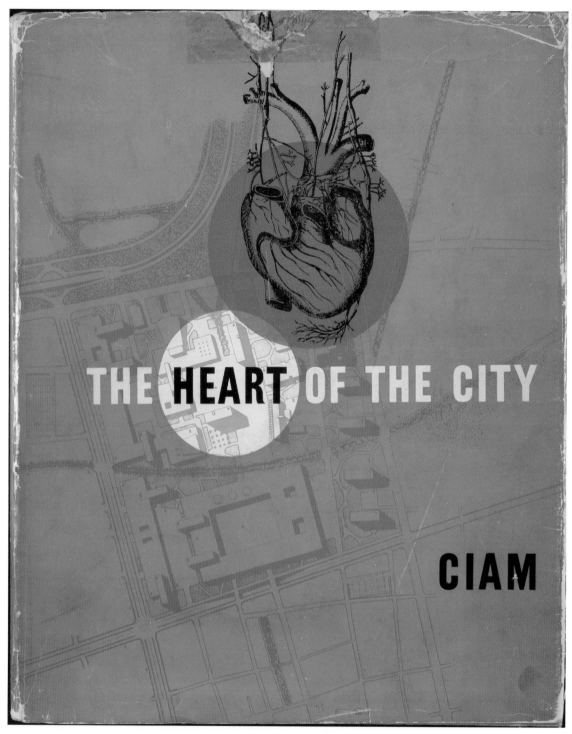

Figure 3.8 Cover of Jaqueline Tyrwhitt, Josep Lluís Sert, and Ernesto N. Rogers, eds., *The Heart of the City*

photographs of crowded plazas, busy markets, and child-filled playgrounds create a rhythm that insists on the city as a useful space for its inhabitants (fig. 3.10).[17] A point of view is evident as one draws connections between the photographs and the architects' emphasis on the use of space, humanization of scale, and the conversion of wasted space into areas for leisure, commerce, and growth.

The camera captures scenes that, when framed by the book, transform the visual data into a description of the role of urbanism in everyday life. The photographs also provide the prelude to the maps and graphs in the book's second half, which comprises statements from numerous CIAM members and projects from CIAM groups across Europe and the United States. Paul Zucker, in his 1953 review of the book for *Progressive Architecture,* praised the book's design: "This volume, with its extraordinary and witty layout, is as pleasing for the eye as it is basic for present and future activities in city planning."[18] It was the connection between the city made visible (through photography) and the analysis of visual data through the use of CIAM proposals that enabled the book's editors to hit a balance between the pleasures of the eye and the work of the mind.[19]

REFLECTING ON MASS COMMUNICATION

Sert included within *The Heart of the City* a revealing commentary on the relation of publishing and promotion to CIAM in general, and to his own work specifically. Prior to Part I appears Le Corbusier's July 1951 text titled "What are you?" In the text, staged as a dialogue, the interlocutor makes an appeal to the Everyman to see in CIAM an advisor to everyday experiences in the world. The town

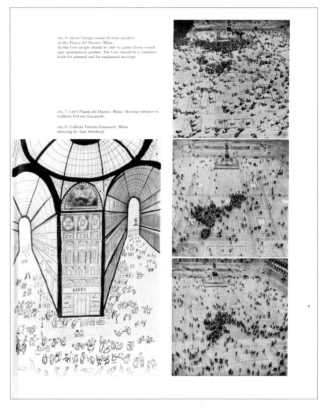

Figure 3.9 From *The Heart of the City*

planners and the architects in CIAM can help, Le Corbusier insisted. Part of CIAM's guidance comes in the form of the publications reproduced alongside the two-page article. The reproduction of CIAM publications within the body of the group's current work was not a novelty, though it may have taken on added importance to Sert, whose most recent book, *Can Our Cities Survive?* was featured on the second page. The cover designed by Bayer stands out among the previous publications and is echoed within *The Heart of the City* by two of Bayer's designs in Paul Lester Wiener's article "New Trends Will Affect the Core." Sert's first American book is now part of CIAM history, part of the proof of the organization's efforts and a demonstration of Sert's leading role in creating useful resources for the future of "modern development."

Closing the book is Le Corbusier's "Description of the CIAM Grid, Bergamo 1949," which reflects on the problem of rising publishing costs and the cumbersome transportation of exhibition materials. Le Corbusier's solution, one that he developed with fellow members of ASCORAL (Association des Constructeurs pour la Rénovation Architecturale), was the rationalization of visual and textual material into the "poetry of classification." The Grid was to

become a "thinking tool" and a means to make the proposal of ideas possible through easy exhibition and publication. He explained, "Here in the Grid the size of each separate sheet has been reduced to the printer's scale. These standard sheets can go straight to press complete with sufficient detail to expound all town planning schemes in all their detail." The Grid provided flexibility, structure, and mobility. While small versions of plans could be stored in a box, the larger-scale Grids could be displayed for consultation and critique. Le Corbusier saw in design a solution to the problems of promoting ideas about urban reform. As Sert argued in

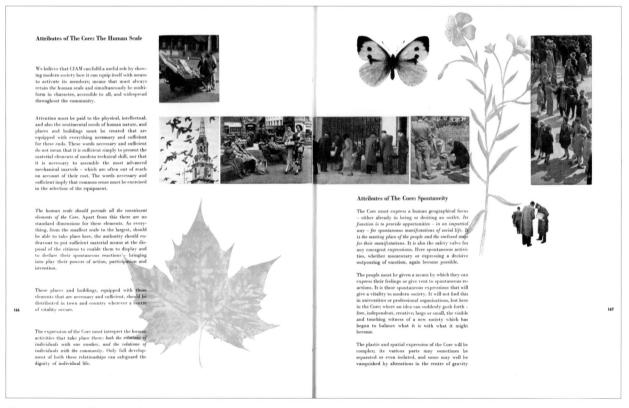

Figure 3.10 From *The Heart of the City*

The Heart of the City, Le Corbusier asserted that if the right information clearly presented could find its audience, the Everyman would agree on the validity and viability of CIAM's proposals.

Sert shared Le Corbusier's belief in the power of the image to make change. He turned to photography continuously throughout his career and repeatedly made use of mass media to introduce his ideas to a general public to gain recognition for his architectural designs. Many leading photographers worked with Sert, from Sala and Michaelis to Francesc Català Roca and Hans Namuth. Sert himself was also a photographer, and there is a large archive of materials from his personal collection awaiting analysis. His understanding of photography as a means to document and diagnose the problems and possibilities of modern architecture and urbanism is partly visible through his use of print culture. But another relationship with photography, perhaps more personal and interactive, is yet to be studied. At the intersection of these two ways of working with images (as a practice and as a critical and promotional tool) lies Sert's contribution to modern architecture's transformation into image, and the use of images to transform modern architecture during the twentieth century.

NOTES

I thank Mary Daniels (Special Collections librarian, Frances Loeb Library, Harvard University Graduate School of Design) and Andreu Carrascal (Arxiu Històric, Col.legi d'Arquitectes de Catalunya) for their generous assistance in the preparation of this essay. It was published in Spanish as "Sert y la imagen," *DC Papeles* (Barcelona) 13–14 (2005): 130–139.

1. For biographical and contextual information about Sert's life and career, I am indebted to Josep M. Rovira, *José Luis Sert,* 1901–1983 (Milan: Electa, 2000).

2. According to Huson Jackson, Sert turned to photography for many reasons: to document and promote, and to record the context of building projects. Although outside the scope of this essay, Sert's later uses of photography are critical to understanding how ingrained photography was in his design process. Email from Huson Jackson to the author, March 1, 2004.

3. "Nuestra inexperiencia ha sido desde luego el primero y principal motivo, de este retraso; pero no dudeis de nuestra voluntad y de nuestro entusiasmo." Letter from J. Torres Clavé to F. García Mercadal, March 10, 1931. GATCPAC Archive, Arxiu Històric, Col.legi d'Arquitectes de Catalunya (COAC).

4. For more on the photographs by Sala and Michaelis, see my "Architecture, Photography and (Gendered) Modernities in 1930s Barcelona," *Modernism/Modernity* 10, no. 1 (January 2003): 141–164.

5. For a full discussion and documentation of Michaelis's work in Spain, see *Margaret Michaelis: Fotografía, vanguardia y política en la Barcelona de la República* (Valencia: IVAM Centro Julio Gonzàlez, and Barcelona: CCCB, 1998).

6. Chris Ealham has examined the mythic construction of Barcelona's fifth district, especially in relation to the place it held for the city's working class, and has called for careful attention to the designation of the district as the Barrio Chino, a name that has often been used unproblematically despite the particular historical complexities that surround the perception of the district as a site of political and social conflict. See Chris Ealham, "An 'Imagined Geography': Ideology, Urban Space and Protest in the Creation of Barcelona's 'Chinatown,' c. 1835–1936," *International Review of Social History* 50 (2005): 373–397.

7. Sert's understanding of photography was no doubt invaluable to his design (with Luis Lacasa) of the exhibition space for the display of Josep Renau's photomurals in the Spanish Pavilion at the 1937 Exposition Internationale des Arts et Techniques dans la vie Moderne in Paris.

8. "José Luis Sert–Architect–Town Planner Biographical Notes," Josep Lluís Sert Collection, Frances Loeb Library, Harvard University Graduate School of Design (JLS).

9. An interesting, earlier connection between Giedion's publications and Sert is in a June 1931 letter from F. García Mercadal to J. Torres Clavé, in which Mercadal suggests: "Sert tiene el librito 'Befreites Wohnen' de Giedion que debía ser traducido y publicado dado lo breve y gracioso de su texto." COAC.

10. Letter from Joseph Hudnut (dean, Graduate School of Design) to Dumas Malone (director, Harvard University Press), November 19, 1941. JLS.

11. Rovira, *Sert,* 110.

12. Letter from Sert to Joseph Hudnut, October 3, 1941. JLS.

13. "Memorandum. January 17, 1941. Notes on the manuscript entitled: 'Should our cities survive?' prepared by Josep Lluís Sert in collaboration with the Congrès Internationaux d'Architecture Moderne." JLS.

14. Letter from Dumas Malone to Joseph Hudnut, November 27, 1942. JLS.

15. Letter from Sert to Serge Chermayeff, February 1, 1951. JLS.

16. Letter from Sert to Jaqueline Tyrwhitt, August 8, 1951. JLS.

17. See, for example, Sigfried Giedion's "Historical Background to the Core," which includes photographs of Aldo van Eyck's playgrounds in Amsterdam. Van Eyck would also actively turn to photography in the preparation of his own presentations, including his Grid panel for CIAM 10, 1956, on "the playground as core and extension of the doorstep." I thank Eric Mumford for pointing out this connection; a reproduction of van Eyck's Grid panel is reproduced in Mumford, *The CIAM Discourse on Urbanism* (Cambridge, Mass.: MIT Press, 2000), 251.

18. Paul Zucker, Review of *The Heart of the City,* in *Progressive Architecture* 34 (February 2, 1953): 174.

19. The dynamic role of photography that emerges in *The Heart of the City,* and has its foundation in earlier publications by Sert and CIAM, would proliferate in later CIAM projects, especially in the work by Team 10.

Part Two

THE LATIN AMERICAN
PLANNING EXPERIENCE

Chapter 4

PLANOS, PLANES Y PLANIFICACIÓN

Josep Lluís Sert and the Idea of Planning

TIMOTHY HYDE

On the company letterhead of Town Planning Associates, the name of Josep Lluís Sert appeared between those of his partners, Paul Lester Wiener and Paul Schulz, who were identified respectively as director of design and architect. Sert's title was town planner.[1] An appellation based less upon realized work than upon a theoretical position Sert had begun to articulate in his prewar projects, the assumed identity of town planner foreshadowed Sert's conception of the role of architecture in postwar modernity. Between 1941 and 1959, Sert and Wiener worked in collaboration to produce nearly a dozen pilot and master plans in Latin America, most of them unrealized.[2] From 1952 until 1959 they developed an array of projects for Cuba that culminated in an unexecuted Pilot Plan for Havana produced for the Cuban government. In 1942, in his book *Can Our Cities Survive?* Sert had argued that the modern city was deteriorating, edging toward crisis. Through his work in Cuba, Sert attempted to demonstrate how architecture might intervene in the

city to help reverse this trajectory of degeneration, establishing the basis for a subsequent role as Josep Lluís Sert, urban designer.

The task of Town Planning Associates in Latin America was planning, which is to say the firm's work was instrumental and programmatic, with legislative, infrastructural, and architectural components all intended to facilitate and advance the process of modernization. Like most of the diverse concepts of planning in circulation at the time, the idea of planning that Sert and Wiener endorsed was motivated by a perceived urban disorder whose manifestations ranged from nagging inefficiency to threatening chaos. This disorder might be overcome by a deliberate pairing of analysis and projection. The Athens Charter had specified, for example, that planning "must foresee the different stages of urban development in time and space. It must coordinate the natural, sociological, economic, and cultural factors." In Cuba, the planner Eduardo Montoulieu defined the neologism *planificación* as a "coordination of conscious efforts and the rational adaptation of methods to obtain results; this entails looking to the future to define objectives and, after having analyzed the past with a fair assessment of the available resources at the time and in the future, setting out to achieve them."[3] Sert and Wiener linked the planning process to social progress. For Sert, planning was the "re-creation of cities to fill man's most urgent needs,"[4] while in Wiener's words, the "fundamental function of planning is to contribute to the cultural and physical betterment of man."[5]

In his definition of planificación, Montoulieu deliberately contrasted the two Spanish words for plan, *plan* and *plano,* arguing that "planificar es mucho más que hacer planos, es hacer planes."[6] His statement pointed to the peculiar relationship between the conceptual program and the representational figure that derived from the primary ambition to legislate order through planning. Conceived as a normative framework, flexible yet controlling, planning implied that intervention at any point would affect all other components of the plan, and that civic order, the prerequisite for social and physical welfare, could be achieved through the realization of formal order. But to what extent might the necessary reciprocity between the formal object, the plano, and the conceptual projection, the plan, constrain the fuller ambitions of planning? Reciprocity licensed Josep Lluís Sert, architect, to become Josep Lluís Sert, town planner, yet the complex exchange between the discursive and the formal in Sert's work reveals that the parallel orders of plan and plano do not necessarily coincide. Instances of these analogous orders in the projects of his Cuba work and the discourse that surrounded them make evident the production of a discursive space for an architecture that reverberates beyond its limits into its urban context, using the relationship of plan and plano as an opportunity to amplify its own effect.

THE ORDER OF PLANNING

In 1953, at CIAM 9, Paul Wiener submitted a paper entitled "Man's Habitat," in which he categorized the human environment at different scales of association.[7] In a later version of the paper published in *Nuestra Architectura* he included a diagram that resolved this environment into four components: the physical habitat, the productive habitat, the social and spiritual habitat, and physical communication (fig. 4.1). It further specified a scalar series linked by these zones, with four squares representing the home, the neighborhood, the city, and the region. These squares were contained in turn by two circles representing the world and the cosmos. Wiener's diagram asserted a clear statement of order. By representing the levels of association from the home to the region as an increase in scale through the concentric squares, it emphasized the continuity between them, suggesting that the same criteria of analysis and prescription could be applied to each. At the scale of the world and cosmos, the graphic changed to a circle, indicating a perceptible distinction. The four zones of the diagram corresponded roughly to the four functions of the city specified in the Athens Charter—the physical to dwelling, the productive to work, the spiritual to leisure, and communication to circulation—but the values assigned by this diagram differed from those in the charter. Not only did the diagram describe the full compass of man's environment, but it also emphasized the relationship between zones more than the categories themselves. The physical and productive zones mirrored one another, forming a background that set the scales into relief; the communicative and the socio-spiritual zones acted as ligatures binding the scales together, with the greater width of the latter band revealing its paramount importance.

Wiener had not been involved in CIAM prior to the war, but afterward his own efforts to situate architecture as a discipline suited for technical consultancies with government agencies were well aligned with the broad CIAM agenda. Wiener made three lecture tours of South America sponsored by the U.S. State Department, during which he advocated a role for architecture to serve private or public agencies in the production of the norms that regulated social progress. In these lectures Wiener described his diagram as part of a projective plan of action, arguing that by representing the natural and social order in which any planning activity would take place, it would "help clarify present problems and signal the guidelines and procedures to be followed in future considerations."[8] Disputing any narrow limitation upon the role of architecture, Wiener insisted that the field would make broad, essential contributions to a new, more adequate human habitat, with an extension of the responsibilities of architecture both represented and enacted by the diagram. "My chart," he claimed, "is a step forward into the human environment to expand the area of [architects'] aspirations and humanistic utility." Its "practical value" lay in its graphic representation of the expanded territory of architecture and its succinct definition of the "basic interrelation of everything that influenced the human environ-

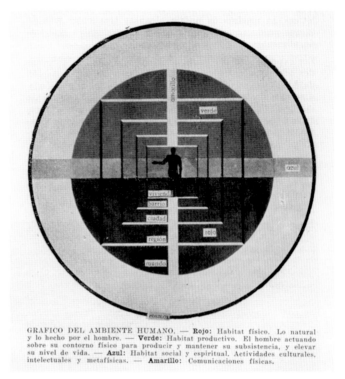

Figure 4.1 Paul Lester Wiener, "Diagram of the Human Environment," *Nuestra Arquitectura* (1953)

ment. In all the levels or cells these are the things that we ought to project in two- or three-dimensional terms, that is to say, the house, the neighborhood, the city or the region."[9]

The cellular scales of Wiener's diagram were not unprecedented. Sert had employed similar categories in his 1944 essay "The Human Scale in City Planning," beginning with the neighborhood unit and ascending through the township, the city, and the metropolitan area to the economic region.[10] Sert continued to regard these as the basic "units" of planning, conceptual elements with a direct relationship to the actual structure of the city. "Every city," he later explained, "is composed of cells," and the role of planning was to orient these "cells or units" in "some kind of system or relationship."[11] For CIAM 8 in 1951 the MARS Group had proposed that the theme of the meeting, the core, or the "Heart of the City," be studied at five "scale-levels" of community: the urban housing group, the urban residential neighborhood, the urban sector, the city, and the metropolis. According to Jaqueline Tyrwhitt's description in the subsequent publication, *The Heart of the City,* each of these scale-levels was a unit of social aggregation that, when combined as an urban environment, created the "area within which a full life can be lived with freedom of opportunity for the development of the potentialities of each individual."[12]

A related diagrammatic instrument, the MARS Grid, provided a standardized presentation format to be used by the Congress delegates to display their

work (fig. 4.2). Six columns organized information pertaining to the core, which existed in some form at each scale-level and thus served as a unifying conceptual element. The first three columns called for the same scalar series as Wiener's diagram, descending from the region to "the place"—which might be city, village, or neighborhood—to the core itself. The fourth column provided spaces for illustrations of the core, and the last two columns coordinated diurnal and historical temporal depictions. Sert, as president of CIAM, likely participated in the development of this presentation format, which illustrated the intention to classify and order disparate and variable elements by enforcing a continuity between scalar relationships and temporal sequences.

In this regard, the MARS Grid was actually a "simplification" of the CIAM Grid designed by Le Corbusier for CIAM 7.[13] Like the MARS Grid, it

Figure 4.2 Town Planning Associates, Project for Chimbote, Peru, presented in the format of the MARS Grid

arrayed standard cells to permit visual comparisons between disparate types of information, but unlike the later version, the CIAM Grid was indexed both vertically and horizontally. The five columns corresponded to the four functions, with an additional miscellaneous category. The horizontal rows encompassed dimensions of planning—from climate and land use to economics and legislation to public opinion. These rows were separated into two groups, one representing the proposition itself and the other representing rational and sentimental public reaction. For presentation, the CIAM Grid was to be displayed horizontally, with its axes inverted, and with the relevant cells filled with maps, drawings, text, or photographs.

Although capable of incorporating information pertaining to any scale, the CIAM Grid did not employ the scalar structure of the previous examples, aiming instead to fix myriad types of data into a coherent schema. The resulting representation portrayed the discrete parts as fungible, homologous elements, so that a relationship between, for example, legislation, climatic conditions, and public enthusiasm would be readily apparent. The organization of the grid suggests that all of the information is made commensurable by the format of the grid itself, a presumption evident in Le Corbusier's descriptions of its efficacy: the two coordinates, he claimed, would accommodate "all forms of analysis and commentary (public opinion, public authority, specialists, sociologists, economists, technicians, etc.)," in effect translating between their different modalities.[14] Its scope, moreover, was comprehensive, spanning "the environment of a kitchen and the environment of a continent,"[15] and the modest

dimensions of the grid, he boasted, were "all the space necessary to contain the graphic presentation of our civilization."[16]

As Wiener would do for his own diagram, Corbusier insisted that his grid was not only an analytical method—a "science of measurement," a "tool for analysis"—but also a projective device—an "instrument for thinking," a "tool for synthesis."[17] "The Grid," he readily conceded, "does not pretend to make fine town planning schemes of itself," but instead imposes a structure upon the dense and disorderly material of a planning problem and enables its user "to construct a mental architecture amid the chaos."[18] Although offered as analytical methods, each of these discursive artifacts contained predispositions toward a particular idea of planning that positioned architecture within a larger matrix of urban activity. More significant than their presumption of universality—evidence of a pervasive insistence upon scientific, rational thought as a shared fact of contemporary life—was the capacity of these diagrams, charts, and orders to connect architecture to the domain of planning. Sert had made this aspiration evident when, in the opening chapter of *Can Our Cities Survive?* he specified the narrative structure of his analysis: "Let us take note of what we see in our city, as a pedestrian would in its streets and parks, or visiting its dwellings, offices, factories, and shops. By assembling our observations, we should arrive at a view of the whole which will help us understand the urban organism in all its functions."[19] The process Sert described was not simply inductive analysis but a stipulation of the interrelationship of scales and modalities that endowed the representational artifacts described above with projective potential. Significantly, each of these artifacts proposed a continuous field of operations, with no points of disjuncture or incommensurability, by deploying two structures of order—one of scale, the other of typological classification—both of which encompassed the full dimensions of planning without interruption. The order of scale traveled from architecture to urban design to the regional plan, while the typological order bound together the heterogeneous content—be it technical, linguistic, visual, or emotional—of any single scalar instance.

The projects in Cuba required the application of these conceptual models to a historical situation of political and social complexities and physical and economic specificities. How could this idea of planning engage the contingencies of a situational context? How did the seamless realm of the plan converge with the formal projections of the plano? Before taking up those questions, it must be emphasized that each of these representational artifacts already contains moments that elude its apparently stable order. In Wiener's diagram, there is the subtle shift between his recoded four functions and those of the Athens Charter; Wiener's differentiation disrupts the causal relationship between physical environment and form to which a technocratic vision would subscribe. The MARS Grid allows the distinction of unconnected categories, as with its break between physical and temporal parameters; the two blank panels in Sert's Chimbote presentation indicate a blind spot in the classification system. In the CIAM Grid, the forced equivalence of "rational" and "sentimental" categories only highlights their incongruence, while the inclusion of both a column and a row categorized as "miscellaneous" strives to contain unanticipated ambiguities. Even Sert's five units of planning, when compared to the MARS Group's scale-levels and to Wiener's cells, show that while scalar logic prevails, the prime component of aggregation is inconstant—the neighborhood unit in one instance, the core in the next, and the home in the last. These equivocal moments in the discursive norms would produce malleable couplings to formal orders, becoming the productive sites for an urban architecture.

THE CODE OF URBANISM

An impulse to analyze and classify was evident in the initial stages of the Pilot Plan for Havana as well. Immediately after being retained as consultants to the Cuban government in 1955, Town Planning Associates assigned extensive research work to the architects, engineers, and draftsmen of the Junta Nacional de Planificación (JNP), the newly created national planning office, requesting that the JNP compile and represent data ranging from climate and land values to family sizes and school attendances. This information was shown in standardized formats, usually in overlays on the map of Havana, to provide a "fair assessment" of existing conditions upon which future objectives could be projected. But to describe this as the beginning of the Pilot Plan is a somewhat fictional account. The JNP did hire Town Planning Associates as consultants in 1955, and the firm did then begin work on the Pilot Plan. And although an orderly process of planning would proceed from analysis to plan to project, events did not actually occur in that sequence.

Sert's professional engagement with Cuba actually began in 1952, when an investor group in New

York commissioned Town Planning Associates to design an entry for the Cuban National Housing Program. Sert and Wiener submitted a neighborhood unit with typical housing, as well a school, a market, and a church. In 1953 another group commissioned the design of a resort hotel on the Isle of Pines off Cuba's southern coast. Early in 1953, Sert joined a rising debate over the need for national planning in Cuba, arguing the advantages of preparing a Pilot Plan for Havana in a telegram sent to Eugenio Batista, who was the head of the Cuban CIAM group ATEC (Agrupación Tectónica de Expresión Contemporánea).[20] In September, Town Planning Associates submitted a formal memorandum to Nicolás Arroyo, another member of ATEC who was then director of the planning office for Varadero, again proposing a Pilot Plan for Havana. In the memo, Sert and Wiener advocated the creation of a metropolitan planning office with their firm as consultant, and also recommended the preparation of regional and national plans for Cuba. These and further efforts to secure a contract failed, but in 1954 Town Planning Associates did become informally involved in the Pilot Plan for Varadero. At the same time, Arroyo offered the firm a collaborative role in a new subdivision called Quinta Palatino, and Sert and Wiener adapted their earlier housing plan to the new site and program.

Sert's personal ties to these Cuban architects and planners could have sustained the impression that Town Planning Associates was working with disinterested technicians; but even though the existence of ministries and a legislature provided a republican cast, Sert and Wiener were aware that the government was the dictatorship of Fulgencio

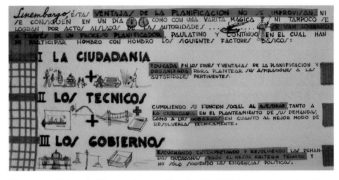

Figure 4.3 Eduardo Montoulieu, outline for "Exhibition on Urbanism," Lyceum y Lawn Tennis Club, Havana, 1943

Batista. However, the advocacy for national planning should not be entirely conflated with Batista's authoritarian regime, which came to power in 1952, more than a decade after the advocacy commenced. The new Cuban constitution of 1940 had provided a model normative structure that influenced a variety of social and institutional practices over the next twelve years, during which Cuba was led by democratically elected presidents. The planner Eduardo Montoulieu, for example, along with other members of Cuba's professional and intellectual associations, implicitly referred to the 1940 constitution in proposing a regimen of planificación to coordinate the interactions of citizens, technicians, and the government (fig. 4.3). Though Sert and Wiener recognized the complicity implied by their work for Batista's government, their institutional colleagues were the associations that had been supporting the project for some years and under different governments.[21] By the end of 1954 the continued lobbying of a diverse group of advocates had reenergized efforts to create a national planning board. Motivated likely by both progressive optimism and professional expediency,

Town Planning Associates gave their strong support to these efforts, and even recruited Charles Haar, professor at Harvard Law School, to review and comment on drafts of the enabling legislation.

In January 1955, when the Junta Nacional de Planificación was officially formed with Arroyo as president and Montoulieu as director, Town Planning Associates had already involved itself extensively in the formation of the planning office. Rather than seeing the Pilot Plan for Havana as the beginning of a planning process, then, it is more accurate to regard it as a consolidation and an extension of earlier trajectories. The carefully graduated presentation sequence of the published Pilot Plan—proceeding from a national program to a metropolitan plan to typical buildings—gives a deceptive impression of methodical formulation. In actuality the plan incorporated much of Town Planning Associates' earlier unrealized work for

Figure 4.4 Town Planning Associates, Pilot Plan for Havana, Metropolitan Area

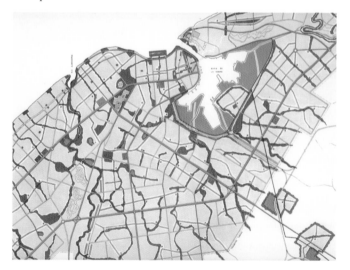

Cuba and for other cities in Latin America.[22] The Pilot Plan was a collation of discrete architectural elements induced into a comprehensive proposition; it supplied as much a retrospective as a prospective framework of order.

The Pilot Plan addressed the entire metropolitan area of Havana, with its dozens of plates illustrating proposals at a variety of scales and in all areas of the city, from the old colonial quarter of Habana Vieja at the mouth of the harbor to the industrial areas clustered around the bay to the expanding perimeter of the city (fig. 4.4).[23] The plan included recommendations for the regulated development of unbuilt areas, the administrative division of the metropolitan area into urban sectors, and the distribution of the four functions of the Athens Charter through new zoning. At an urban scale, it described a new organization of linear parks and linked "civic nuclei" laced throughout the existing city. The plan offered architectural propositions as well, such as an artificial island and new buildings to be raised on landfill along the Malecón adjacent to Habana Centro, the reconfiguration of the Plaza Cívica already under construction south of Vedado, and the extensive reconstruction of Habana Vieja.

Sert and Wiener sought to provide a consistent framework that was at the same time flexible enough to engage the varied urban morphology of Havana. The *intramuros* district of Habana Vieja, with streets only a few meters wide, colonial *palacios,* and hardly any tall structures, was very different from Vedado, platted on a grid with wide boulevard streets in the early twentieth century and housing dozens of high-rise condominium buildings. Elsewhere, the Pilot Plan had to accommodate topographical particularities, such as the Almendares river that separated Vedado from the Miramar district; the ridge occupied by the Universidad de la Habana, between Vedado and Habana Centro; the Loma de los Catalanes, a small hill upon which the new Plaza Cívica was located; and the sweeping coastline facing the ocean and the inner harbor. The physical fabric of Havana registered the differentiations of historical periods and institutional singularities, but the aim of the Pilot Plan was to contain these within a legible conceptual order.

Perhaps the most important new element proposed in the Pilot Plan was an extensive road system for the city and its environs. This road system supplied the armature of all of the plates in the published plan, even those of existing conditions, suggesting that the network was its crucial ordering gesture.[24] It would certainly have had the most significant effect on the existing city, and its orderly arrangement concealed the inevitable violence of cuts through the existing fabric. But the plan emphasized not the routes—some were new, some followed existing roads, others were only "suggestions"—but rather the classification of the roads according to the Rule of the 7V, Le Corbusier's hierarchical system of circulation proposed in 1950 for the Bogotá plan that he produced in collaboration with Town Planning Associates.

The Rule of the 7V classified roadways according to speed, attempting a decisive separation of pedestrian and vehicular environments. V1 was the classification for limited-access expressways, allowing the frictionless flow of traffic required by a modern city, while V7 identified a pedestrian route, guaranteeing the maintenance of a "human scale" in the

urban environment. The five remaining categories spanned between these two to create a harmonious order of circulation. This abstraction of the circulatory function offers yet another example of smooth scalar transposition, but the Rule of the 7V also contained an encounter with existing urban patterns. The V4, lined with shops and streets according to Le Corbusier's detailed description, followed "existing bridal paths, easy, and usually winding roads, not made by human genius, but by the passage of much traffic."[25] By incorporating these established routes into the overall classification, Corbusier argued, the 7V created a rational system adequate to new urban conditions but permitted "life [to] continue to flow along its old traditional route."[26] Sert and Wiener made this same distinction in their Pilot Plan, introducing new expressways and improving existing roads but also identifying existing "Main Streets" to serve as V4 roads. Their text specified that "these main streets . . . follow the winding lines of the old roads opened between the property lines of the sugar plantations and large farms; they were never meant for the transportation means of today or those of tomorrow."[27] In their plans, V4 roads wind unevenly through the new circulatory grid, disrupting the sequential order of scale with the inconsistencies of use and habit (fig. 4.5).

Typological order was undermined here as well in the contrast of the principle of the 7V with the statistical methods of traffic engineering. On behalf of the JNP, Sert and Wiener retained experts in relevant fields and were responsible for integrating their expertise into the plan. Engineering recommendations were provided by the firm of Seeyle, Stevenson, Value and Knecht, which in 1956 helped

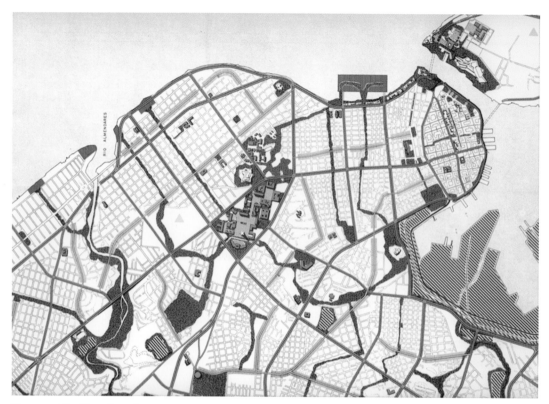

Figure 4.5 Pilot Plan, Central Area

devise the road network superimposed upon the existing city; this preliminary layout indicated road types but did not follow the Rule of the 7V. Their detailed proposal, based upon calculations of existing and anticipated traffic densities, included four road types, with typical roadway sections modified from the standards the same engineers had developed for the Bogotá plan. By 1958 the road layout remained untouched, but the engineers' classifications had been replaced with the 7V classifications. The road sections were keyed according to both systems, so that, for example, road type D-D was also captioned as type V4. The two classifications, however, did not actually correspond, and diagrams showed the V4 as a single street whereas the engineers proposed a divided roadway. A memo from Paul Schulz to Sert on the subject of road widths in Habana Vieja confirmed this malleability: "We used the Bogota V3 standard. The Havana V3 standard . . . I thought too wide."[28] These details expose a willingness to reconcile the conceptual system to existing conditions and, more important, the insuperable incommensurability of two modalities, one mathematical and the other figural.

The proposed reorganization of streets would have required significant physical interventions throughout the city but would undoubtedly have had the greatest impact upon Habana Vieja, for which the Pilot Plan proposed extensive reconstruction (fig. 4.6). The plan called for the extension of the new road system into its compact, dense urban fabric, with two new broad avenues dividing the district into four sectors. Within these sectors, streets newly dedicated to pedestrian use alternated with streets widened for vehicular traffic; the narrower streets would maintain the "traditional small scale street of Havana" while the wider ones eased the congestion of traffic. Sert's and Wiener's concern for the relationship of old and new was evident in the proposed preservation of monuments in old Havana, including intact "clusters" of buildings that could "form charming streets, beautiful in scale, recalling the origins of the city."[29] But in sharp contrast to these

"archeological zones," the plan proposed tall towers for a new financial area along the central axis of the district. This complex, to have housed the banking institutions historically located in Old Havana, bears no relationship to the surrounding fabric; its motivation was to encourage those institutions to remain in the old district rather than join the westward sprawl.[30] The Pilot Plan attempted to reconcile two disparate elements: the historical contingencies of the existing Habana Vieja, and the normative order of an overall conceptual plan. In fact, the plan tempered an earlier proposal in which Old Havana and much of the adjacent Malecón was to be demolished and reassembled into superblocks with widely spaced high-rise slabs.

Figure 4.6 Pilot Plan, Habana Vieja

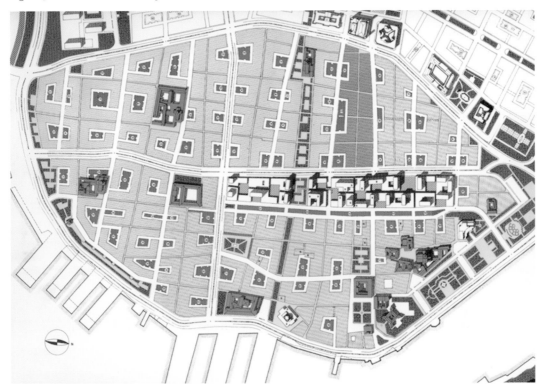

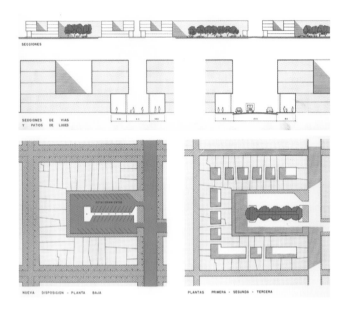

Figure 4.7 Pilot Plan, typical cuadra configuration for Habana Vieja

A series of sketches produced by Wiener in 1955 began the transformation of the proposal for Habana Vieja from a cluster of superblocks into an articulated layout resembling the final plan devised by Sert with Mario Romañach, the Cuban architect in charge of the JNP office responsible for the Pilot Plan. Wiener's sketches suggest the considered restitution of existing elements: studies of the overall district restored specific streets to the central area, and his notations recorded the idea of "integrating" an historic zone with recreational and residential areas; tracings of the southern half showed the superblocks eroded by interior streets, and ultimately returned to the existing *cuadra* outlines. The cuadra, the block of the traditional Latin American city, signified the continuity of urban morphology and could serve as an iterable unit to be adapted to different densities and programs

(fig. 4.7). In Old Havana, Sert and Wiener proposed the cuadra as a "typical" element, suggesting that its interior be opened to create a central patio, or courtyard, and its perimeter built directly against the pedestrian and vehicular streets, with the first floor carved away by an arcade. They indicated that the central patios could have many uses; in commercial areas, parking would be most practical, but in areas of greater residential density the patios should be gardens, play spaces, and parks—the detailed plans showed more sheltered patios in the residential area for just this reason. The typical plans also suggested that existing lot lines might be maintained, and the cuadras might also have incorporated existing buildings, as they were to have done in Bogotá. For Sert and Wiener, their proposal for Old Havana was not a wholesale demolition but rather a calibration of existing and modern elements within a new structural order, a structural order itself inspired by the ideal order of the foundational cities of Latin America. The cuadra solution evidences the manner in which a formal component was produced to complement the conceptual order through the careful screening and manipulation of existing components and criteria.

In the plan, the typical cuadra defined an overall mass and a relationship to street and to patio. These factors would be subject to *condicionales,* or height and setback requirements, with which Sert was evidently preoccupied. His notes, for example, included data on setbacks at several new subdivisions in the city, as well as dimensions from colonial buildings. Historic areas, he conceded, might have unique requirements, but he proposed that existing typical buildings could "be used as measuring units and help toward the determination of lot sizes, clearances between buildings, setbacks from street lines, and yard spaces." The intention was to define "standards that . . . fit as well as possible into the established customs of the country."[31] For the cuadra configurations of Old Havana, the plan illustrated specific condicionales. The pedestrian streets maintained the narrow width of the original streets; the vehicular streets were dimensioned for their new traffic flow requirements. The height of the cuadra, however, was set in proportion to the width of the street by an angle derived from Le Corbusier's Modulor; the complementary angle determined the dimensions of the interior patio openings.

The incorporation of the Modulor, perhaps as a drafting shorthand, was hardly surprising given its prominence at the time. Corbusier published *Modulor 2* in 1955, and according to Sert's own account, he had actually been using the scale since its preliminary introduction in 1948.[32] Sert supplied no fewer than three separate testimonials for Corbusier's volumes. The first, written in 1948, exclaimed, "Working on a job for Lima (a town plan), I have tried out the 'Modulor.' What a wonderful find! In urbanism and all large-scale projects, it is a most valuable aid. With it, you can determine standard heights, dimensions and limit volumes, and by doing so lay the foundations for a legal code of urbanism."[33] The Modulor offered yet another instance of scalar logic, now explicitly formal rather analytical in function. It is familiar enough that its details need not be rehearsed, but three points should be emphasized: the first is that the Modulor was a scalar system without any breaks or points of singularity—it did not begin from zero, but from

a geometric relationship that enabled it to increase or decrease infinitely; the second is Corbusier's assertion that the Modulor reconciled disparate systems of measurement and proportion, overcoming the frictions between metric units, English units, and the human body, and uniting them into a coherent scale that provided a harmony of parts at any perceptual dimension—a synthesizing ambition that paralleled the typological binding of his grid; and third, that the Modulor was based on a small but real mathematical mistake, the incorrect presumption of a geometric relationship between its two proportional series.[34]

The presence of this mistake, and the further compromise of the famously arbitrary adjustment of the "typical" height of the male figure, are moments of instability that betray the ambition of the Modulor—the attempt to imagine and construct a continuous field that united distinct elements. The Modulor, claimed its author, "is a flawless fabric formed of stitches of every dimension, from the smallest to the largest, a texture of perfect homogeneity."[35] But he offered the Modulor as more than an abstract concept; it was an instrument of design that could translate between classificatory analysis and objects of built form. When Sert declared that the Modulor could "lay the foundations for a legal code of urbanism" by governing condicionales, he expressed his desire for an operative correspondence between a conceptual and a social order. But if the mandate for condicionales expressed his desire for embodied order, his advocacy for the incorporation of existing practices into new standards acknowledged the possibility that such ordering systems would establish norms, not universal absolutes. The explicit contrast, for example, between one street dimensioned with the Modulor and another by historic fact demonstrated the inevitable and deliberate modulation of his discursive ideal. But such transformations, while they forestalled claims to universality, did not entirely restrain the normative ambitions expressed discursively in diagrams and charts.

THE ENCLOSURE OF ARCHITECTURE

The conceptual orders of Sert's idea of planning that encompassed the urban configurations of the Pilot Plan also supply a lens through which to examine the architectural components of the Pilot Plan and to understand their relation to the urban context. Beginning with their 1948 Chimbote project in Peru, Sert and Wiener devoted much effort to the design and elaboration of their innovative model of carpet housing, creating an extensive inventory of typical solutions. The last of their housing projects was the Sector Typico proposed in the Pilot Plan. This "typical neighborhood sector" was actually the

Figure 4.8 Pilot Plan, typical neighborhood unit

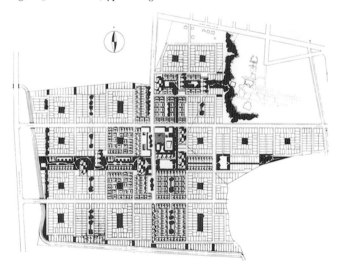

Quinta Palatino project developed previously with Arroyo and his colleagues, which was itself a project that Sert and Wiener adapted from their 1952 submission for the Cuban National Housing Program. The "typical" solution had emerged from a series of proposals that addressed different and particular circumstances.

Quinta Palatino, one of many subdivisions rapidly expanding the metropolitan area, had been commissioned as a speculative venture, but Sert and Wiener saw it as a proposal well suited to the environmental, social, and urban conditions of Havana—a typical neighborhood unit. Almost all of their projects in Latin America incorporated such a component, and by 1953 two distinct models had evolved: neighborhood units that maintained the formal organization of the cuadra, whose grid was readily incorporated into other elements of the plan, and neighborhood units in which the aggregate of the carpet housing defined the texture of the whole, punctuated by community buildings such as schools. Although the cuadra model expressed a more apparent order, the ideal order of the grid, it was in fact a concession to the influence of colonial tradition, while the carpet model employed in the new towns was an unadulterated expression of Sert's ideal plan.

In their housing schemes in Cuba, Sert and Wiener deployed both of these models. One drawing from the Pilot Plan showing Quinta Palatino as a typical sector represented the actual proposal for the unrealized speculative venture.[36] Here, neither the cuadra grid nor the carpet texture determined the overall layout, which was configured according to existing exigencies of subdivision. The facing page, however, offered another version, this one with the systematic organization of the cuadras (fig. 4.8). In this configuration, patios appeared within houses, at the center of the cuadras, and as public plazas surrounded by communal buildings. Here, and more fully in the typical neighborhood unit of the Cuban Housing proposal, where the carpet model organized the design, the patio manifests the significant conceptual imperative that Sert assigned to it.[37] This particular plan was the subject of the 1953 article "Can Patios Make Cities?" in which Sert elaborated the urban role of the patio that he had first announced in his contribution to CIAM 8.[38] Sert had described the patio as a fundamental element of civic space that could define a core at any scale level. In the article, Sert refers to the patio as a "module," extending its range to reflect Wiener's diagram of the human habitat, linking the home ("patio house") and the city ("patio civic center") and organizing parks, community buildings, and neighborhoods as well (fig. 4.9). The article captures the proposition that an architectural element be used as an instrument of urbanism and measured along a continuous scale.

By 1957, Sert and Wiener were describing this concept as the "rebirth of the patio" and considering it a central conceit of their urban plans: "The patio becomes the predominant architectural feature in these designs. They range from the patio for the one-family dwelling to those between apartments or row houses, to the public neighborhood patios of the small local square, or the larger patio of the local core, and finally the series of patios or squares of the main urban or metropolitan cores."[39] Once again, this statement presumed the smooth flow of a scalar progression, and in doing so concealed a cru-

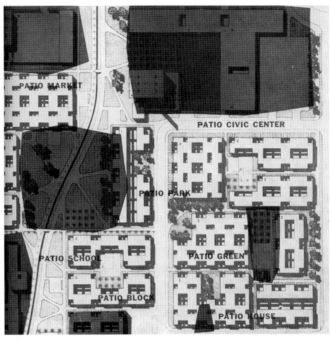

Figure 4.9 Detail plan from "Can Patios Make Cities?" *Architectural Forum* (August 1953)

cial moment of transition from the private realm of the individual to the social realm of the collective. Sert, interested on the one hand in the formal figure of the patio, and on the other in the social potential of the civic center, did not remark any conflict between the scaling of the formal type and the equivalent scaling of the social context. But his designs and writings made clear that the patio served two distinct purposes—at the scale of the house, exclusion; at the scale of the core, inclusion—a distinction that occurred along a seam in the graduated logic.

The patio houses that Sert and Wiener developed consisted of only three spatial zones: "areas cerradas, areas cubiertas, areas cercadas"—closed spaces, covered spaces, and enclosed spaces. The enclosed space, the patio, provided an outdoor room in which the family would enact daily life shielded from the public space of the street. Sert regarded this emphatic separation as essential, explaining that "if these outside spaces are not enclosed in patio form there will be no privacy and they will be useless."[40] In all of the housing types, a patio was located at the front of the house, with the street walls punctured only by doors or block screens. The private, protected interior is "contained within the walls. . . . Behind them, once you enter the house, you can be in a different world—the world that each family can build for itself."[41]

At the civic scale, on the other hand, the patio was inclusive, drawing together and integrating the disparate elements of community. It remained an enclosed space, encircled by buildings such as the library, market, and church, but it now was the symbolic and actual unity of these elements. The patio, Sert believed, could render an awareness of interdependence, acting "both as a setting for the expression of this sense of community and as an actual expression of it."[42] Its civic role prompted a different state of enclosure in the civic patio, with a more permeable boundary and more differentiated space than at the scale of the house. Programmatic requirements influenced this change, of course, but Sert's elaboration of the patio enclosure conveyed greater significance than just functional complexity. While exclusion could be accomplished with a wall, Sert achieved the goal of inclusion by staging a sequential relationship between central space and articulated programs. In the case of buildings such as the market or the school in the original Cuban Housing proposal, later presented as "typical" civic elements in the Pilot Plan, a repetition of patios supplied the

required mediation. At the school, for example, Sert used a boundary wall to demarcate the overall patio of the school complex, and individual patios placed adjacent to every classroom to subdivide the interior domain. In its simplest manifestation, the enclosure—the central object of Sert's architectural experimentation in his Latin American projects—consisted of the wall alone. In the context of the patio house, the articulation of the wall surface began moving toward his distinctive architectural idiom. His elaborate sketches documented attempts to control the relationship between interior and exterior—not, as in earlier works, by simply connecting the two, but by balancing the penetration of light, air, and views against the need for decisive boundaries. By the early 1950s the maturation of his architectural idiom enabled a conception of enclosure as a mediating boundary formed at any scale by wall and patio together to connect interior and exterior spheres while still preserving their specificities.

The implication of this architectural mediation for Sert's idea of planning may be illustrated with a final, unexecuted element of the Pilot Plan: the proposed presidential palace, the Palace of the Palms (fig. 4.10). It is impossible to consider this project without recalling that it was commissioned by the dictator, Fulgencio Batista. The association colors most aspects of the project—for example, Sert's attempt to prove the suitability of the building's scale by comparing it with other executive residences was more transparent flattery than analytical rigor. Yet the design merits consideration as a resonant example of Sert's architectural and urban intentions, and precisely because its coarse political instrumentality suggests the fragility of Sert's projec-

tions of architectural operations in urban scales
and contexts.

The project began in 1955, when Town Planning
Associates was commissioned in collaboration with
Cuban architects Mario Romañach and Gabriela
Menendez. Sert recruited Hideo Sasaki as landscape
architect and Felix Candela as structural engineer.
The palace was to house three functions—the presidential ministry, the presidential residence, and the
official reception halls. "The dominant problem,"
wrote Sert, "was to form an architectural unity from
the agglomerate parts and yet retain in each part the
character and expression appropriate to its function.
The repeated module of the structure . . . gives a
rhythm to the whole, but the most positive unifying
element . . . is the concrete shell roof."[43] Candela
helped to design this dense cluster of individual
parasols fashioned to evoke royal palm trees, a "symbol of Cuba." Sasaki was responsible for the articulation of the exterior gardens that extend outward the
four distinct orientations anchored by the central
patio of the palace. The eastern façade overlooked a
"traditional" Plaza de Armas—also a civic patio in
Sert's terms—to be used for public ceremonies. Two
entrances flanking a central balcony for presidential
appearances and the columns guarding the line of
the wall evoke a neoclassicism extremely unusual for
Sert. On the opposite façade, a single volume for the
reception hall with adjacent terraces balanced the
aggregate pieces of the residential quarters overlooking a private informal garden. An elevated terrace in
the middle joined the central patio to the expansive
view of the city of Havana. The result is unmistak-
ably similar in scale, organization, and potential to
the proposed typical cuadra.

Figure 4.10 Josep Lluís Sert, Mario Romañach, Gabriela
Menendez, Felix Candela, Hideo Sasaki, Palace of the Palms
(presidential palace), Havana, 1956–58, model

The basic premise of the palace project was a
calibration of independent elements and coherent
whole through an ordering device, in this case the
roof. This is very much the premise, and the promise, of Sert's idea of planning, which deployed formal mechanisms to reconstitute a civic order. The
desire to forge civic order through planning com-
pelled the parallel between the conceptual orders of
planning and the formal orders evident in his projects, and required from both the possibility of containing, comparing, and combining incommensu-
rable elements. Many of the resulting formal strategies, such as the cuadra, the patio, the Modulor, and
the road system, appear in the design of the palace
and its surroundings. Each of these normalizing
strategies proposes and permits the figurative extension of the building or the projection of its architectural effects. This projection is simultaneously lit-

eral, in the gardens that expand the distinct characters of the four façades; symbolic, in the presentation of tropes of civic expression such as the column grid that resolves into a monumental colonnade, and the national symbol of the royal palm; and, most important, normative, in the use of typical elements to place the architecture within scalar series and typological classifications and connect the palace to patios and cuadras manifested at other sites and scales. These elements also situate the palace within Sert's idea of planning, an uninterrupted discursive space in which an object realized at any one point subsequently reverberated up or down scalar sequences or through typological classifications.

The conceptual order of planning also facilitated the careful negotiation of the myriad contingencies of the Cuban context. The apparent frictions that confronted the constitution of a physical and social civic order—such as the existing circulatory patterns, the historical past and its artifacts, the economic exigencies of speculative development—could be subsumed within the normative framework of the plan. Sert and Wiener fashioned their practices of planificación from a reciprocal exchange between plan and plano; the chronology of the Cuba projects, in which many of the individual elements preceded the plan, evidences not, or not only, expediency on the part of Sert and Wiener, but the invention of a fabric of integration to encompass previously independent architectural objects. The inherent formal character of the patio or cuadra spanned between these independent figures and the environment represented in Wiener's diagram or the CIAM Grid. Together, these devices offered a mechanism for urban design whereby a singular architectural instance could be rendered legible at multiple scales and through the interpretive modes of multiple disciplines.

Sert's idea of planning, with its conjunction of discursive norms and architectural technique, was an idea situated as much within architecture as outside of it. And while the presidential palace project exemplifies the promise of this idea, it also makes visible its fragility. No other aspect of the plan accentuated so sharply the contradictions between the progressive ambitions and intentions of planning and the repressive social realities of Batista's Cuba. Viewed in the historical context of its design, the palace was removed from the fabric of the city by the narrow channel to the bay and segregated from its social context by its occupant's need for security. It repudiated the emancipatory intentions of planificación with its appropriation of progressive norms as symbols of power. It is difficult to imagine the project transcending the corrupting contingencies of its situation, although the connection between architecture and the project of normalization initiated by the 1940 constitution holds out such a possibility. In spite of their creator's aspirations, the conceptual orders supporting Sert's idea of planning were not "flawless fabrics." They contained elusive moments that provided potent architectural elaborations but also elided discordant transpositions. These moments did not all prove to be sites of invention but were productive flaws in the fabric, engagements between plan and plano that outlined the possibility and the limitations of an urban design.

NOTES

1. These denominations also appeared in publicity for the firm. The *New York Times* of March 26, 1945, in an article on the firm's proposal for prefabricated housing, referred to Wiener as designer, Schulz as architect, and Sert as city planner. But all three partners had been trained as architects, and although there was a division of responsibilities within the firm, it did not necessarily correspond to their official titles. Wiener, while maintaining an interest in industrial and exhibition design from his prewar activities, collaborated with Sert in the design and supervision of the firm's planning projects. Sert took design responsibility for most of the firm's architectural projects. Paul Schulz had primarily an administrative role in the firm. The three partners formed Town Planning Associates in 1942, although Sert and Wiener had been affiliated the previous year in a group called Planning Associates, composed of Sert, Wiener, and the architectural firm Morris & O'Connor. Sert and Wiener also worked independently for individual clients even during the period of their partnership.

2. The work of Town Planning Associates in Latin America is placed within the overall context of Sert's career in Josep M. Rovira, *José Luis Sert, 1901–1983* (Milan: Electa, 2003), and Josep M. Rovira, Eric Mumford, and Octavio Borgatello, eds., *Sert, 1928–1979: Half a Century of Architecture—Complete Work* (Barcelona: Fundació Joan Miró, 2005). The significance of the Latin American projects in their relation to CIAM urbanism is presented in Eric Mumford, "CIAM and Latin America," in Xavier Costa and Guido Hartray, eds., *Sert, arquitecto en Nueva York* (Barcelona: ACTAR, 1997), and in Patricia Schnitter, "José Luis Sert y Colombia: De la carta de Atenas a una carta del hábitat" (Ph.D. diss., Universitat Politécnica de Catalunya, 2002). The projects for Cuba that are the focus of this essay have received less attention.

3. Folder Addenda/TPA, Josep Lluís Sert Collection, Frances Loeb Library, Harvard University Graduate School of Design (JLS). Some material in this collection has been recatalogued, and the folder designations indicated here may have changed. All translations are by the author.

4. Josep Lluís Sert, *Can Our Cities Survive? An ABC of Urban Problems, Their Analysis, Their Solutions* (Cambridge, Mass.: Harvard University Press, 1942), 2.

5. Paul Lester Wiener, "El Ambiente humano y el urbanismo," *Nuestra Arquitectura* 320 (1956): 20.

6. "To plan is much more than to draw plans, it is to make plans of action" (Folder Addenda/TPA, JLS).

7. Wiener did not attend CIAM 9, but he submitted his paper to be read at the meeting. Wiener's participation in CIAM was likely initiated by his partnership with Sert, but consisted of quite individual contributions on his part. It began in 1944, when he joined the CIAM Chapter for Relief and Postwar Planning, and continued with his attendance at CIAM 6 and CIAM 7. His essay "New Trends Will Affect the Core" was published as part of the proceedings of CIAM 8. Wiener's concepts of planning and the environment, laid out in the context of CIAM, were components of the discourse that he and Sert jointly articulated in the work of Town Planning Associates.

8. Wiener, "El Ambiente humano y el urbanismo," 21. Wiener visited Brazil during the war and made extended lecture tours in South America in 1945, 1953, and 1956. The texts of his lectures are contained in Box 11, Paul Lester Wiener Collection (PLW), Special Collections, Knight Library, University of Oregon.

9. Ibid.

10. Josep Lluís Sert, "The Human Scale in City Planning," in Paul Zucker, ed., *New Architecture and City Planning* (New York: Philosophical Library, 1944), 398. Sert certainly did not invent these conceptual categories—the idea of the neighborhood unit can be traced to Clarence Perry's contribution to the Regional Plan of New York, and Patrick Geddes elaborated the significance of the region in his earliest writings—but the crucial point here is Sert's reliance upon the sequence as contiguous formal categories.

11. Josep Lluís Sert, "The Architect and the City," in H. Warren Dunham, ed., *The City in Mid-Century* (Detroit: Wayne State University Press, 1957), 21.

12. Jaqueline Tyrwhitt, "Cores Within the Urban Constellation," in Jaqueline

Tyrwhitt, ed., *The Heart of the City* (New York: Pellegrini and Cudahy, 1952), 105. Sert's close involvement with the publication is documented in his extensive correspondence with Tyrwhitt regarding the format, text, and illustrations for the volume.

13. Ibid. The thematic focus of CIAM 8 on the core placed an emphasis upon the representation of the core as a formal object in relation to a context, which permitted the distillation reflected by the format of the MARS Grid. Both the MARS Grid and the CIAM Grid are illustrated in *The Heart of the City*. For an examination of the epistemological presumptions of the grid format at CIAM Congresses alongside those of the scalar associations proposed as an alternative by Alison and Peter Smithson and other members of Team X, see Annie Pedret, "Dismantling the CIAM Grid: New Values for Modern Architecture," in Max Risselada and Dirk van den Heuvel, eds., *Team 10, 1953–81: In Search of a Utopia of the Present* (Rotterdam: NAI, 2005), 252–257.

14. Le Corbusier, "Grille CIAM d'urbanisme," *l'Architecture d'aujourd'hui*, January 1949, p. 12.

15. Le Corbusier, "Description of the CIAM Grid, Bergamo 1949," in *Heart of the City*, 172–174.

16. Le Corbusier, "Tools of Universality," *Transformations* 1 (1950): 42.

17. Corbusier, "Description of the CIAM Grid, Bergamo 1949," 174; Corbusier, "Tools of Universality," 42.

18. Corbusier, "Description of the CIAM Grid, Bergamo 1949," 172.

19. Sert, *Can Our Cities Survive?* 10.

20. During his temporary residence in Cuba in the spring of 1939, Sert himself had encouraged the establishment of ATEC. Its members included Nicolás Arroyo, Eduardo Montoulieu, Mario Romañach, and Rita Gutierrez, all of whom played a direct role in the planning proposals examined below.

21. The engagement between representational practices and political agency in Cuba cannot be neatly categorized either as dissociative or as inherently corrupting, the two tendencies of much postrevolutionary historiography. Cuba differed from other nations in which Town Planning Associates worked as consultants because it possessed, in its constitution of 1940, a conceptual structure independent of governmental and disciplinary prerogatives. Nicolás Quintana, who worked with Sert in the JNP, recalls that Sert disapproved of Batista's regime but was optimistic it would be short-lived. (Nicolás Quintana, interview by author, June 9, 2005, Miami.) In 1959, shortly after the Cuban Revolution, Wiener mentioned to his colleague Charles Haar the awkwardness of his and Sert's position: "Here we are good liberals and democrats and are probably identified in the minds of some people as Batista men." Letter, Wiener to Haar, February 13, 1959 (Box 13, Folder 15, PLW).

22. Town Planning Associates, *Plan piloto de la Habana: Directivas generales, diseños preliminares, soluciones tipo* (New York: Wittenborn, 1959). The *Plan piloto de la Habana* was published as an oversize volume with dozens of color and black-and-white plates illustrating the various aspects of the plan described by an accompanying Spanish text. An English translation was also included, but it differed in several passages from the Spanish version.

23. The Pilot Plan was considered a prelude to the "more precise definitions" of a Master Plan, but it could and did contain rather detailed recommendations. Both plans were understood to be "flexible" structures capable of adapting to changes in and new analyses of the conditions of the city. The Pilot Plan offered, at all scales, a "preliminary" proposal for the future structure of Havana. See ibid., 4–6 (English text).

24. Sert apparently did consider it the central component of the plan. For example, in Sigfried Giedion's 1958 seminar at Harvard on the "Human Scale in Design," Sert was scheduled to present the Pilot Plan and to discuss the role of its road system in restoring harmony to the civic realm of the city.

25. Le Corbusier, *Oeuvre complète, 1946–1952* (Zurich: W. Boesiger, 1953), 110.

26. Ibid.

27. Town Planning Associates, *Plan piloto de la Habana,* 14 (English text).

28. Memo from Schulz to Sert dated September 1, 1956 (Box 13, Folder 8, PLW).

29. Town Planning Associates, *Plan piloto de la Habana,* 40 (English text).

30. The proposals pertaining to Habana Vieja have long been the target of the most pointed criticism of the Pilot Plan. From the standpoint of contemporary practices of historic preservation, and more broadly in relation to contemporary cultural practices, such criticisms are certainly warranted. But an accurate and productive assessment of the plan requires consideration of the historic context. Sert and Wiener unquestionably understood the unique historic character of the old city and believed that their plan maintained it; but they also believed that its severely dilapidated housing demanded extensive renewal and argued that the renovated district could arrest the accelerating decentralization of the city. Moreover, some components of their proposals—such as the creation of a financial center and the construction of high-rise buildings along the Malecón—did not originate with Sert and Wiener. The banking institutions promoted the former, and the Horizontal Property Law of 1952 had already spurred the first manifestations of the latter. Two distinct perspectives on the Pilot Plan for Havana make for an illuminating but reductive comparison: Sigfried Giedion's introduction to Knud Bastlund, *José Luis Sert: Architecture, City Planning, Urban Design* (Zurich: Les Editions d'Architecture, 1967), and Roberto Segre's critique through the lens of revolutionary Marxism in "La Habana de Sert: CIAM, ron y cha cha cha," *DANA* 37/38 (1995): 120–124.

31. Folder Addenda/TPA/Havana Master Plan, JLS.

32. Sert had probably been introduced to the Modulor even earlier. Wiener likely saw Le Corbusier's presentation of the Modulor at the 1947 convention of the American Designers Institute, at which Wiener was also a speaker. By 1953, Sert was definitely using the Modulor in architectural projects. See, for example, his designs for the church in Puerto Ordaz and the hospital at Maracaibo, both in Venezuela.

33. Le Corbusier, *The Modulor* (Cambridge, Mass.: Harvard University Press, 1954), 210.

34. Le Corbusier derived the numerical series of the Modulor from a sequence of geometric diagrams, in which a right triangle fixed the positions of two contiguous squares. These diagrams were inaccurate, in that only one of the resulting squares was in fact a square while the other was almost imperceptibly rectangular. For Le Corbusier, such a minute discrepancy had no practical implication, however. "In philosophy . . . I suspect that these six thousandths of a value have an infinitely precious importance: the thing is not open and shut, it is not sealed; there is a chink to let in the air; life is there, awakened by the recurrence of a fateful equality which is not exactly, not strictly equal . . . and that is what creates movement." Ibid., 235.

35. Ibid., 84.

36. The project was commissioned by the Abreu family, which owned the land and an adjacent hacienda. The hacienda, which was to be preserved along with its grounds, is visible in all of the versions of the plans. None of the TPA proposals were carried out, although the firm was credited in publications of the final version of the subdivision, renamed Santa Catalina. Under the direction of Emilio del Junco, a small portion of the speculative project was actually built, including a half-dozen of its streets and a series of attached houses designed by Mario Romañach.

37. Sert used the word *patio* to describe an enclosed or semi-enclosed courtyard or pedestrian plaza.

38. See Josep Lluís Sert, "Centres of Community Life," in *Heart of the City*.

39. Paul Lester Wiener and Josep Lluís Sert, "The Work of Town Planning Associates in Latin America, 1945–1956," *Architectural Design* (June 1957): 191.

40. Town Planning Associates, "Housing, Cuba: A Proposal for Community Planning," *Architects Yearbook* (1955): 83.

41. José Luis Sert, "The Rebirth of the Patio," in Bastlund, *José Luis Sert,* 135.

42. Sert, "Centres of Community Life," 6. In this passage, Sert is quoting the Congress invitation, which he probably helped formulate.

43. Folder Addenda/TPA/Palace of the Palms, JLS.

Chapter 5

JOSEP LLUÍS SERT'S EVOLVING CONCEPT OF THE URBAN CORE

Between Corbusian Form and Mumfordian Social Practice

MARDGES BACON

Toward the end of World War II, the architect and planner Paul Zucker noted that the "ordering principle" in architecture would soon shift from prewar functionalism to postwar social practice. For public buildings, as well as dwellings and entire settlements, the postwar compass would be increasingly drawn to "human values" and "social understanding and feeling."[1] In *New Architecture and City Planning*, a volume of essays he edited, Zucker not only expressed his own views but also helped to circulate those of recent European émigrés, including Josep Lluís Sert, Sigfried Giedion, Joseph Albers, Serge Chermayeff, and László Moholy-Nagy, who had participated in prewar CIAM Congresses, along with those of American architects, planners, and urban sociologists.[2] Largely opposed to decentralist policies, on the one hand, and the isolated and programmatically homogeneous New Deal housing projects, on the other, the émigré authors were united in advocating more diverse urban interventions dedicated to community and civic identity. They wanted

to bring to North American cities the vitality of the European cities they had left behind.

Sert projected his aspirations for postwar urbanism in an essay, "The Human Scale in City Planning." He saw the aftermath of the war as an opportunity to transform the "actual inorganic shape of our cities into an organic and living body."[3] If the prewar city was mechanistic and functional, the postwar metropolis would take on a natural morphology and become more socially responsive. Sert called on urban planners to take into account the needs of both individuals and the larger community, thereby reflecting a "democratic way of living."[4] This evolving approach to urbanism reflects a shift in attitude away from the "functional city," which dominated such prewar Congresses as CIAM 4 (1933), toward an emphasis on the social structure of the urban core expressed as the "heart of the city" at CIAM 8 (1951).[5] In this essay I will explore Sert's efforts to marshal these objectives toward redefining the civic dimensions of the urban core both in his

77

writings and in his Latin American planning projects. In doing so, I will examine the formative role of Le Corbusier's theory and design and follow the arc of Sert's Americanization under the sway of the social historian and critic Lewis Mumford. From the late 1920s to the postwar period, that path will take us from Barcelona and Paris to New York and Latin America. Situated between Corbusian form and Mumfordian social practice, Sert's concept of the urban core, its representation in his Brazilian project for the Motor City (Cidade dos Motores; fig. 5.1; 1944–47), and its further refinement in his project for the Peruvian town of Chimbote (fig. 5.2; 1946–48), mark a critical juncture in the development of urban design as both discipline and practice.[6]

LE CORBUSIER AS MENTOR

The mentor-protégé relationship between Le Corbusier and Josep Lluís Sert has been the subject of much commentary by historians as well as archi-

Figure 5.1 Josep Lluís Sert and Paul Lester Wiener, civic center, the Motor City (Cidade dos Motores), near Rio de Janiero, 1944–47

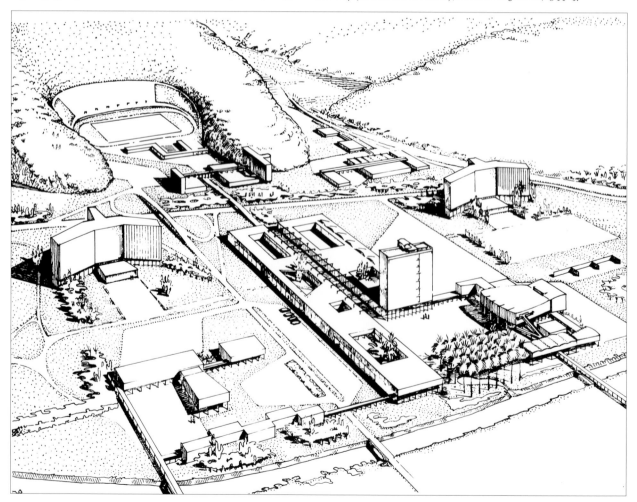

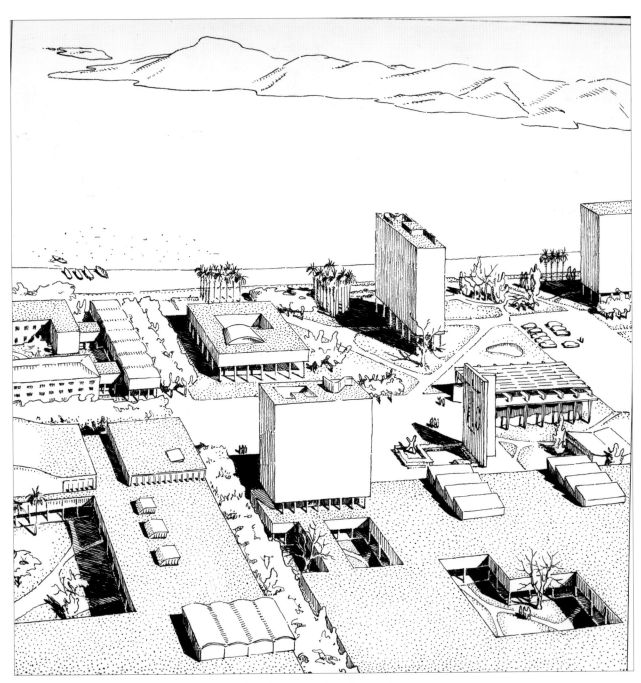

Figure 5.2 Josep Lluís Sert and Paul Lester Wiener, Civic Center, Chimbote, Peru, 1946–48

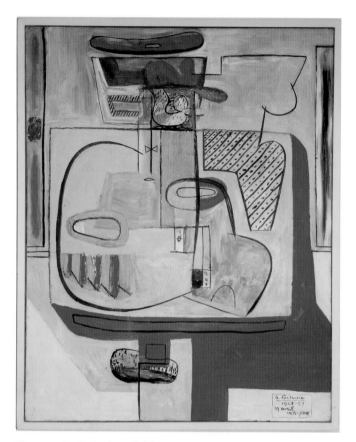

Figure 5.3 Le Corbusier, still-life painting inscribed to Sert, 1947:
"1928–47 / 19 Avril / New York"

tects.[7] From apprentice to colleague and collaborator and then to client, Sert's personal and professional relationship with Le Corbusier traversed the turbulent decade 1929–39, largely in Barcelona and Paris, and then through wartime exile and postwar reconstruction in New York during the 1940s, and finally to Cambridge, Massachusetts. More than a seminal force in the development of Sert's ideas on architecture and planning, Le Corbusier was also a kindred spirit who shared an affinity for the vitality and poetic character of Spanish culture. In 1947 Le Corbusier inscribed a painting to Sert "1928–47 /

19 Avril / New York" (fig. 5.3), affirming a long friendship from their first meeting in Barcelona in 1928 to their postwar reunion in New York, where Le Corbusier worked with an international team of architects on the design of the United Nations Headquarters.[8] Although Sert served as an apprentice in the Le Corbusier atelier (1929–30), he transcended that role in an unprecedented way. Their collaboration with José Torres Clavé and a Catalan group of architects on the Plan Macià for Barcelona (see fig. 2.1) led to future joint projects. For his Casa Bloc housing development, one of his executed buildings in Barcelona, Sert used the Corbusian typology of dense slab blocks called *maisons à redents* (indented houses or set-back apartment blocks), which appeared in his Radiant City housing program.[9] Later Sert (with Paul Lester Wiener) and Le Corbusier would work together on the plan for Bogotá (1949–53; fig. 5.4). Toward the end of Le Corbusier's professional career, Sert, in his role as dean of the Graduate School of Design at Harvard University, managed to deliver to his mentor the commission for the Carpenter Center for the Visual Arts (1959–63). It was both Le Corbusier's only American building and the pair's final collaborative effort.

SERT IN AMERICA

Sert's maturation as an architect, urban designer, and teacher coincided with his arrival in the United States in June 1939 as an exile, following the collapse of the republican government in Spain. When the Franco regime declared him "unfit to practice architecture," Sert wrote to CIAM secretary Sigfried Giedion that there was "nothing for me to do in

Europe after the last events in Spain." As war approached, his future in Paris became untenable.[10] Inevitably, Sert's emigration helped to distance him not only geographically but also ideologically from the orthodoxy of Le Corbusier's thinking. Sert devoted his early years in New York City to research on and the selection of illustrations for the CIAM book *Can Our Cities Survive?* This involved him in a transatlantic discourse on the issue of civic identity and the urban core, a topic that he had helped to raise at CIAM 5 (1937) in Paris on the theme of "Logis et loisirs" (dwellings and recreation).[11] From at least as early as 1935 Sert had taken charge of a publication under the working title *The Functional City*, which would contain the proceedings of CIAM 4 (1933), including the Town Planning Chart laying out a "doctrine of urbanism" known as the Athens Charter, as well as some of the CIAM 5 research and commentary. Sert had intended the book to be a chronicle of the CIAM 4 meeting, elucidating the "four functions" of urbanism: dwelling, recreation, work, and transportation. With the help of Giedion, who was already in the United States giving the Norton lectures at Harvard University (1938–39), and the expectation of a forthcoming CIAM meeting in New York the following fall, Sert had made his

Figure 5.4 Paul Lester Wiener, Le Corbusier, and Josep Lluís Sert, Bogotá, 1950

Figure 5.5 Josep Lluís Sert, center, and Lewis Mumford, tribute to Mumford, Harvard University, 1979

way to North America with the manuscript and documents. During the next two years Sert would work with Giedion, Walter Gropius, and Joseph Hudnut, dean of Harvard's Graduate School of Design, as well as others, to bring the book to press. As Josep Rovira explains, Sert and CIAM had aimed the manuscript, including its graphs and images, at a European audience. Now that it was directed toward both the American layperson and professional, the manuscript needed to make vital connections between urban problems on two sides of the Atlantic. With the aim of crafting a provocative and didactic book in the service of the CIAM cause, Sert told Gropius that he was determined for it to advance a "general line of action." But Giedion advised Sert to eliminate all "propaganda," such as photomontages of slum conditions in European cities, and adapt

instead to American customs without "compromising the text," which Giedion instructed to be in English. Sert told Gropius that he would consult with Lewis Mumford. Gropius subsequently wrote to Mumford on Sert's behalf.[12]

IN PURSUIT OF MUMFORD'S SOCIAL VISION AND ENDORSEMENT

Why did Sert and Gropius seek Mumford's support? In the mid-1930s Sert developed what would become an enduring admiration for the social critic (fig. 5.5). It began with Sert's reading of Mumford's *Technics and Civilization* (1934) in conjunction with research in Paris for a projected book on urbanism.[13] "For the first time," Sert recalled of the experience, "the structure and development of cities was exposed and explained." Although Sert had lost his personal library during the Spanish civil war, he still had Mumford's volume in Paris. "When I crossed the Atlantic in 1939 with very few books," Sert later recollected, "*Technics and Civilization* was one of them." In time, as Sert acquired Mumford's *Culture of Cities* (1938), he discovered a more inclusive definition and a deeper understanding of the city as "a geographic plexus, an economic organization, an institutional process, a theater of social action, and an esthetic symbol of collective unity." Throughout his professional life Sert continued to value Mumford's social vision promoting human rights. Moreover, he appreciated Mumford's ability to contextualize both architecture and the city: architecture within an urban landscape, and the evolution of cities governed by social, economic, and technological forces.[14]

Gropius and Giedion shared Sert's high regard for Mumford. Indeed, from the 1920s Mumford's writings were well known and respected in Germany; a German edition of *Sticks and Stones* was published in 1925.[15] Mumford's involvement in the work of the Deutscher Werkbund, through Walter Curt Behrendt, who edited its journal *Die Form,* secured him a European platform from which to advance modernism as a social imperative.[16] Following the publication of *The Culture of Cities,* Gropius sent a copy to Giedion who, in turn, advised Sert in Paris that it was "important for our work," presumably because he thought that it accorded with many CIAM initiatives.[17] Giedion's *Space, Time and Architecture* (1941) not only included discussions of the work of Frank Lloyd Wright and the Chicago School, studies pioneered by Mumford, but also drew on *The Culture of Cities* for an analysis of urban form and its evolution.[18] During Gropius's first visit to the United States in 1928 he met Mumford, and they remained esteemed friends. But things were different with Giedion. Mumford's relationship with him remained problematic. In 1940, when Mumford received from Giedion what he termed a "pathetic letter" asking him to review *Space, Time and Architecture,* he would not oblige.[19] For Mumford shared the opinion of his colleague Frederic Osborn, the British planner and fellow disciple of Ebenezer Howard, whose severe review of Giedion's book, in Osborn's words, "put it in its place as a contribution to planning and aesthetic theory."[20] Notwithstanding "what an effort it has cost him to move away from the purely abstract esthetic position he once occupied," Mumford wrote of Giedion in 1942, he feared that his reputation as a "good historical scholar" would lend "authority . . . to his very shallow pronouncements on the nature and task of mod-

ern city planning," as it was framed within the CIAM enterprise.[21] Frank Lloyd Wright joined Mumford in his opposition to Giedion.[22]

Sert, Giedion, and Gropius shared a pragmatic reason for seeking Mumford's backing of Sert's manuscript. They knew that an endorsement from one of America's foremost public intellectuals and its leading critic of the city would facilitate publication and ensure the book's critical reception and commercial success.[23] Following a meeting with Mumford in early December 1940, Sert sent him the manuscript and accompanying illustrations.[24] Sert asked Mumford to write the introduction. Although Mumford declined, he offered encouragement mixed with sharp but constructive criticism. He commended Sert for "the skill and wisdom" he brought to "establishing the guiding principles about modern town planning." However, the social critic felt that the CIAM program, limited to its four functions, was seriously flawed by its failure to take into account the political, educational, and cultural context of buildings and urban planning. Mumford cautioned that these were "the *distinguishing* marks of the city," adding that "all the economic organs of the city exist, ultimately, to support this civic nucleus."[25] Privately he was more candid. To Osborn, Mumford objected that Sert "in accordance with CIAM instructions" had written his draft of *Can Our Cities Survive?* "without a single reference to the functions of government, group association or culture."[26] In a subsequent letter to Gropius, Mumford did offer his support, judging Sert's text "the best statement of the method and objective of modern city planning that anyone had made." Sert then relayed to Gropius that he had told Mumford of their agreement "to complete the manuscript as he suggests." Sert proposed not to circulate it further "before the work with Mumford is over."[27] Throughout the next year Sert revised the manuscript, with Mumford supporting a proposal to the Carnegie Corporation for its subvention. When the proposal was rejected, Hudnut and Gropius prevailed upon Harvard University Press. By December 1941 Sert had completed the layout and submitted the final manuscript, with revisions far in excess of the press's contractual agreement.[28] The text, Giedion emphasized in his Introduction to *Cities*, was "exclusively the work of Mr. Sert."[29]

The question remains, how did Sert revise the manuscript in response to Mumford's criticism? The answer sheds new light on the evolution of Sert's urbanism during the 1940s, with its shift of emphasis from the "functional city" to the urban core, a change that would significantly inform CIAM thinking on the postwar city. The manuscript submitted to Mumford, as well as the complete final manuscript draft and the dummy of *Can Our Cities Survive?* do not appear to have remained intact.[30] However, the contents of the Athens Charter (La Charte d'Athènes), another version of the record of the CIAM 4 Congress on the functional city that Le Corbusier and the CIAM-France group published in 1943, suggest that Mumford would have had a similar objection to it. Like the 1940 draft of *Cities*, it too contains no program for civic centers and little discussion of a city's political, economic, cultural, and social organs.[31] Yet *Can Our Cities Survive?* specifically addresses civic enterprise in Mumfordian language, particularly in the last chapter, "Toward the Functional City." Picking up on Mumford's

criticism, Sert revised the manuscript accordingly. In it he directs his readers to consider not only the economics of speculative building enterprise "in the heart of the city" but also those "organs" that benefit the community (a theme that prefigures the CIAM 8 Congress in 1951). For a city, he emphasizes, "should be composed of something more than a sum of neighborhoods, industrial and recreational areas, business centers, and connecting highways. . . . Visible expression of man's higher aspirations should be . . . conceived in a nucleus of many urban activities, grouped to form *the civic center*." Moreover, this "civic center, nucleus of urban culture," Sert argued, would give "the skyline of the city its distinctive character."

Sert's preferred models, as with Mumford and others, were the towns and free cities of the middle ages, where cathedrals, public squares, marketplaces, town halls, and other institutions served as hubs for public gatherings and civic life. These cathedral and market towns, organized around a civic center, were cities with strong pedestrian cores. Their streets, though narrow, easily accommodated the movement of people and vehicles. In such cities, social functions, as well as commercial ones, were closely integrated. Cathedrals and towers may have dominated a dense core, but they were spread far enough apart to provide an open space suffused with light and air. These symbols of power gave meaningful expression to urban order while the space in between was used for religious festivities, as well as for commerce, political gatherings, and recreation. Moreover, these compact towns were close to nature. "No modern city," Sert claimed, "has maintained this relationship."[32] Thus the modern planner could look to medieval town planning principles, just as Le Corbusier could base the Cartesian towers of his Radiant City on the "white" cathedrals of the middle ages and its cities as models of renewal, both physical and spiritual.[33] But Le Corbusier stops short of addressing the public realm of the medieval urban core. Rather, drawing on Mumford, especially *The Culture of Cities,* and making a connection, as Giedion had done, between buildings and the morphology of the city, Sert observed that changes in "civic centers have followed those of a cultural, social, economic, or political nature."[34] For Mumford the cities of the middle ages offered models of "organic planning and building," which could help to promote civic values, social cohesion, and aesthetic order in modern ones. Bell towers would "synchronize activities," while cathedral spires towering over the surrounding buildings produced a "crescendo movement in vertical space," contrasting the sacred and collective with the secular and individual.[35] Eliel Saarinen also recognized the importance of the medieval city, where a town hall, a cathedral, and public buildings, together with their surrounding public squares and plazas, formed a nucleus and its plan embodied a "functional organism." Yet, in contrast to Sert, Le Corbusier, and most other modernists, Saarinen used the medieval city to build a case for its "physical decentralisation," which sat well in Mumford's camp.[36] Like Mumford and Giedion, Sert also looked to other historical examples. In Renaissance cities, whose identities were shaped by national and imperial interests, civic centers generally developed in linear formation along with public buildings and other symbolic monuments to power.[37] But for most modernists the cen-

tralized medieval town remained the chief paradigm.

It is important to emphasize Sert's preoccupation with a related theme in *Can Our Cities Survive?* Sert accepted the idea that cities underwent a cyclical process of evolution: "Cities as living organisms." This premise, so evident in Mumford's theory of urban development as a progression of stages, owes much to Mumford's mentor, the Scottish planner Patrick Geddes, specifically his book *Cities in Evolution* (1915), which had been so influential in Europe during the 1920s. Recognizing the consequences of such evolution for the planner, Sert held that if cities, like living organisms, are "born . . . develop, disintegrate, and die," then "city planning has become obsolete." Modern planning needed to reform by adopting the methods of the sciences and social sciences to construct what Sert called "urban biology or the study of the life of cities and of the living conditions within them."[38] Of course, Mumford had also drawn on Geddes's vision of the city as an "organ of social transmission," reflecting the character of a civilization.[39] Although Le Corbusier's publication of the Athens Charter had addressed biological and psychological factors, a reflection of Radiant City ideas, Sert's view of the city suggests closer ties to Mumford and Geddes.[40] Sert's criticism of outdated planning models and methods led the émigré architect Serge Chermayeff to concur in 1943 that "strictly speaking there is no planning profession as yet." Leaving Mumford aside, Chermayeff, who practiced architecture in Britain during the 1930s and was both versed in British planning history and a participant in the MARS group before immigrating to the United States, identified this organic synergy and "common purpose" between Sert and Geddes. In calling for an "urban biology," an allusion to the cycle of all living things, Chermayeff noted that Sert "joins hands with Professor Geddes across thirty-eight years." Chermayeff's voice is important because he would later attend CIAM 8 and accept an appointment at Harvard, where he participated in the first Urban Design Conference (1956), which named the new discipline.[41]

Sert was predisposed to Lewis Mumford's worldview and to his suggestions, leading him to make changes in the *Cities* manuscript. He himself had long advocated both the civic center and an expansion of the four functions. In developing the Plan Macià for Barcelona, Sert and Le Corbusier provided for residential, commercial, and industrial sectors, and also planned a civic center on the site of the demolished Barrio Chino district. Their program featured an administrative center on a mall-like parcel of land measuring 400 by 1,200 meters, and it included schools, museums, libraries, trade union halls, and cooperatives. As Rovira has shown, the most comprehensive design for the civic center of the Plan Macià (see fig. 2.1) was worked out in Le Corbusier's office in January 1935 from Sert's drawings.[42] Moreover, at CIAM 5 in Paris (1937), devoted to "Logis et loisirs," specifically in the presentation of the Plan Macià ("Application Case: Cities"), cities were to be zoned according to function, featuring provisions for civic and administrative centers with areas devoted to physical and cultural leisure.[43]

Sert must have felt confident that his revisions to the *Cities* manuscript would please Mumford because he discussed with him the matter of a book review.[44] The social critic appeared to be sufficiently satisfied, writing a positive review in the *New Republic*. Mumford may have extended himself in part because he looked upon Sert as a "very decent fellow" who had made an effort to respond to his criticism. But Mumford was still ambivalent about the book, and his judgment of CIAM remained unforgiving. In his review he acknowledged Sert's efforts to broaden the discussion of the four functions by directing them toward social and cultural objectives. He endorsed Sert's premise for urban reconstruction that would lead, in Sert's words, to the "better fulfillment of the cultural role of cities." Such "human insight," Mumford underscored, would "distinguish it from some of the earlier doctrinaire formulations by individual members of the CIAM group." Most likely this was a reference to the Giedion-dominated CIAM positions Mumford disdained and also to Le Corbusier's rationalist vision of the city that, on the whole, he vigorously opposed. However, Le Corbusier's master plan for the town of Nemours in Algeria (1934) was an exception. In 1935 Mumford had seen a model of the Nemours project when it was exhibited in Le Corbusier's first solo exhibition of his architecture and planning at the Museum of Modern Art in New York. Writing to Le Corbusier a few years later, Mumford called it "the best, I think, that anyone has produced for contemporary urban design." In *The Culture of Cities* Mumford not only illustrated the Nemours model but also endorsed Le Corbusier's socially responsive and open-ended project, which he considered "one of the marks of the new urban order." The Nemours plan was important for Sert because it not only exemplified a rare convergence of Corbusian and Mumfordian thought but it served as a model for several of Sert's Latin American projects a decade later. Yet Mumford's *New Republic* review served largely as a platform for advancing his own agenda. He claimed that World War II was evidence of "an organic expression of a disintegrating society." Postwar reconstruction, therefore, could not be successfully achieved through the "mechanical activity" of technocracies and industrial capitalism with their "indifference to human measure and human purpose."[45] Privately, again to Osborn, Mumford was more blunt in his appraisal. Although Mumford recognized that Sert's "amended version at least made verbal acknowledgment" of civic and cultural functions, such "pallid efforts" to address fully his criticism remained "an indication of the sociological superficiality of the CIAM analysis."[46]

In his teaching and in his professional practice with Town Planning Associates, which he founded with Wiener in 1941, Sert would remain in Mumford's camp. Following the publication of *Can Our Cities Survive?* Sert traveled to the Midwest in the spring of 1943 to lecture on "Urbanism and Suburbanization"—more specifically on the role of the four functions in postwar reconstruction. The first was held in Detroit (March 18) and the second in Chicago at the Institute of Design (March 22) at the invitation of its director, László Moholy-Nagy. For two spring semesters (1943 and 1944) Sert served as a visiting critic in the department of architecture and also gave several lectures at Yale University, where the discipline of city planning was under the direction of the French planner Maurice Rotival. Sert's Yale lecture in fall of 1943, "Human Scale in Planning," was one of several on that theme, which reflected Mumford's influence.[47] The follow-

ing year his important essay titled "The Human Scale in City Planning" appeared in the Zucker volume. It provides further evidence of the shift in Sert's thinking. Rather than representing postwar cities as "abstractions . . . in which the machine would be the sole transforming agent," Sert argued, they should be "shaped by social, political and economic conditions."[48] Cities required a more "organic social structure," one that would reunite man with nature. Increased light, open space, and trees would foster human interaction in cities, an idea drawn not only from the writings of Mumford and Le Corbusier during the 1930s but also from his association with Henry Churchill, author of *The City Is the People* (1945). The architect, housing specialist, and city planner Churchill had been one of the prime movers, along with Mumford, Henry Wright, and Albert Mayer, in a private civic group called the Housing Study Guild. Like Mumford and other guild members, Churchill called for a multifaceted approach to the problem of redevelopment, especially public housing, which emphasized social concerns. Churchill also served as one of the associated architects of Queensbridge Houses (with William F. R. Ballard, chief architect, and Frederick G. Frost, Sr., and Burnett C. Turner), a large New Deal project in Queens, New York (1936–40), which employed attached Y-shaped "units plans" around the perimeter of superblocks with central courts.[49] Notwithstanding Sert's criticism that Queensbridge was planned for the wrong site, he shared ideas with Churchill and relied on his expertise and professional support.[50]

For Sert, who had joined the republican cause in Spain and witnessed its defeat in 1939, social

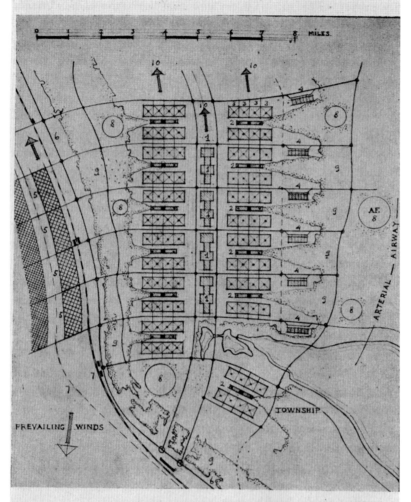

Diagramatic plan for a city composed of twelve township units (about 960,000 inhabitants). Such a city could grow by increasing the number of townships. Each new township would correspond to an additional section in the civic nucleus and the industrial areas. The city would grow like a plant does, in an organic manner. This planned organic growth would be the opposite of the anarchial expansion of our cities as they have developed in the last hundred years.

INDEX TO DIAGRAM

1. Civic Center	6. Main Highways
2. Township Center	7. Railways
3. Neighborhood Unit	8. Air Fields
4. Light Industry	9. Green Belt
5. Heavy Industry	10. Directions of Future Growth

Figure 5.6 Josep Lluís Sert, drawing of a civic nucleus

questions were inextricably linked to political and economic ones. The allied victory of 1944, he thought, would assure the growth of democracy and with it planning that reflected the values of a community as well as the individuals in it.[51] If the social structure of cities needed to be more "organic," so did their political structure need to be strengthened by community development. Following up on both CIAM 4 themes and Radiant City ideas, Sert called for cities to be zoned according to function, which would provide viable alternatives to suburbanization. Toward that objective Sert articulated a program of cohesive neighborhood units organized around a civic center. This provided fine-grained differentiations of scale. Sert's principal model remained the medieval walking city, as it had been for Mumford. But he also looked to comprehensive housing programs, notably Clarence Perry's "neighborhood unit," with a community center and a civic center planned around a common or square.[52] Indeed, by 1934 Clarence Stein and Catherine Bauer had identified the neighborhood community as the "basic unit of city building."[53] To illustrate the progression in Sert's thinking about the neighborhood unit in his 1944 essay in the Zucker anthology, he offered several diagrams, one with a centrally located civic nucleus linked to social services but still close to industry (fig. 5.6). Sert would further develop the neighborhood unit in his Latin American planning projects. Like Mumford, Sert warned against the dangers of "civic disintegration." But he distanced himself from Mumford when he faulted decentralization and suburban commuting, a pervasive trend that Le Corbusier had vigorously opposed in his books *La Ville radieuse* (1935) and *Quand les cathé-*

drales étaient blanches: Voyage au pays des timides (1937).[54] Sert's vision of the city rejected not only decentralized planning but also an economic and social model founded on individualism, self-sufficiency, and an emerging consumerism, which underscored Frank Lloyd Wright's project for an agrarian community, Broadacre City (1929–35). While Sert's economic base relied on local production, it was nonetheless dependent on the vitality of the region. His appeal to reshape the postwar city into an "organic and living body" also drew on some of the ideas that Giedion had adopted from Mumford and Geddes.[55] Such reshaping, Sert advocated, would require the kind of redefined social structure offered by Saarinen's method of dividing urban patterns into incremental functional units. Modeled on the configuration of single cells and "cellular tissue," town-planning principles could provide "organic order." For both Sert and Saarinen, planning whole communities composed of units, and basing them on the structure and "expression" of living cells, offered a plan of action to curb urban decline, notwithstanding Saarinen's call for a more decentralized and incremental dispersal of the units.[56]

MONUMENTALITY AND METAPHOR

A metaphorical view of the city enriched Sert's pragmatic approach. In addition to well-designed communities, postwar cities required effective symbolic expression. Sert's essay, like Giedion's "Need for a New Monumentality," also in the Zucker volume, grew out of their earlier collaboration with Fernand Léger on a program of architectural expression and planning for postwar democracies. This resulted in their joint paper "Nine Points on

Monumentality" (1943), a revisionist piece rejecting the modernist repudiation of monuments. Indeed, monumentality had defined the character of prewar cities, shaped in Europe by Beaux-Arts architecture and planning, as well as totalitarian schemes, and in North America by Beaux-Arts architecture and City Beautiful planning.[57] Mumford, as Giedion recognized, had promoted the idea of a modern monument as an oxymoron: "If it is a monument it is not modern, and if it is modern, it cannot be a monument."[58] Like Mumford, most prewar modernists regarded monumentality as moribund and elitist. However, the war transformed the modernist project. Anticipating a postwar period of political stability, modernists now championed monuments as meaningful symbols of human ideals and collective forces for both new and redefined democracies. Monuments, they claimed, were "the expression of man's highest cultural needs." To redress postwar chaos and enrich the social, cultural, and civic life of cities and communities, Sert, Léger, and Giedion called for the integration of buildings and urban fabric while reserving monuments as "powerful accents."[59] To do so, Giedion counseled in his solo essay, political and civic leaders needed "emotional or artistic training." Such instruction would correct the prewar schism between thinking and feeling, which Giedion had earlier identified as a modern malady.[60] To these voices on the new monumentality may be added that of Carol Aronovici, an experienced housing specialist whose essay on "Civic Art" in the Zucker anthology raised similar concerns. Critical of urban mass housing and slum clearance programs, on the one hand, but determined to redirect modernism away from commercialism and

civic enterprise of "monstrous size," on the other, Aronovici called for a new civic art that embodied democratic, communal, humanistic, emotional, and spiritual expression.[61]

LATIN AMERICAN PLANNING PROJECTS: THE MOTOR CITY

Sert's ideas on the importance of human scale, social interaction, housing, and green spaces in the urban core, combined with his call for enriching the cultural life of cities through symbolic expression, informed his postwar urban planning work in Latin America. In projects for several aspiring democracies—ironically, ones still largely controlled by authoritarian regimes—Sert and Wiener helped to demonstrate the new civic impulse. These projects have been the subject of recent scholarly analysis.[62] The earliest two, a plan for the Motor City (Cidade dos Motores) near Rio de Janiero (1944–47; see fig. 5.1) and a project for Chimbote, Peru (1946–48; see fig. 5.2), show a course of planning based on social practice. They represent the progressive principles that Sert projected in *Cities,* his essay on monumentality, and his 1944 essay "The Human Scale in City Planning": a strong urban core with provisions for dwellings close to industry near the periphery (thereby precluding the need for suburbs), a balance between civic buildings and open spaces, an urban biology governing both structure and growth, access to nature, and a vital social agenda with institutions that affirm both individuals and community. While more fully developed in Chimbote, both plans show Sert's use of organic planning models with well-defined civic centers and neighborhood units, which Mumford, Giedion, Perry, Saarinen, and also

Geddes had advocated. Their respective programs to strengthen the urban core would lead to Sert's attempts to revise the CIAM agenda, as Eric Mumford has demonstrated.[63] For the Motor City and Chimbote projects Sert also drew on local culture, climate, topography, and indigenous traditions. Yet these plans still distinguish Sert as a disciple of Corbusian form. Although not executed, Sert's two designs synthesize organic expression and formal-functional elements, thereby defining his postwar strategy.

The Motor City plan marks the first of more than eight Latin American projects designed by Sert and Wiener.[64] Like the others, the Motor City was conceived within a larger political and economic agenda. In an effort "to counter Axis influence" during the war, as Eric Mumford and Rovira have determined, the United States extended its sphere of influence and promoted capitalist enterprise, policies that continued after the war. In brief, during World War II the Brazilian government, under the leadership of President Getúlio Vargas but backed by American capital, embarked on an ambitious program of modernization and industrialization, nationalizing the production of iron and steel. In May 1943 the Brazilian Airplane Factory Commission and its chief, Brigadier-General Antonio Guedes Muñiz, called on Sert and Wiener to design a new town in conjunction with an existing airplane engine plant. Located twenty-five miles from Rio de Janiero, the new town was envisioned as part of Vargas's strategy to promote popular reform. The plan called for the construction of a new tractor factory alongside the airplane factory. The manufacture of tractors for use in agriculture and road construction would help

to increase food production and distribution in a country coping with malnutrition.[65]

Based both on Le Corbusier's Radiant City principles and the tenets of CIAM 4, Sert and Wiener's master plan for the Motor City provided functional zoning for industrial, agricultural, and urban development, as well as for dwellings, recreation, and work. Like the plan for Barcelona, the Motor City design situated factories in an industrial sector. Located to the northwest and connected to nearby rail lines, they were still close to workers' housing. While neighborhood unit principles, such as Perry's, structured the city and its projected development, the focus was on a "civic nucleus" with three zones: one for administration, amusement, and commerce; a second for culture; and a third for sports. Within the Motor City's core Sert sought to ensure the vitality of civic life and promote its "democratic" expression. Consulting vernacular traditions of the Americas, Sert set out to restore the civic center along the lines of Latin American town squares (*praças*) and promenades (*passeios*), which had been "laid out according to the town planning charter of Philip II of Spain" in 1573 at a time when Portugal was subject to Spanish rule. Like New England village greens, these Latin civic centers would serve as places of public assembly.[66] Such town squares also demonstrated a fusion of modernism and local identity.

According to Rovira's detailed analyses, Sert and Wiener developed the Motor City in three phases.[67] Although the civic center appeared in all three iterations of the project, it was most fully developed in an undated perspective rendering and plan, which Sert first published in 1946 (fig. 5.7; see also

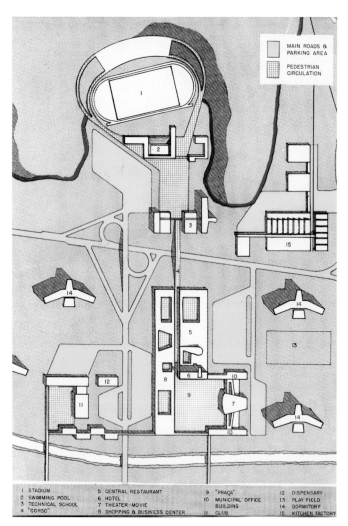

MAIN ROADS &
PARKING AREA

PEDESTRIAN
CIRCULATION

I STADIUM	5 CENTRAL RESTAURANT	9 "PRAÇA"	12 DISPENSARY
2 SWIMMING POOL	6 HOTEL	10 MUNICIPAL OFFICE	13 PLAY FIELD
3 TECHNICAL SCHOOL	7 THEATER-MOVIE	BUILDING	14 DORMITORY
4 "CORSO"	8 SHOPPING & BUSINESS CENTER	11 CLUB	15 KITCHEN FACTORY

Figure 5.7 Josep Lluís Sert and Paul Lester Wiener, plan of civic center, the Motor City (Cidade dos Motores), near Rio de Janeiro, 1944–47

fig. 5.1).[68] Toward the mountains to the west, a sports stadium and swimming pool were linked to the pedestrian promenade (*corso*) leading to a shopping and business center with a restaurant. An expansive shopping arcade raised on *pilotis* (supporting columns) was punctuated with landscaped patios. The civic center was planned around a town square and promenade. Its most figural and decidedly Corbusian elements were a wedge-shaped movie theater and the vertical slab of the hotel. An auditorium, supported by pilotis and connected by ramps, framed one side of the town square, with a shopping center, hotel, and municipal office building on the others. To the south a clubhouse had its own enclosed court. These typologies combined with the social and political character of the civic center, which informed all of Sert and Wiener's Latin American plans and would become the central theme of the 1951 CIAM 8 Congress "Heart of the City," draw on a number of sources. For Sert especially, the civic center was a vital component linking modernism and Spanish republican ideals. Although the early collaboration of Sert and Le Corbusier on the Plan Macià for Barcelona called for a civic center, this section was unresolved. The invention of civic forms and three-dimensional spatial composition on an urban scale had preoccupied Le Corbusier since the League of Nations competition (1926–27), which grouped building masses with different functions. Sert's use of an acoustical shell for the auditorium, which ultimately derived from the research of Gustave Lyon, was indebted to the auditoriums of Le Corbusier's projects for the League of Nations and the Palace of the Soviets (1931–32), as well as of his Centrosoyuz in

Moscow (1928–30).[69] Moreover, Sert's use of connecting ramps also suggests those of the Palace of the Soviets. Sert's understanding of civic programs was also informed by the Nemours project, which called for the schematic development of a civic center with a city hall and other public buildings, a church, and an auditorium. Although not developed in detail, the figural elements in the Nemours plan were grouped on a prominent sloping site along an axial route to the industrial and residential zones.[70]

Understandably, Sert would draw more closely on Le Corbusier's Latin American projects. The Ministry of Education in Rio de Janeiro (1936), designed by Lúcio Costa and Oscar Niemeyer with Le Corbusier, is the earliest of these (fig. 5.8). Le Corbusier envisioned its vertical slab raised above a terrace site on pilotis, which Niemeyer then expanded to ten meters. Serving as a model for the hotel in Sert's Motor City, the ministry was set at right angles to a connecting portico on one side

and a wedge-shaped conference hall (similar to the Motor City theater-lecture hall) on the other.[71] Le Corbusier also designed the master plan for the Cité Universitaire of Brazil in Rio de Janiero (1936), in which intersecting slabs and porticos raised on pilotis extended along a "distribution platform." With schools devoted to the humanities, law, medicine, and the arts, the program called for a library and museum, theaters, and auditoriums, each with their own Corbusian typologies.[72] Le Corbusier's master plan for Buenos Aires (1938), designed in collaboration with Jorge Ferrari Hardoy and Juan Kurchan, specified two civic centers, one for the city and one for the state, with a similar deployment of typology. His plan (*plan directeur*) reconfigured the "molecular structure" of the existing city, based on the *cuadra,* or square (100 × 100 meters), whose conditions were so congested, he claimed, that there were "no more arteries, nor lungs, nor defined organs."[73]

Figure 5.8 Le Corbusier, drawing of the Ministry of Education, Rio de Janeiro, by Lúcio Costa and Oscar Niemeyer with Le Corbusier, 1936

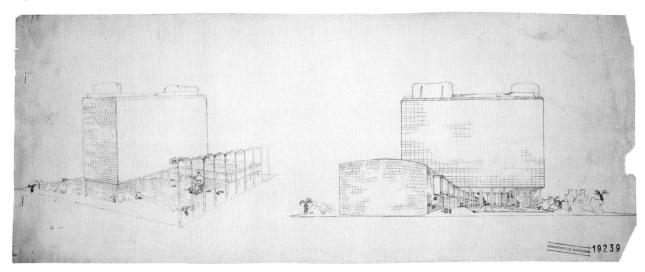

At the same time that Sert was planning the Motor City, Le Corbusier was at work on a master plan for the reconstruction of Saint-Dié (1945), a town in the Vosges region of eastern France whose historic core had been destroyed by the Germans during World War II (see fig. 8.2). Le Corbusier designed this walking city on a scale of one kilometer. His plan for the new civic center, which he described as both "the heart of the city" and "its heart and its brain," was his most fully developed urban core to date.[74] Sited on a spreading pedestrian plaza along a central axis from the Meurthe River to the old cathedral, a high-rise tower would serve as an administrative center for municipal offices, the prefecture of police, courts, and other civic affairs. Lozenge-shaped in plan, this skyscraper was similar to his recent project for the Admiralty Building for the Quartier de la marine in Algiers (1938–42).[75] Le Corbusier envisioned the Saint-Dié tower, like others he proposed for North America, as not only the focus of the civic center but also a template for renewal. The reconstruction plan called for other functional units dispersed on the plaza, including a horizontal slab containing shops and cafés, a wedge-shaped community center, and a building typology with a square spiral plan, which he called "a museum of unlimited growth." These units were also raised on pilotis.

In 1945 Sert, who was then in the throes of the third and final design for the Motor City, must have encountered the Saint-Dié plan at an exhibition in New York City. That September Saint-Dié was included in a Rockefeller Center show of Le Corbusier's work as a painter, architect, planner, and writer. Two months later it was published in the

French architectural press.[76] Between the second and third projects for the Motor City the urban core emerged as a pedestrian thoroughfare with a civic center and figural elements drawn from familiar Corbusian typologies. A decade later Sert acknowledged that Saint-Dié's "pedestrian center was the first physical expression of the emerging idea of the 'core.'" Clearly it had a significant impact on the evolution of Sert's work and of the urban core in general.[77] Yet for all of their similarities of scale, siting, typological form, and formal planning, Saint-Dié's civic center distributed individual buildings across a monumental plaza while the Motor City civic center sought more communitarian focus and vernacular expression, allowing the town square and promenade to anchor its buildings.

To account for the design of the Motor City's civic center, its integration with a neighborhood shopping center, and its horizontal slabs, wedge-shaped auditorium, and pilotis, we must reach beyond Le Corbusier's conceptual and formal precedents. The courtyard configuration, compact focus, and figural elements are drawn in part from the emerging typology of the mixed-use art, cultural, and community center of the late 1930s. Impington Village College, Cambridgeshire, England (1936–39), by Walter Gropius and E. Maxwell Fry, which served as a secondary school by day and a community center for adult education at night, united an assembly hall, workshop, classrooms, and covered walks in a courtyard scheme. The architects achieved greater clarity in the merger of auditorium and courtyard in another project for a Papworth School for Tuberculous in Cambridge, England (1936).[78] Similar courtyard configurations appear in design entries

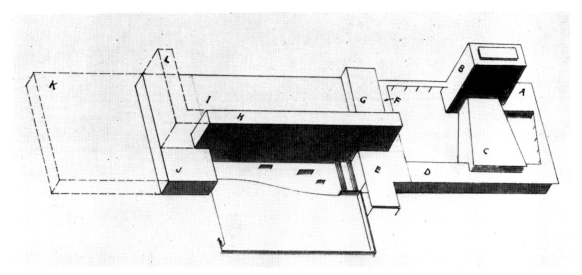

Figure 5.9 Eliel and Eero Saarinen (with J. Robert F. Swanson), isometric drawing (winning entry) in the competition for a gallery of art, Smithsonian Institution, 1939

for three North American open competitions of the late 1930s: an art center for Wheaton College in Norton, Massachusetts (1938); a festival theater and fine arts center at the College of William and Mary in Williamsburg, Virginia (1938–39); and an art gallery for the Smithsonian Institution in Washington, D.C. (1939). The programs for the three North American projects were conceived as multipurpose cultural institutions serving the arts. Each had provisions for a theater (auditorium), administration offices, classrooms, studios, galleries, and a library.[79] Many leading American modernists submitted entries to at least one of the competitions. The office of Eliel and Eero Saarinen entered all three.

Walter Gropius and Marcel Breuer's entry in the Wheaton College competition is of special interest because it signifies the maturation of the courtyard scheme. By rotating Impington's assembly hall 180 degrees, Gropius and Breuer integrate their Wheaton auditorium with the horizontal slabs of its two courtyards.[80] A similar use of typologies and massing informed many entries in all three competi-

tions. The winning design in the William and Mary competition, by Eero Saarinen, Ralph Rapson, and Frederic James followed Gropius and Breuer's model.[81] Instructed to observe a "strict adaptation to function," entrants in the Smithsonian competition refined these typologies and their massing. Isometric drawings for the winning design by Eliel and Eero Saarinen (with J. Robert F. Swanson; fig. 5.9) and a third-prize entry by G. Holmes Perkins show the emergence of a prominent vertical slab for the stage house of the auditorium, which dominated the courtyard's horizontal slabs raised on pilotis.[82] But Sert did not model his plan for the Motor City (or Chimbote) directly on any one of these competition projects. However, published designs for all three competitions, which established the formal and conceptual components of the modern cultural center— courtyard, wedge-shaped auditorium, vertical and horizontal slabs, and pilotis—were widely discussed by Mumford and published in the professional press at the time of Sert's arrival in New York in the summer of 1939. They were also exhibited at the

Museum of Modern Art. The Modern even organized traveling exhibitions consisting of thirty-four winning entries from the three, which circulated to thirty-six institutions.[83]

In response to the social deficit of the Great Depression during the 1930s, both New Deal programs (especially in conjunction with social housing) and enlightened private initiatives focused on community buildings, some at the intersection of modernism. The Carl Mackley Houses in Philadelphia, designed by the German-born American architect Oscar Stonorov (with Alfred Kastner and W. Pope Barney) and completed by the Public Works Administration in 1935, employed housing *à redents* (indented) around a perimeter block while forming three courtyards. Social amenities included a swimming pool, playground, auditorium, kindergarten, and communal laundry.[84] Stonorov's received ideas from European modernism on the importance of social ethics, together with New Deal planning initiatives, also shaped his design for a community center. Planned in conjunction with the Architects, Painters and Sculptors Collaborative, his project demonstrated a synthesis of the arts. A model of Stonorov's community center was exhibited at the Museum of Modern Art in the summer of 1938. Although predating Sert's arrival in North America, the exhibition received much attention. Museum of Modern Art director Alfred Barr called the center "architecturally far more advanced than any yet built in America." Designed with the idea that it could be part of the 1939 New York World's Fair, the project organized buildings around a colonnade decorated with murals and

sculpture, which encompassed an outdoor swimming pool. Barr recommended that "this spontaneous conjunction of the three arts should be studied as a precedent whenever American communities undertake public buildings."[85]

Unlike the design of the Impington complex and many of the entries in the North American competitions that would develop from it, the formal-figural aspects of Stonorov's community center probably had little to do with Sert's Latin American planning. But Stonorov's project to repair "shapeless community life" through "the establishment of integrated neighborhoods around the cells of community centers," combined with his use of modernist design principles, encouraged new forms of civic and community centers as social condensers and may also have been a model for prewar shopping centers.[86] Stonorov's subsequent collaboration on a wartime housing community called Bomber City (1943) is an early example. Designed for workers near the Ford aircraft plant at Willow Run (outside Detroit), the project included a progressive town plan with a community center and shopping center designed by Saarinen and Swanson (fig. 5.10), and housing by Stonorov and Louis Kahn, as well as by Skidmore, Owings, Merrill & Andrews. The entire project, which *Architectural Forum* called "the most workable and most human guide to the integrated community produced to date," was not built.[87] However, the design of the town center, which included a bell tower as a functional and symbolic tool for civic cohesion, and its lucid plan for separating pedestrians and vehicles must have influenced Sert.

In addition to the civic center, Saarinen and Swanson's project emphasized the increasing role of

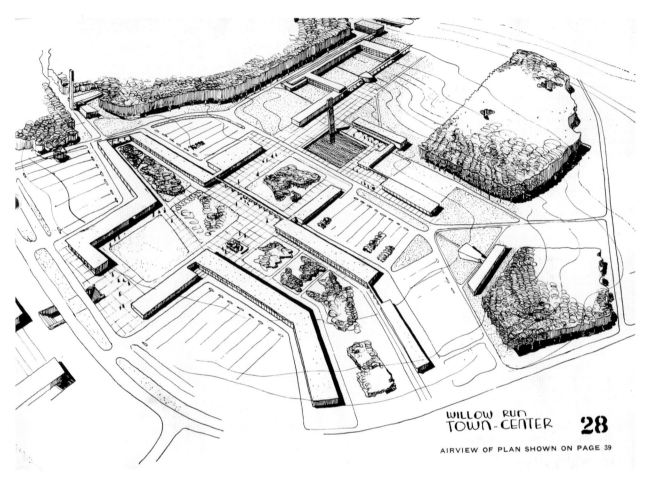

WILLOW RUN
TOWN-CENTER **28**

AIRVIEW OF PLAN SHOWN ON PAGE 39

Figure 5.10 Saarinen and Swanson, "Willow Run Town Center" project, aerial view, 1942–43

the shopping center in town planning, a role that Sert recognized in *Can Our Cities Survive?* and continued to study. Sert undoubtedly agreed with Stein and Bauer's view that "the economic success of a neighborhood community and the well-being of its inhabitants depend to a great extent on the planning of the neighborhood shopping center."[88]

Many of Sert and Wiener's Latin American projects, which successfully integrate community shopping centers and civic centers within the neighborhood unit, appear to be formulated in terms

of North American models. Two cogent examples of shopping centers, as Eric Mumford points out, are Pietro Belluschi's McLoughlin Heights in Vancouver, Washington (1942; planned in conjunction with FPHA war housing), and Linda Vista, near San Diego (1943–44), both designed around a landscaped central court with covered pedestrian walkways.[89]

The Smithsonian competition as well as both Stonorov's project for a community center and Saarinen and Swanson's design for a civic-community shopping center are noteworthy because they helped to shape the discourse on monumentality and promote modern monuments as an expression of democracy. These issues concerned Sert deeply. The Smithsonian was conceived as a gallery for the exhibition of contemporary art as well as an institution with an educational mission to redress the schism between modernism and the public at large. Sponsored by the government and intended for a prominent site on the Mall, the projected modern monument embodied the New Deal philosophy that an institution devoted to the work of living artists might enrich the "cultural life of the community all over the United States."[90] At the intersection of social, cultural, and political expression, the Smithsonian project would help not only to revitalize civic life but also to democratize the avant-garde. Saarinen and Swanson's Willow Run project, whose design was informed by their earlier Smithsonian entry, was deemed "one of the best . . . planned communities" and "a model for post-war planning" and recognized at the time as especially influential.[91] In her 1944 exhibition catalogue essay "Built in U.S.A.—Since 1932," Museum of Modern Art curator Elizabeth Mock affirmed that "modern architecture has its roots in the concept of democracy." In order to distance itself from totalitarianism and also symbolize the codependence of the individual and society, Mock argued, "democracy needs monuments," which the Saarinens' design epitomized.[92] Such projects as Stonorov's community center, the North American competition entries, and Willow Run stimulated debate on the civic role of buildings serving art, culture, and society.[93] No critic was more engaged in that discourse than Mumford.

Because modernists in the three North American competitions used different building masses to define discrete but spatially integrated functional components, they inevitably engaged the domain of urban design. Le Corbusier called such modern urbanism a "new three-dimensional science." What Le Corbusier most admired in Sert's project for the Motor City was this same play of masses in space where "geometry has supplied a wealth of combinations." At the same time, he valued Sert's sensitivity to the character of the region—its climate, geography, and topography. Today one might add to that Sert's appreciation for the rhythms of Latin daily life. Anticipating the electronic age, Le Corbusier proposed that "if we study in detail the plans and sections, we virtually walk in this city."[94] Indeed, like Le Corbusier's urbanism, the Motor City separates pedestrians from cars. Yet embedded in both Le Corbusier's and Sert's sectional approach is a paradox, because, even though Saint-Dié and the Motor City are each defined as a walking city, their superblocks are designed on the scale of the automobile.[95]

This brings us back to the central feature of Sert and Wiener's Motor City plan and the modernist concept of three-dimensional space intersecting with local influences. Sert's civic center attempted to do all things. It was a site of civic and cultural life, democratic assembly, and commerce. It was also the social space of quotidian habits. In the expansive shopping center, described as a "continuous parasol-like elevated slab on posts [that] protects the strollers from the hot sun," Sert sought a resolution between modern design and vernacular practice. Imparting both human scale and ventilation to the superblocks, Sert used a geometry of cutout forms.

Threading through the shopping center and neighborhoods, these concrete slabs suggested Corbusian three-dimensional planning. In section, for example, they resembled the first phase in the development of the Avenida 9 de Julio in Buenos Aires, whose excavations in the fall of 1937 for a subterranean pedestrian passageway and underground parking garage were widely published. Hardoy and Kurchan began the project in 1938 and were soon joined by Le Corbusier.[96] While drawing on modernist design, whether in Rio de Janeiro, Buenos Aires, or elsewhere, Sert's patio courtyards also looked to the traditional Latin American city square, which earlier Le Corbusier had helped to transform in conceptualizing the Ministry of Education building in Rio (see fig. 5.8).[97] Moreover, Sert and Wiener's covered passageways offered the same "free architectural arrangement" as in the Arab bazaar, a vernacular source known to Sert from its prevalence in Moorish Spain. In the end, Sert based his Latin American urban planning on a rich fusion of modernism and the vernacular, which he later elucidated in his CIAM 8 essay "Centres of Community Life."[98]

One other figural element of the Motor City has long been associated with Le Corbusier: a slab, Y-shaped in plan. A group of nine-story dormitories, to accommodate 801 "bachelors" each, stood on the western edge of the city close to the civic center (see figs. 5.1 and 5.7). The Y-formation first appeared in the office towers of the Plan Macià for Barcelona. In 1930 Le Corbusier used this typology for a new sixty-story Cartesian skyscraper, a variant of the cruciform design. By the mid-1930s Le Corbusier had employed the Y-formation for both housing (*unités d'habitation*) and office projects in Europe and the

United States. Oriented toward the path of the sun, its façade received excellent exposure to light. In 1935 Le Corbusier proposed a project for New York City, one that reconfigured its grid into superblocks and called for business and housing high-rises employing Y-shaped plans. Privately, Le Corbusier acknowledged his debt to Sert. In his 1935 *Agenda*, Le Corbusier referred to the Y-formation as a *modèle type Sert,* thus attributing the typology to his Macià collaborator and revealing Sert's contribution to Corbusian planning.[99] There has been speculation on the origin of the Y-shaped plan, which was used in Europe and the United States during the 1920s and 1930s. Sert most likely looked to an American source, Alden Park, a cooperative apartment complex in Germantown, Pennsylvania (1926–28), designed by Edwin Rorke. In March 1930, *Architectural Record* published an aerial photograph of the thirteen-story towers of Alden Park. Sert reproduced the photograph in both *Can Our Cities Survive?* and his avant-garde journal *A.C.* (*Documentos de actividad contemporánea*) to illustrate the advantages of high rises in a park.[100] Sert and Le Corbusier's designs helped to promote towers in Y-formation on both sides of the Atlantic.

While suggesting North American precedents, Sert's Motor City projected a more ambitious scale and integration of civic and neighborhood shopping centers within a regional plan. Following its publication in professional journals in 1946 and subsequent exhibition at the Museum of Modern Art, the Motor City helped to transmit Sert's vision of neighborhood planning to North American commercial developers and their architects. Sert's design approach, for example, influenced the architect and planner

Morris Ketchum, who concluded in 1948 that "regional shopping facilities should be planned as a part of a larger group of civic and institutional buildings." To Ketchum, the Motor City layout demonstrated not only the "tremendous possibilities of this approach to regional planning" but also the idea that "organized recentralization is a good antidote to planless decentralization." Ketchum would draw on Sert's thinking in his designs (with Gina & Sharp) for the business district of Rye, New York (1946), North Shore Center near Beverly, Massachusetts (1947), and Shoppers' World in Framingham, Massachusetts (1949–51).[101]

LATIN AMERICAN PLANNING PROJECTS: CHIMBOTE

The civic center (with its shopping component), broadly defined as a pedestrian space in the heart of the city, approached maturity in the master plan for Chimbote in Peru (1946–48; see fig. 5.2). Here Sert joined Corbusian form and Mumfordian social practice to the new monumentality, which synthesized architecture, painting, and sculpture. During World War II the redevelopment of the port town of Chimbote was conceived within a larger plan to industrialize the Santa Valley. With loans from the U.S.-backed Import and Export Bank (as in the case of the Motor City project) and funds from the Peruvian government, a hydroelectric power station was built on the Santa River to provide both power and irrigation to the valley. The abundant supply of electricity made possible the construction of a new port facility and an industrial complex to process and store Peru's natural resources, which included coal, iron, and other metals. When the new port opened in 1945, the Peruana del Santa

Corporation charged Wiener with the task of preparing a "long range Master Plan of Chimbote and surroundings," which Town Planning Associates submitted in 1948.[102]

At Chimbote, Corbusian modernism further intersected with vernacular and regional practice. Breaking away from the small-scale grid (cuadra) of the existing city, the Chimbote project called for the large-scale blocks of Sert and Le Corbusier's Plan Macià and of the Motor City project, as well as the separation of cars from pedestrians, greater plasticity, and three-dimensional planning. "Designed organically," Sert and Wiener maintained, their plan could be potentially extendable. Following CIAM principles, Chimbote was zoned by the "four functions" with an emphasis on industry and neighborhood units, each with its own nucleus. Like the Motor City, the focus at Chimbote was on the civic center with its shopping plaza, this time facing the waterfront (along the lines of Macià's civic center site). Similar to but more ambitious and resolved than the Motor City program, Chimbote's civic center also called for an enriched complement of buildings and public works, largely derived from Corbusian typology (although eliminating the wedge-shaped auditorium in favor of retaining an existing cinema). Influenced by Saint-Dié (see fig. 8.2), Chimbote's civic center (see fig. 5.2) emerged fully formed as an ensemble of Corbusian figural elements. Indeed, the Chimbote project shares much with Saint-Dié: a walking city with a pedestrian bridge to connect the civic center to other sectors; buildings framed by green spaces and raised on pilotis to provide "uninterrupted pedestrian circulation"; vertical slabs (with roof gardens) to advance

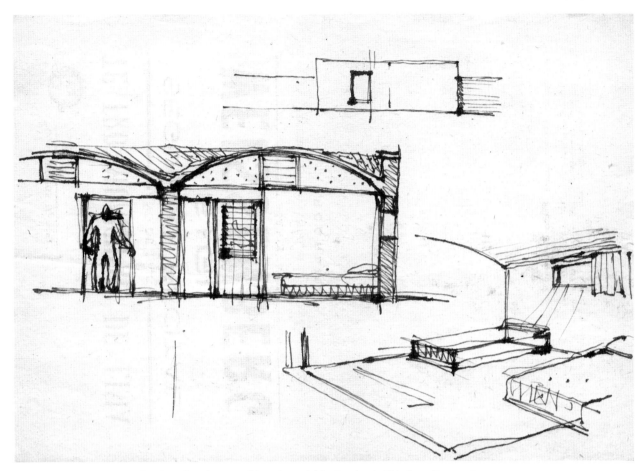

Figure 5.11 Josep Lluís Sert, drawing of interior, type C housing, neighborhood unit, Chimbote, Peru, 1948

the tensional relationships of the modernist enterprise; and a museum in close proximity to the municipal building. On the one hand, Chimbote's civic center expresses a freer and even more three-dimensional composition than that of the Motor City, undoubtedly inspired by Saint-Dié. On the other hand, Chimbote's civic center is concentrated around a single common square, while that of Saint-Dié disperses figural elements in a field. Promising an "architectural monumental whole," Sert and Wiener modeled their civic center after the colonial Plaza de Armas instead of the North American "main street," which they claimed had "proven disastrous in all U.S. cities."[103]

Sert further distanced himself from Corbusian poetics by addressing the social sphere of daily life, one that inevitably consulted local traditions. A church and its bell tower dominate Chimbote's pedestrian core.[104] Sert integrated commercial and civic functions through expansive shopping arcades with patio courtyards providing human scale. Moreover, he consulted the *genius loci* of pre-Columbian traditions. Anticipating the eventual surge in population (from 12,000 up to 50,000 inhabitants), largely indigenous Peruvians coming down to the valley from the adjacent mountains, Sert's plan incorporates the valley's new irrigation system, based on the Tennessee Valley Authority (TVA) model of harnessing the river to provide a source of inexpensive electrical power and transform soil into fertile land, thereby increasing food production. Indeed, as Mumford had envisioned, large-scale planning, as was used by the TVA, was becoming a postwar paradigm.[105] It demonstrated that by means of government intervention and a powerful synergy between man and machine, an entire region could be transformed and thereby, in Sert's words, "revalorized."[106] The Chimbote master plan also specified the "collective cultivation of land," a local tradition since the time of the Incas. The civic center called for a stream to run through the town center with branches fanning out to provide irrigation, along the lines of an ancient system employed by both Arab and Incan cultivators.[107] Such vernacular methods interested Sert but were overshadowed by his modernist vision. However, this diversion of the stream does parallel an organic process to convert Chimbote's existing grid into a stem-and-branch system of neighborhood clusters with open blocks for housing and green spaces, following the so-called townless highway model, invented by Benton MacKaye and promoted by Regional Planning Association of America members Clarence Stein, Mumford and, later, by Gropius. Such regional planning reflected Sert's contributions to the CIAM agenda from his book *Can Our Cities Survive?* to the Bridgwater CIAM Congress in 1947 and beyond.[108]

In combining rural, regional, and ancient traditions with modern building techniques, Sert also followed a dedicated path that Le Corbusier had initiated in the 1930s. For the civic center and neighborhood units of the Chimbote plan introduce one final vernacular element drawn from Islamic, Catalan, and Incan traditions: brick vaults. These vaults crown the single-story concrete slabs of the civic center. They also serve the neighborhood units, specifically the one-story patio houses identified as type C (fig. 5.11), which provided one of several low-rise, high-density solutions. Here shallow brick vaults capped with flat roofs resembled the adobe huts that these houses were intended to replace.[109] Chimbote's type C model would lead to Sert's design for the neighborhood units of the Quiroga sector in Bogotá (1951), which called for patio houses integrating suites of thin-shell concrete vaults and a surrounding wall. Such configurations suggested projects by Le Corbusier, most notably his "Residence inside an Agricultural Estate near Cherchell, North Africa" (1942; fig. 5.12). Earlier the shallow concrete vault had been used both by Auguste Perret for warehouses at Casablanca (1914–16) and by Le Corbusier in his project for the Monol Houses (1919). Le Corbusier specified similar vaults for his project for a cooperative village called the Radiant Farm (1934) and for the Weekend House (Petite Maison de Weekend, or Villa Félix), Celle-Saint-Cloud (1935). These anticipated such later projects as Sainte-Baume and the Roq and Rob vacation housing at Cap Martin (1949).[110] An executed building, the Weekend House, shared with Sert's vaulted structures similar references to Islamic and Catalan vernacular traditions, especially

Figure 5.12 Le Corbusier, drawing, residence inside an agricultural estate near Cherchell, North Africa, 1942

Figure 5.13 Associated Architects, Lower Plaza, Rockefeller Center, New York City, 1929–40

as Antoni Gaudí interpreted them. For Sert it was as much a return to his roots as a projection of modernism. "My first modern design at the school in Barcelona," he later recalled, "was a building with a vaulted roof because in Catalonia these . . . very thin brick vaults had been very well developed in Barcelona by the local craftsmen."[111]

With increasing clarity Sert's plans for the Motor City and Chimbote helped to define not only the civic center but also a stronger synergy between architecture and urbanism.[112] These city planning projects for postwar countries of the Americas, oscillating between authoritarian rule and democratic aspirations, assimilated both Corbusian form and Mumfordian social practice at the same time as they embodied the alliance of pre-industrial culture and modernism. The urban core that emerged in the projects for the Motor City, Saint-Dié, and elsewhere came to maturity at Chimbote. For Sert this meant grafting Corbusian physical form to a matrix of local traditions. Sert's insistence on responding to the practical needs, social formation, and symbolic expression of Latin American communities, however, distanced him from Le Corbusier's proscriptive emphasis on aesthetics and emotions. Le Corbusier and Sert's divergent attitudes toward the urban core are best examined in their respective presentations at the CIAM 8 Congress (1951), "The Heart of the City," where each architect employed the metaphor of theater. Both called for more three-dimensional and plastic expression engaging a synthesis of the arts, one that Sert, as well as Giedion and Le Corbusier, had envisioned at the CIAM 6 and 7 Congresses. But Le Corbusier saw the urban core as a proscribed stage for popular theater in the tradition of commedia dell'Arte or Punch and Judy. Such performance had the capacity to intensify life, Le Corbusier thought, leading to a "form of poetry" where "art is revealed."[113] By the time Sert envisioned the urban core as a theater of experience, he had already turned to Mumford's social concept of civic space as a platform for drama, rather than a formal stage set. Sert built on Mumford's concept of the city as a spatial matrix creating "differentiated opportunities for a common life and a significant collective drama" when he defined the task of the architect-planner to "build the frame or container within which this community life could take place."[114] Although both architects called for spontaneity, Le Corbusier associated it with artistic spectacle, which divided actor from audience, while Sert embedded it in the organic life of the city, enfranchising the populace as participants. For Sert, the core was both a utilitarian and symbolic space "preserved from being built

upon and . . . available for spontaneous manifestations by the populace."[115] Indeed, Sert's idea of the city center as a generative social space, a site of purposeful public assembly as well as random encounters, was bound up with the destiny of the postcolonial democratic state. In the Motor City and Chimbote cores Sert incorporated the modernity of the North American urban plaza, such as New York's Rockefeller Center (fig. 5.13), with the vernacular tradition of the colonial town square. It was there that a "New York crowd spontaneously took over" to celebrate prematurely the liberation of Paris, Giedion later recalled in *The Heart of the City*.[116] Based on these models, Sert and Wiener's city plans for future Latin American democracies could provide places of assembly and experience, evincing what Mumford called a city's "associative life."[117] To European observers, Sert's urban projects, which were suffused with organic life, embodied Frank Lloyd Wright's architecture of democracy.[118] Drawing on Corbusian form and Mumfordian social practice, Sert developed a richly figurative and human-centered concept of the urban core at the Motor City and Chimbote, which would shape subsequent Latin American projects, future CIAM debates, and the emerging discipline of urban design.[119]

NOTES

I wish to express my thanks to Mary Daniels, special collections librarian, Frances Loeb Library, Harvard Design School, for generously sharing her expertise on Josep Lluís Sert's work and career. I am also indebted to Inés Zalduendo, archivist at the Loeb Library, who assisted me with translation and shared her knowledge of Le Corbusier's master plan for Buenos Aires. Judith Ann Schiff, Laura Tatum, and Diane Kaplan, archivists at Yale University Library, and Nancy Shawcross, archivist at the Van Pelt Library, University of Pennsylvania, provided invaluable help. I remain grateful to Robert Wojtowicz. Arnaud Dercelles, librarian and archivist at the Fondation Le Corbusier in Paris, and Laura Muir, curator at the Busch Reisinger Museum at Harvard University, kindly assisted me with illustrations, as did Mina Marefat. I extend special thanks to Eric Mumford for reading the manuscript and offering critical comments and editorial suggestions. I am also greatly indebted to Hashim Sarkis for his editorial judgment and for giving me the opportunity to contribute to this volume.

1. Paul Zucker, *New Architecture and City Planning* (New York: Philosophical Library, 1944), 8–9.

2. The participants were drawn from a range of disciplines in the social sciences, humanities, and, most notably, the arts. They also included Charles Abrams, George Howe, Albert Kahn, Louis Kahn, Lawrence Kocher, and Richard Neutra.

3. Josep Lluís Sert, "The Human Scale in City Planning," in Zucker, *New Architecture and City Planning*, 398.

4. Ibid., 394.

5. On the CIAM congresses, see Martin Steinmann, ed., *CIAM: Dokumente 1928–1939* (Basel: Birkhäuser, 1979). Giorgio Ciucci, "The Invention of the Modern Movement," *Oppositions* 24 (Spring 1981): 68–91. Eric Mumford, *The CIAM Discourse on Urbanism, 1928–1960* (Cambridge, Mass.: MIT Press, 2000).

6. I owe a strong debt of gratitude to the work of other scholars, most notably Josep M. Rovira, *José Luis Sert* (Milan: Electa, 2000), and Eric Mumford, "CIAM Urbanism After the Athens Charter," *Planning Perspectives* 7 (1992): 391–417; Mumford, "CIAM and Latin America," in Xavier Costa and Guido Hartray, eds., *Sert: Arquitecto en Nueva York* (Barcelona: Museu d'Art Contemporani de Barcelona, 1997), 48–75; and Mumford, *CIAM Discourse on Urbanism*.

7. Maxwell Fry referred to Sert as Le Corbusier's "disciple." See his essay "Le Corbusier at Chandigarh," in Russell Walden, ed., *The Open Hand: Essays on Le Corbusier* (Cambridge, Mass.: MIT Press, 1977), 357.

8. For Sert's comments on Le Corbusier's contributions to the planning of the United Nations Headquarters, see Josep Lluís Sert, "U.N. Headquarters," *Progressive Architecture* 28 (October 1947): 96, 98, 100, 102. For a brief discussion of Le Corbusier's role in the design and planning of the U.N. Headquarters, see Mardges Bacon, *Le Corbusier in America: Travels in the Land of the Timid* (Cambridge, Mass.: MIT Press, 2001), 304–308.

9. On the Casa Bloc housing development, see Rovira, *Sert*, 70–73; Carolina B. Garcia, "Casa Bloc," in Josep M. Rovira, ed., *Sert, 1928–1979: Half a Century of Architecture—Complete Work* (Barcelona: Fundació Joan Miró, 2005), 45–48. On the typology of Corbusian housing à redents, see Le Corbusier, *La Ville radieuse* (Paris: Editions de l'Architecture d'aujourd'hui, [1935]); *The Radiant City*, Pamela Knight, Eleanor Levieux, and Derek Coltman, trans. (New York: Orion, 1967), 156–164.

10. Joan Ockman, "The War Years in America: New York, New Monumentality," in Costa and Hartray, eds., *Sert: Arquitecto en Nueva York*, 22. Letter, Josep Lluís Sert to Sigfried Giedion, March 21, 1939, as quoted in Rovira, *Sert*, 101. John Peter, *The Oral History of Modern Architecture: Interviews with the Greatest Architects of the Twentieth Century* (New York: Harry N. Abrams, 1994), 253.

11. Josep Lluís Sert, *Can Our Cities Survive?* (Cambridge, Mass.: Harvard University Press, 1942). Steinmann, *CIAM*, 192. CIAM, *Logis et loisirs, 5e Congrès CIAM Paris 1937* (Boulogne-sur-Seine: Editions de l'Architecture d'aujourd'hui, 1938), 35. Rovira, *Sert*, 84–87; Mumford, *CIAM Discourse on Urbanism*, 104–116.

12. Eric Mumford offers an insightful

account of *Can Our Cities Survive?* as propaganda in his *CIAM Discourse on Urbanism,* 131–142. For a full historical account of Sert's book see Rovira, *Sert,* 93–111. See Letters, Josep Lluís Sert to Walter Gropius, January 27 and October 9, 1940; Sigfried Giedion to Josep Lluís Sert, February 3, 1940; and Lewis Mumford to Walter Gropius, November 25, 1940 (WGP, HL, HU).

13. Lewis Mumford, *Technics and Civilization* (New York: Harcourt, Brace, 1934).

14. Josep Lluís Sert, "Lewis Mumford," October 1979 (JLSC, SC, FLL, HDS); Lewis Mumford, *The Culture of Cities* (New York: Harcourt, Brace, 1938), 480.

15. Lewis Mumford, *Von Blockhaus zum Wolkenkratzer: Eine Studie über Amerikanische Architektur und Zivilisation,* M. Mauthner, trans. (Berlin: Bruno Cassirer Verlag, 1925). Robert Wojtowicz, *Lewis Mumford and American Modernism* (New York: Cambridge University Press, 1996), 85.

16. For a comprehensive and insightful view of Mumford's role in shaping the German discourse on the modern movement, see M. David Samson, "Unser Newyorker Mitarbeiter, Lewis Mumford, Walter Curt Behrendt, and the Modern Movement in Germany," *JSAH* 55 (June 1996): 126–139.

17. Letter, Sigfried Giedion to Josep Lluís Sert, May 16, 1939 (JLSC, SC, FLL, HDS). First editions of *The Culture of Cities* and *Technics and Civilization,* along with other Mumford publications, appear in an inventory of Sert's library (JLSC, SC, FLL, HDS). Paul Lester Wiener, Josep Lluís Sert, and Paul Schulz include *The Culture of Cities* in their unpublished "Bibliography on Regional and City Planning" [1953] (PLWC, SC, UOL).

18. Sigfried Giedion, *Space, Time and Architecture: The Growth of a New Tradition* (Cambridge, Mass.: Harvard University Press, 1941).

19. Letters, Sigfried Giedion to Lewis Mumford, September 20, 1940 (LMP, SP, VPL, UP), and Lewis Mumford to Walter Gropius, November 25, 1940 (WGP, HL, HU).

20. Letter, Frederic J. Osborn to Lewis Mumford, July 30, 1942, in Michael R. Hughes, ed., *The Letters of Lewis Mumford and Frederic J. Osborn* (Bath: Adams and Dart, 1971), 31. See F[rederic]. J. Osborn, "Planning for Pictures," *Town and Country Planning* 38 (Summer 1942): 42–47.

21. For Mumford's view of Giedion, see his letter to Frederic J. Osborn, November 27, 1942, in Hughes, *Letters of Mumford and Osborn,* 34.

22. Wright wrote to Mumford that "such history as I've read (by Gideon [*sic*], say) and from many pens is so specious a pretense of knowledge—that *my gorge* rises as I read." Letter, Frank Lloyd Wright to Lewis Mumford, January 10, 1952, in Bruce Brooks Pfeiffer and Robert Wojtowicz, eds., *Frank Lloyd Wright and Lewis Mumford: Thirty Years of Correspondence* (New York: Princeton Architectural Press, 2001), 206–207.

23. Letters, Josep Lluís Sert to Lewis Mumford, November 20 and 28, 1940 (Arensberg Archives, Philadelphia Museum of Art), and Lewis Mumford to Josep Lluís Sert, November 23, 1940 (JLSC, SC, FLL, HDS).

24. In early 1940 Sert changed the name of the manuscript from *The Functional City* to *Should Our Cities Survive?* See letter, Sigfried Giedion to Le Corbusier, February 20, 1940 (Sigfried Giedion Archive 43-k-1941-2-20 [6]), as quoted in Rovira, *Sert,* 111 n.217.

25. Letter, Lewis Mumford to Josep Lluís Sert, December 28, 1940 (JLSC, SC, FLL, HDS).

26. Letter, Lewis Mumford to Frederic J. Osborn, May 5, 1945. Earlier Mumford had written to Osborn that "when I saw the book in ms. I discovered that, though it dealt with recreation, it had no other reference to the civic and social functions of the city: hence I refused to give it the blessing of an introduction"; letter, Mumford to Osborn, November 27, 1942, both in Hughes, *Letters of Mumford and Osborn,* 34, 83.

27. Letters, Lewis Mumford to Josep Lluís Sert, December 28, 1940; Walter Gropius to Josep Lluís Sert, January 8, 1941; and Josep Lluís Sert to Walter Gropius, January 13, 1941 (JLSC, SC, FLL, HDS).

28. "Memorandum, Notes on the Manuscript Entitled: 'Should Our Cities Survive?' Prepared by Josep Lluís Sert, in Collaboration with the Congrès Internationaux d'Architecture Moderne," January 17, 1941. Letters, Walter Gropius and Joseph Hudnut to

F. P. Keppel (president of the Carnegie Corporation), January 17, 1941; Dumas Malone to Joseph Hudnut, September 26 and October 7, 1941; Josep Lluís Sert to Joseph Hudnut, October 3, 1941, and January 7, 1942; Dumas Malone to Joseph Hudnut, November 27, 1942; and Memorandum of Agreement, October 7, 1941 (JLSC, SC, FLL, HDS). Letter, Josep Lluís Sert to Walter Gropius, April 20, 1941 (WGP, HL, HU).

29. Sigfried Giedion, "Introduction," in Josep Lluís Sert, Can Our Cities Survive? x.

30. Some photographs and other illustrations from Can Our Cities Survive? are contained in the Sert Collection (JLSC, SC, FLL, HDS). No dummy has been located among the Sigfried Giedion Papers and CIAM Archive documents in the GTA Archives at the ETH Zurich or in the Herbert Bayer Collection and Archive at the Denver Art Museum. I wish to thank Reto Geiser for his generous help with the CIAM Archive documents and Gwen F. Chanzit, curator of the Bayer Collection, for her assistance.

31. Le Corbusier, La Charte d'Athènes (Paris: Plon, 1943); Le Corbusier, The Athens Charter, Anthony Eardley, trans. (New York: Grossman, 1973).

32. Sert, Can Our Cities Survive? 228–232. For Mumford's comments on the civic nucleus, see Culture of Cities, 133, 478.

33. See Le Corbusier, La Ville radieuse and Quand les cathédrales étaient blanches: Voyage au pays des timides

(Paris: Librairie Plon, 1937), 3–11. On Le Corbusier's use of the medieval cathedral as a model for his Cartesian skyscraper, see Bacon, Le Corbusier in America, 228–236.

34. Sert, Can Our Cities Survive? 230.

35. Mumford, Culture of Cities, 20.

36. Eliel Saarinen, The City: Its Growth, Its Decay, Its Future (Cambridge, Mass.: MIT Press, 1943), 40. See letter, Frederic J. Osborn to Lewis Mumford, June 19, 1944, in Hughes, Letters of Mumford and Osborn, 55.

37. Sert, Can Our Cities Survive? 232.

38. Patrick Geddes, Cities in Evolution (1915; rpt. New York: Oxford University Press, 1950). A 1949 edition of the book appears in Wiener, Sert, and Schulz, "Bibliography of Regional and City Planning" and also in the "Sert Library Inventory" (JLSC, SC, FLL, HDS). See also Volker M. Welter, Biopolis: Patrick Geddes and the City of Life (Cambridge, Mass.: MIT Press, 2002), 92–99. Sert, Can Our Cities Survive? 2, 4.

39. Mumford, Culture of Cities, 6–7.

40. Le Corbusier, Athens Charter, 44–45. On Le Corbusier's biological and psychological analogies, see his Quand les cathédrales étaient blanches, 248–249, 273–291; When the Cathedrals Were White: A Journey to the Country of Timid People, Francis E. Hyslop, Jr., trans. (New York: Reynal and Hitchcock, 1947), 54, 61–63, 169–170. For a discussion of these analogies, see Bacon, Le Corbusier in America, 72–73, 141–146, fig. 3.8.

41. Serge Chermayeff, "Planning: Urns

or Urbanism?" Pencil Points 24 (February 1943): 74. Sert noted this passage in his own copy (JLSC, SC, FLL, HDS). See Eric Mumford, Chapter 8 of this volume; Mumford, CIAM Discourse on Urbanism, 204. On Chermayeff's appointment and the early years of the program, see Anthony Alofsin, The Struggle for Modernism (New York: Norton, 2002), 250–257. For the published conference report, see "Urban Design," Progressive Architecture 37 (August 1956): 97–112.

42. H. Allen Brooks, ed., The Le Corbusier Archive, vol. 12 (New York: Garland and Fondation Le Corbusier, 1983), #13204, 90. Letter, Le Corbusier to Josep Lluís Sert, January 22, 1935 (FLC H3 13 30), as quoted in Rovira, Sert, 78–79; see also Francesc Roca, El Plan Macià (Barcelona: La Magrana, 1977).

43. Josep Lluís Sert, "Cas d'application: Villes," Logis et loisirs, 32–41, reprinted in Steinmann, CIAM, 192. Indeed, as developed in a preliminary meeting in Amsterdam of June 9–13, 1935, for CIAM 5, the four zones had been expanded to six (housing, production, provisions, leisure, community life, and transport). Rovira, Sert, 80–86, 91.

44. In the spring of 1942, Mumford told Sert that he would review the book. Letter, Josep Lluís Sert to Joseph Hudnut, October 29, 1942 (JLSC, SC, FLL, HDS). The following January Mumford apologized to Sert for the delay in "reviewing your admirable book." Letter, Lewis Mumford to Josep

Lluís Sert, January 18, 1943 (JLSC, SC, FLL, HDS).

45. Lewis Mumford, "How Can Our Cities Survive?" review of *Can Our Cities Survive? New Republic* 108 (February 8, 1943): 186–187. Letter, Lewis Mumford to Frederic J. Osborn, November 27, 1942, in Hughes, *Letters of Mumford and Osborn,* 34. Letter, Lewis Mumford to Le Corbusier, September 18, 1937 (FLC). Mumford, *Culture of Cities,* [437], fig. 30. On Mumford's views of Le Corbusier's urban vision, see Bacon, *Le Corbusier in America,* 240–241, 381n.14.

46. Letter, Lewis Mumford to Frederic J. Osborn, May 5, 1945, in Hughes, *Letters of Mumford and Osborn,* 83.

47. "News," *Pencil Points* 24 (March 1943): 23. "Mr. Sert to Speak," *Chicago Sun,* March 21, 1943, and Sarah Brown Boyden, "Higher Buildings, Fewer of Them, Sert's Solution to Cliff Dwelling," *Chicago Sun,* March 23, 1943, newspaper clippings in Sert Scrapbook (JLSC, SC, FLL, HDS). In the spring of 1943, Sert was invited to serve as a visiting critic and make six visits to Yale. Letter, Everett V. Meeks to Josep Lluís Sert, March 29, 1943; see also telegrams, Everett V. Meeks to Josep Lluís Sert, March 19 and 22, 1943. In the spring of 1944 Sert was invited again to give a lecture (March 30) and serve as visiting critic in a city planning studio, for which eight visits were projected. Letters, C. [Carroll] L. V. Meeks to Josep Lluís Sert, February 17, 1944, and March 21, 1944 (JLSC, SC, FLL, HDS). Letter, Judith

Ann Schiff to Mardges Bacon, July 19, 2005 (Manuscripts and Archives, Yale University Library).

48. Sert, "Human Scale in City Planning," 392.

49. New York City Housing Authority, *Fifth Annual Report, 1938,* 13; Richard Plunz, *A History of Housing in New York City* (New York: Columbia University Press, 1990), 238–241; Richard Pommer, "The Architecture of Urban Housing in the United States During the Early 1930s," *JSAH* 37 (December 1978): 253–258.

50. See Henry S. Churchill, *The City Is the People* (New York: Reynal and Hitchcock, 1945). This book appears in Wiener, Sert, and Schulz, "Bibliography of Regional and City Planning." Sert entered Henry Churchill's name as a professional reference in his 1947 report to the architectural registration board. "Experience and Record in Professional Practice Submitted to the National Council of Architectural Registration Boards," February 21, 1947 (JLSC, SC, FLL, HDS). See also Sert, *Can Our Cities Survive?* 38–40.

51. Sert, "Human Scale in City Planning," 394.

52. Sponsored by the Russell Sage Foundation, Perry articulated a set of neighborhood planning principles, some based on British town planning models (and promoted by Mumford), which Sert acknowledged in his essay "Human Scale in City Planning," 408, 411–412n.8. Clarence Arthur Perry, *Housing for the Machine Age* (New

York: Russell Sage Foundation, 1939). Wiener, Sert, and Schulz include Perry's book in their "Bibliography of Regional and City Planning," 13.

53. Clarence S. Stein and Catherine Bauer, "Store Buildings and Neighborhood Shopping Centers," *Architectural Record* 75 (February 1934): 175. The article appears in Wiener, Sert, and Schulz, "Bibliography of Regional and City Planning."

54. Sert, "Human Scale in City Planning," 393. For Le Corbusier's opposition to suburbanization, see *La Ville radieuse,* 104–111; *Quand les cathédrales étaient blanches,* 273–291; *When the Cathedrals Were White,* 186–201.

55. On Giedion's concept of "architecture as an organism," see *Space, Time and Architecture,* 19–23.

56. Sert, "Human Scale in City Planning," 398n.6; Saarinen, *City: Its Growth, Its Decay, Its Future,* 8–18.

57. Sigfried Giedion, "The Need for a New Monumentality," in Zucker, *New Architecture and City Planning,* 549–568. In 1956 Giedion first published the "Nine Points on Monumentality" with an explanation of its origin and authorship. S[igfried] Giedion, *Architektur und Gemeinschaft* (Hamburg: Rowohlt, 1956), 25–26, 40–42; *Architecture, You and Me: The Diary of a Development* (Cambridge, Mass: Harvard University Press, 1958), 48–51. Joan Ockman reprints the essay and provides an introduction that contextualizes it, both in her edited

volume *Architecture Culture, 1943–1968: A Documentary Anthology* (New York: Rizzoli, 1993), 27–30.

58. Mumford, *Culture of Cities*, 438.

59. Giedion, *Architecture, You and Me*, 48–49.

60. Giedion, *Space, Time and Architecture*, 584–585.

61. Carol Aronovici, "Civic Art," in Zucker, *New Architecture and City Planning*, 366–391. A professor at the School of Architecture at Columbia University, Aronovici was director of the Housing Orientation Study at Columbia and an associate of Henry Wright, Churchill, Mayer, and Mumford.

62. Rovira, *Sert*, 113–161; Josep M. Rovira, "Cidade dos Motores" and "Chimbote" in *Sert, 1928–1979*, 116–126, 129–137; Mumford, "CIAM and Latin America" and Maria Rubert de Ventós, "Cities in Latin America: The Work of Town Planning Associates, 1943–1956," in Costa and Hartray, *Sert: Arquitecto en Nueva York*, 48–75, 76–101.

63. Mumford, "CIAM and Latin America," 58, 72.

64. Other Latin American plans include Lima in Peru (1947–48), and Medellín, Cali, Tumaco, and Bogotá (the latter with Le Corbusier) in Colombia (1949–53). Sert and Wiener were also engaged in additional projects in Venezuela and Cuba. See "Urbanisme en Amérique Latine," *l'Architecture d'aujourd'hui* 21 (December 1950–January 1951): 1–55; "Five Civic Centers in South America" (recent work by Paul Lester Wiener and Josep Lluís Sert), *Architectural Record* 114 (August 1953): 121–136; Paul Lester Wiener and Josep Lluís Sert, "The Work of the Town Planning Associates in Latin America 1945–1956," *Architectural Design* 27 (June 1957): 290.

65. See Mumford, "CIAM and Latin America," 48. Sigrid de Lima, "Brazil Builds a New City," *American Journal of Economics and Sociology*, 343 (JLSC, SC, FLL, HDS).

66. Paul Lester Wiener and Josep Lluís Sert, "A City Measured by Its People," in "Brasil Builds a New City: Cidade dos Motores," *Progressive Architecture* 27 (September 1946): 58, 74. In the colonial cities of the New World, new civic centers replaced traditional cathedral squares. Citing provisions in the royal charter, Sert explained: "The main plaza shall be of an oblong form . . . which is best for fiestas in which horses are used . . . ; a moderate and good proportion is six hundred feet long and four hundred feet wide. . . . *Building lots shall not be assigned to individual persons in the plaza* where the buildings of the church and royal houses and the public land of the city are placed." Royal Ordinances for New Towns Given by King Philip II of Spain in San Lorenzo of the Escorial, July 3, 1573. Sert, *Can Our Cities Survive?* 232n.5.

67. Rovira, *Sert*, 113–127; Rovira, "Cidade dos Motores" in Rovira, *Sert, 1928–1979*, 116–126.

68. Wiener and Sert, "A City Measured by Its People," 58, 59.

69. On Le Corbusier's appreciation of Gustave Lyon's design of the acoustical shell for the Salle Pleyel in Paris, see Le Corbusier, "La Salle Pleyel, une preuve de l'évolution architecturale," *Cahiers d'art* 2 (February 1928): 89–90.

70. Mumford endorsed Le Corbusier's Nemours project because he considered it socially responsive, in contrast to his visionary projects. Le Corbusier, *La Ville radieuse*, 310–318; *The Radiant City*, 310–318. Mumford, *Culture of Cities*, [437], fig. 30.

71. See also the drawings reproduced in Le Corbusier and Pierre Jeanneret, *Oeuvre complète, 1934–1938*, Max Bill, ed. (Zurich: Girsberger, 1939; rpt. 1964), 81.

72. Le Corbusier and Jeanneret, *Oeuvre complète, 1934–1938*, 42–45.

73. Ibid., 58–59. Le Corbusier "Plan Director para Buenos Aires," *La Arquitectura de Hoy* 4 (April 1947). Brooks, *Le Corbusier Archive*, 13: 3–10.

74. Le Corbusier, *Oeuvre complète, 1938–1946*, W. Boesiger, ed. (Zurich: Editions d'Architecture, 1946), 133; Le Corbusier, "A Plan for St. Dié," *Architectural Record* 100 (October 1946): 80.

75. Le Corbusier, *Oeuvre complète, 1938–1946*, 48–65.

76. "Le Corbusier Show," *Architectural Forum* 83 (October 1945): 11. Edward Alden Jewell, "Le Corbusier Art on Display Today," *New York Times*, September 21, 1945. See also "News," *Pencil Points* 22 (October 1945): 16; "Le Corbusier Has Exhibit,"

Architectural Record 98 (November 1945): 160. "Un Plan pour Saint-Dié," *l'Homme et l'architecture* no. 5–6 (November–December 1945): 39–44.

77. Josep Lluís Sert, caption to Le Corbusier's rendering of Saint-Dié, "Urban Design," report of conference, Graduate School of Design, Harvard University, April 9–10, 1956, *Progressive Architecture* 37 (August 1956): 100–101.

78. "The Village College Idea" and "Impington Village College," *Architectural Review* 86 (December 1939): 225–234; "Impington Village College, Cambridgeshire," *Architect's Journal* 90 (December 21, 1939): 734–740. Although misidentified as the "Village College in Cambridgeshire," a perspective rendering of the Papworth School for Tuberculous appeared in *Architect's Journal* 86 (November 4, 1937): 705. See also Sigfried Giedion, *Walter Gropius: Work and Teamwork* (New York: Reinhold, 1934), 130–132.

79. The Museum of Modern Art cosponsored the first two, and Thomas Mabry, its executive director, served as "technical adviser" for the Smithsonian competition. In 1936 Wallace K. Harrison prepared two master plans for a Municipal Art Center in conjunction with the Museum of Modern Art and a northern extension of Rockefeller Center, which included a new museum, opera house, and other cultural buildings organized around a plaza site. Sert may have known of the plans through Le Corbusier, who expressed his interest in collaborating with Harrison. The plans are discussed and illustrated in Bacon, *Le Corbusier in America,* 198–200.

For each of the competition programs, see James D. Kornwolf, ed., *Modernism in America, 1937–1941: A Catalog and Exhibition of Four Architectural Competitions* (Williamsburg, Va.: Muscarelle Museum of Art, College of William and Mary, 1985), 225–227, 233–241.

80. Walter Gropius and Marcel Breuer's design won second prize in the competition. The programmatic components of Percival Goodman's design were also well integrated. Sert's later partner Paul Wiener, along with Pierre Bezy and John W. Stedman, Jr., won third prize in the Wheaton competition. These entries appear in Kornwolf, *Modernism in America,* 44–46, 48–49, 264, figs. 41–46, 49–51; and Talbot F. Hamlin, "Competitions: [Art Center for Wheaton College, Norton, Mass.]," *Pencil Points* 19 (September 1938): 551–565, and "Report of the Jury," *Architectural Forum* 69 (August 1938): 143, 148–149, 150, 152.

81. See especially Rapson's perspective rendering of September 15, 1938. Kornwolf, *Modernism in America,* 146–151, figs. 137–144; *Architectural Record* 85 (April 1939): 61–62.

82. Kornwolf, *Modernism in America,* 182, 198–201, 212–213, figs. 178–181, 192–193. Joseph Hudnut served as professional advisor to the Smithsonian Gallery of Art Commission and chairman of the jury, which oversaw the competition.

Hudnut, "Smithsonian Competition Results," *Magazine of Art* 32 (August 1939): 456–459, 488–489. The jury commended the Saarinen design for its "remarkable clarity of composition in mass" and the G. Holmes Perkins plan as "exceptionally well organized." For the report and illustrations of the winning designs, including the Saarinen and the Perkins isometric perspectives, see "Smithsonian Gallery of Art Competition," *Architectural Forum* 71 (July 1939): 10–11ff. See also Mina Marefat, "When Modern Was a Cause: The 1939 Smithsonian Art Gallery Competition," *Competitions* 1 (Fall 1991): 36–49.

83. For Mumford's criticism of the Wheaton, William and Mary, and Smithsonian competitions, see "The Skyline: Notes on Modernism," *New Yorker* 14 (October 22, 1938): 73–74; "The Skyline: The American Tradition," *New Yorker* 15 (March 11, 1939): 47–48; "Reflections on Modern Architecture," *Twice a Year* 2 (Spring–Summer 1939): 35–41; "The Skyline: Growing Pains; The New Museum," *New Yorker* 15 (June 3, 1939): 40–42; "The Skyline: Shade and Sunlight," *New Yorker* 15 (December 2, 1939): 73–75; "The Skyline: Millions for Mausoleums," *New Yorker* 15 (December 30, 1939): 45–46. For the Museum of Modern Art exhibition of the Wheaton art center competition, see "An Architectural Competition," *Bulletin of the Museum of Modern Art* 5 (February 1938): 2–3; the College of William and Mary competition,

see *Bulletin of the Museum of Modern Art* 6 (1939); and the Smithsonian, see "Smithsonian Architectural Competition," *Bulletin of the Museum of Modern Art* 6 (January 1940): 7; Kornwolf, *Modernism in America*, 265.On the Modern's traveling exhibitions entitled "Competition for an Art Center at Wheaton College," "Competition for a Festival Theatre in Williamsburg, Virginia," and "Competition for a New Smithsonian Gallery of Art, Washington, D.C.," see *Bulletin of the Museum of Modern Art* 7 (September 1940): 13. Kornwolf, *Modernism in America*, 3.

84. On the Mackley Houses, see "The Carl Mackley Houses in Philadelphia," *Architectural Record* 78 (November 1935): 289–298; Albert Mayer, "A Critique of the Hosiery Workers' Housing Development in Philadelphia," *Architecture* 71 (April 1935): 189–194. Richard Pommer, "The Architecture of Urban Housing in the United States During the Early 1930s," *JSAH* 37 (December 1978): 240.

85. "Summer Exhibition," *Bulletin of the Museum of Modern Art* 4 (July 1937): 7–8. See also F. A. Gutheim, "Architecture, Art, Life," *Magazine of Art* 30 (May 1937): 306–309.

86. Cynthia Wentworth, "Leisure and the Community Center," *American City* 52 (August 1937): 66–67. Hugh Potter's River Oaks Shopping Center in Houston (1938), which called for semicircular retail units with stuccoed brick walls and steel windows, may be drawn from Stonorov's project. This well-publicized community shopping center appears in many of the books and articles listed in Wiener, Sert, and Schulz, "Bibliography on Regional and City Planning." See especially "Suburban Shopping Centers," *National Real Estate Journal* 39 (December 1938): 29, and "Community Shopping Centers," *Architectural Record* 87 (June 1940): 102, 114–118.

87. Alan Mather, "The Battle of Willow Run," *Common Sense* 12 (February 1943): 40. For an analysis of the project from the perspective of Stonorov and Kahn, see David B. Brownlee and David G. DeLong, *Louis I. Kahn: In the Realm of Architecture* (New York: Rizzoli, 1991), 30–31. See also Hermann H. Field, "The Lesson of Willow Run," *Task*, no. 4 (1943): 9–21. "Willow Run," *Architectural Forum* 78 (March 1943): 37, 41. See also William H. Jordy, "Fiasco at Willow Run," *Nation* 156 (8 May 1943): 655–658.

88. Sert, *Can Our Cities Survive?* 71, 233. Wiener, Sert, and Schulz include neighborhood shopping centers in their "Bibliography of Regional and City Planning." Stein and Bauer, "Store Buildings and Neighborhood Shopping Centers," 175.

89. See Eric Mumford, "Sert and Hofmann at Chimbote" in *Hans Hofmann: The Chimbote Project* (Barcelona: Museu d'Art Contemporani, 2004), 58, 75n.23. On McLoughlin Heights, see Meredith L. Claussen, *Pietro Belluschi: Modern American Architect* (Cambridge, Mass.: MIT Press, 1994), 115–117. On Linda Vista, see "'Grass on Main Street'

Becomes a Reality," *Architectural Forum* 81 (September 1944): 81–93, 178; Richard Longstreth, *City Center to Regional Mall: Architecture, the Automobile, and Retailing in Los Angeles, 1920–1950* (Cambridge, Mass.: MIT Press, 1997), 296–298.

90. Hudnut, "Smithsonian Competition Results," 457.

91. Morris Ketchum, Jr., *Shops and Stores* (New York: Reinhold, 1948), 271.

92. Elizabeth Mock, "Built in U.S.A.— Since 1932," in Elizabeth Mock, ed., *Built in USA: 1932–1944* (New York: Museum of Modern Art, 1944), 25.

93. For a list of subsequent American community buildings, organized by region, see "Brief Geographical Directory of Recent Community Buildings," in *Architectural Record* 99 (May 1946): 112.

94. Le Corbusier, "Architecture and Urbanism," *Progressive Architecture* 28 (February 1947): 67–68.

95. Ada Louise Huxtable, "Two Cities: Planning in North and South America," *Bulletin of the Museum of Modern Art* 14 (June 1947): 3–11.

96. Ferrari Hardoy worked in Le Corbusier's Paris atelier in 1938. On the plan for Buenos Aires, see "Le Corbusier Plan Director para Buenos Aires," *La Arquitectura de hoy*, fig. 24. See also "Esta Cobrando Expresion La Avenida 9 de Julio," *La Nacion* (September 26, 1937) (Jorge Ferrari Hardoy Collection, Special Collections, Frances Loeb Library, Graduate School of Design, Harvard University).

97. Le Corbusier and Jeanneret, *Oeuvre*

complète, 1934–1938, 81.

98. Wiener and Sert, "Brasil Builds a New City," 58. J. L. Sert, "Centres of Community Life," in J. Tyrwhitt, J. L. Sert, and E. N. Rogers, eds., *CIAM 8. The Heart of the City: Towards the Humanisation of Urban Life* (London: Lund Humphries, 1952), 3–16.

99. Sert illustrates a model of Le Corbusier's Cartesian skyscraper in *Can Our Cities Survive?* 149. Le Corbusier employed the Y-shaped plan for housing blocks in his projects for a Rome suburb (1934) and Bat'a industries at Hellocourt in France (1935). In 1937 he used this typology for housing blocks in his Bastion Kellermann project for the Exposition Internationale "Arts et Techniques" in Paris. He also employed the Y-shaped plan for offices in his projects for Antwerp (1933) and Algiers (1938). Le Corbusier, *Radiant City,* 218–219, 270–287, 304; Le Corbusier and P[ierre] Jeanneret, *Oeuvre complète de 1929–1934,* Willy Boesiger, ed. (Zurich: Girsberger, 1935; rpt. 1964), 156–159. Le Corbusier and Jeanneret, *Oeuvre complète, 1934–1938,* 36–37, 74–77, 103, 148–151. Le Corbusier, *Agenda* [November 6, 1935], marginal notes, 140 (FLC).

100. For example, Hans Poelzig's project for a skyscraper on the Friedrichstrasse in Berlin of 1921 employed a Y-shaped plan, as did two American projects published in 1929: St. Cloud Hospital near Minneapolis and Casa Riviera Apartments in Long Beach, California. For discussions of the use of the Y-shaped plan in Europe and the United States, see Eric Mumford, "The

'Tower in a Park' in America: Theory and Practice, 1920–1960," *Planning Perspectives* 10 (1995): 21–22; Bacon, *Le Corbusier in America,* 154–156, 172–174. On Alden Park, see Henry Wright, "The Place of the Apartment in the Modern Community," *Architectural Record* 67 (March 1930): 212; *A. C.* 25 (June 1937): 35; Sert, *Can Our Cities Survive?* 69. See also letter, Josep Lluís Sert to Joseph Hudnut, April 23, 1942 (JLSC, SC, FLL, HDS).

101. Ketchum illustrates two plans and an axonometric drawing of the Motor City in *Shops and Stores,* 281–285. See also "Shopping Center," *Architectural Forum* 85 (August 1946): 76–79; Longstreth, *City Center to Regional Mall,* 325–330, 332–333.

102. Paul Lester Wiener and Josep Lluís Sert, "Report on the Master Plan of Chimbote," December 31, 1948 (PLWC, SC, UOL). Barton Jones, an American engineer who had previously worked for the TVA, supervised the project. Rovira, "Chimbote," in Rovira, *Sert, 1928–1979,* 130–131.

103. Paul Lester Wiener and Josep Lluís Sert, "Pilot Plan for the Town of Chimbote," February 14, 1948, and "Report on the Master Plan of Chimbote," December 31, 1948 (PLWC, SC, UOL).

104. In 1950 Sert collaborated with the German-born American artist Hans Hofmann on a design for the Chimbote bell tower, which was not constructed. See Mumford, "Sert and Hofmann at Chimbote" (and other essays) in *Hans Hofmann: The Chimbote Project,* 52.

105. "Five Civic Centers in South

America," 123. On the objectives of the TVA from the perspective of authority board member David E. Lilienthal, see his *TVA: Democracy on the March* (New York: Harper, 1944), a book that appears in Wiener, Sert, and Schulz, "Bibliography on Regional and City Planning." For Mumford's views on TVA as a "great project in socialized planning" with its system of dams as "agents of regional development," see *Culture of Cities,* 324–325, 400.

106. Sert, *Can Our Cities Survive?* 217.

107. Wiener and Sert, "Report on the Master Plan of Chimbote," December 31, 1948 (PLWC, SC, UOL). Tyrwhitt, Sert, and Rogers, *CIAM 8,* 129–130. Sert's library contained such books as Hiram Bingham, *Lost City of the Incas* (1948); Garcilaso de la Vega, *Comentarios Reales de los Incas,* vols. 1 and 2 (1945); Walter Lehmann, ed. *The Art of Old Peru* (1924); *Arte Prehispánico de México* (1946). See "Sert Library Inventory."

108. Mumford, *Culture of Cities,* 489. Wiener, Sert, and Schulz's "Bibliography on Regional and City Planning" includes the article by Benton MacKaye and Lewis Mumford, "Townless Highways for the Motorist," *Harper's Magazine* 163 (August 1931): 347–356; Clarence Stein, *Towards New Towns for America* (Liverpool: Liverpool University Press, 1949); Clarence Stein, "City Patterns—Past and Future," *Pencil Points* 23 (June 1942): 53. See also Walter Gropius, *Rebuilding Our Communities* (Chicago: Paul Theobald, 1945), which reproduced Clarence Stein's diagram of the "town-

less highway" with its clusters of neighborhood units (page 19) (PLWC, SC, UOL). On national and regional planning at CIAM 6 and 7, see S[igfried] Giedion, *A Decade of New Architecture* (Zurich: Girsberger, 1951), 23–24.

109. For a description of Chimbote's type C housing, see P. L. Wiener and J. L. Sert, "4 Pilot Plans for South-American Cities," in "Urbanisme en Amérique Latine," *l'Architecture d'aujourd'hui* 21, no. 33 (December 1950–January 1951): 1–55. An aerial perspective of the neighborhood unit in the Quiroga sector in Bogotá (1951) is incorrectly identified as Chimbote, in Rovira, *Sert, 1928–1979,* 137. I thank Mary Daniels for drawing this to my attention.

110. Le Corbusier, *Oeuvre complète, 1938–1946,* 116–117. On the increasing importance of the patio in the Latin American town planning projects of Wiener and Sert, see their "Can Patios Make Cities?" *Architectural Forum* 99 (August 1953): 124–131. Perret's warehouses at Casablanca are illustrated in Roberto Gargiani, *Auguste Perret* (Milan: Gallimard/Electa, 1994), 292, fig. 31. On the Monol Houses, see Le Corbusier and Pierre Jeanneret, *Oeuvre complète, 1910–1929* (Zurich: Girsberger, 1937; rpt. 1964), 30. On the Radiant Farm, see Le Corbusier and Jeanneret, *Oeuvre complète de 1929–1934,* 186–191. For illustrations of the Weekend House, see Le Corbusier and Jeanneret, *Oeuvre complète, 1934–1938,* 124–130. On the Roq and Rob project, see W. Boesiger and H. Girsberger,

Le Corbusier, 1910–65 (London: Thames and Hudson, 1967), 132–133.

111. On Sert's knowledge and appreciation of Gaudí's work, see James Johnson Sweeney and Josep Lluís Sert, *Antoni Gaudí* (London: Architectural Press, 1960). See Peter, *Oral History of Modern Architecture,* 249.

112. Sert noted that although CIAM Congresses since the early 1930s had studied the integration of architecture and planning, the 1947 CIAM 6 Congress at Bridgwater recognized that the two disciplines had moved closer together as a consequence of postwar reconstruction. Sert, "Centres of Community Life," in Tyrwhitt, Sert, and Rogers, *CIAM 8,* 3, 6.

113. Le Corbusier, "Core as a Meeting Place of the Arts," and Sert, "Centres of Community Life," both in Tyrwhitt, Sert, and Rogers, *CIAM 8,* 3–16, 41–52. For the emergence of poetic and aesthetic issues as well as a synthesis of the arts in the CIAM debates, see S. G. [Sigfried Giedion], "Architect, Painter and Sculptor" and "The Bridgwater Questionnaire," both in Giedion, *Decade of New Architecture,* 30–37. See also Mumford, *CIAM Discourse on Urbanism, 1928–1960,* 180, 192–193, 196. On Le Corbusier's interest in a synthesis of the arts combined with postwar planning, see Christopher Pearson, "Le Corbusier's 'synthesis of the major arts' in the context of the French Reconstruction," in Karen Koehler, ed., *The Built Surface,* vol. 2 (Aldershot, U.K.: Ashgate, 2004), 209–227.

114. Mumford, *Culture of Cities,* 479, 481, 484. Sert, "Centres of Community Life," in Tyrwhitt, Sert, and Rogers, *CIAM 8,* 8.

115. "Conversation at CIAM 8," in Tyrwhitt, Sert, and Rogers, *CIAM 8,* 36.

116. S[igfried] Giedion, "The Heart of the City: A Summing-Up," in Tyrwhitt, Sert, and Rogers, *CIAM 8,* 161; see also vii, 4, 5.

117. Mumford, *Culture of Cities,* 482.

118. Frank Lloyd Wright, "Démocratie et architecture" [excerpts from Wright's *When Democracy Builds,* Stéphanie Chandler, trans. (Chicago, 1944)], *Chantiers* 1 (December 1946): 3. A reference to Sert and Wiener's work, which appears in the *Chantiers* excerpts, is found in neither the first edition of 1944 nor the revised edition (Chicago: University of Chicago Press, 1945). The citation to the 1944 edition prompted Wiener to inquire of Pierre-Louis Flouquet, technical director of *Chantiers,* whether this was a mistake or "an insertion authorized later by Frank Lloyd Wright." Letter, Paul Lester Wiener to P. L. Flouquet, February 6, 1947 (PLWC, SC, UOL).

119. In 1959 Sert told John Peter: "I've always been interested in architecture as an extension of human problems, not only technical, but human problems. I'm very interested in this side, of how this is an expression of a way of living and of certain approaches to life." Peter, *Oral History of Modern Architecture,* 256.

Part Three

THE PARAMETERS
OF URBAN DESIGN

Chapter 6

BREAKING COMMON GROUND

Joseph Hudnut and the Prehistory of Urban Design

JILL PEARLMAN

Though this book names Josep Lluís Sert as the architect of urban design, largely for his having created the urban design program in 1960 at Harvard's Graduate School of Design, the groundwork for that program had been set nearly two decades before Sert arrived at Harvard. Indeed, one must look back to the beginnings of the GSD, to 1936, when Joseph Hudnut founded the school, and to Hudnut's subsequent sixteen years as dean alongside his prize hire, Walter Gropius.

While Gropius needs no introduction, it is Hudnut's fate that he still probably does. Not unlike others who had worked in partnership with the charismatic Gropius—Adolf Meyer, Maxwell Fry, and Konrad Wachsmann come to mind—the Bauhaus master greatly overshadowed Hudnut during their years together at Harvard. Nonetheless, it was Hudnut (and not Gropius) who founded the GSD, and although he never quite used the words that Sert often did, Hudnut founded the school as a "common ground" for the disparate fields of architecture, landscape architecture, and city plan-

ning. Before 1936, the three fields had been housed in separate schools at Harvard (as at other universities), with little contact among them. But Hudnut brought them together in the new GSD to tackle the ultimate design problem—the city. Seventeen years before Sert arrived at Harvard, Hudnut had broken common ground by founding the GSD to confront the issue of urban design.

To grasp Hudnut's aims in founding the GSD, a comparison to Gropius's idea for the Bauhaus program seems useful. At the opening of the German design school in 1919 Gropius had claimed that "the arts exist in isolation, from which they can be rescued only through the conscious cooperative effort of all craftsmen." Moreover, he declared, "the ultimate aim of all visual arts is the complete building."[1] For Hudnut at the GSD, the ultimate object of cooperation among the fields that he brought together was the city. Sert seemed to agree with Hudnut rather than Gropius on this issue, for, as he claimed a few years into his own GSD dean-ship, "Architecture is often called the mother of the

Figure 6.1 Joseph Hudnut in his GSD office, 1946

changeably. On numerous occasions, Hudnut and Sert also substituted the term "city planning." For both deans, civic or urban design referred to that part of city planning that addressed the physical form of the city. Hudnut would agree with Sert's definition of urban design as "the most creative phase of city planning and that in which imagination and artistic capacities can play a more important part."[3]

Hudnut had been interested in civic design well before he came to Harvard. While "civic" may conjure visions of grand city centers or majestic monuments (Sert avoided the word for this reason[4]), Hudnut meant otherwise. This is not to imply that Hudnut favored the "functional city" that Sert promoted so vigorously in *Can Our Cities Survive?* and as CIAM's president. In fact, Hudnut did not promote any particular type of urban form because he believed that there were many possible ways to restore humanity to the city. By the start of the postwar era, however, he had become less open-minded. As much as he disliked imperial civic form, he had come to disdain the functional city as sterile and inhuman and to lean toward the kind of urbanism that Jane Jacobs would later promote (fig. 6.1). Hudnut was all for the crowded, dense, mixed-use centralized city, where streets served as key public places.[5] And yet, while Hudnut and Sert ultimately differed on the kind of form the city should take, they both regarded the "activity" of civic or urban design in much the same way. They also shared similar views on educating practitioners to take part in this activity. Indeed, Sert would carry through with the program that Hudnut had begun laying out during his years at the GSD.

arts, but it is the city that deserves that title. The city has united the arts."[2] Creating an urban pattern that worked to foster social harmony and to satisfy individual needs and the needs of the human spirit in a world increasingly shaped by industrialization, by cars, by suburbanization—this was the focus of Hudnut's efforts at Harvard and the reason he founded the GSD. He grew more adamant about this as planning for the postwar city got under way.

Though Hudnut preferred "civic design" to Sert's "urban design," the terms were used inter-

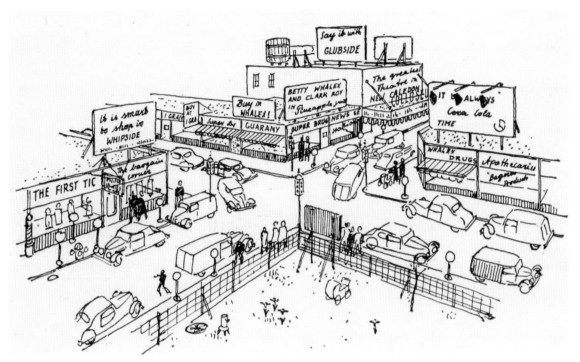

Figure 6.2 "Shops and markets, with their colored letterings, bright windows, neon lights and the murmur of crowds . . . that is precisely what is needed." Sketch by Wilhelm von Moltke for Hudnut's "The Art in Housing," *Architectural Record* 93 (January 1943).

When Sert published *Can Our Cities Survive?* in 1942, the volume that was intended to promote the CIAM urbanistic agenda in the United States, Hudnut wrote the book's foreword. Hudnut did not come out in favor of the CIAM agenda, nor did he even consider any formal aspects of the group's urbanistic goals. Instead, Hudnut focused on what he and Sert shared when it came to the question of city design: a belief in the importance of the activity or "*processes* by which material things are shaped and assembled for civic use." Those processes, Hudnut explained, should be guided "not only by those intellectual forces which seek to bend natural law to human betterment but also by those spiritual forces which throughout human history have left repeated imprints upon the human environment."[6] In effect, Hudnut was arguing for the restoration of "art" to the process of designing cities. This argument would find its way into the many essays that Hudnut would publish on the subject of city design.

HUDNUT AND CIVIC DESIGN

Hudnut had come to the activity of civic design quite by accident. He had trained as a Beaux-Arts architect at Harvard, Michigan, and Columbia, where he received his master's degree in 1917.

VIEW DOWN LAKE VIEW AVENUE, ACROSS HOLLAND SQARE, WYOMISSING, *showing* PROPOSED HOUSES
HEGEMANN AND PEETS, CITY PLANNING AND LANDSCAPE ARCHITECTS, MILWAUKEE AND WYOMISSING NOV. 7 1917

Figure 6.3 Joseph Hudnut, drawing of "View Down Lake Avenue, Across Holland Square, Wyomissing," 1917

Until 1926, when he turned to full-time teaching, he ran a gentlemanly practice in New York and later in Charlottesville, Virginia, designing houses and churches, some with a Georgian twist, others with a Gothic, Greek Revival, or Tudor aspect (figs. 6.2 and 6.3). Hudnut had the good fortune in 1917 to encounter the German city planner and theorist Werner Hegemann. Intrigued by Hegemann's intellectual depth and social commitment, Hudnut signed on as his assistant. In tandem with his own practice, Hudnut assisted Hegemann in creating two picturesque residential communities, one in Milwaukee and the other near Reading, Pennsylvania, using the historic styles of architecture common to each region. Hudnut helped his mentor order street systems, public squares, vistas, and extensive parks in these communities to accentuate the beauty and irregularity of their natural settings. As he did so, Hudnut began to question all that he been taught about architecture and its practice. His work with Hegemann proved to be a life-shaping experience.[7]

Today Hegemann is best known for having written *The American Vitruvius: An Architect's Handbook of Civic Art* with Elbert Peets in 1922, reissued to popular acclaim in 1989.[8] As readers of that book know, Hegemann was by no means a modernist, and he did not belong to CIAM. In fact, Hegemann had been critical of CIAM planning ideas and of Le Corbusier's "ghastly" skyscrapers, fearing that they might actually come to pass, "not because they are desirable, healthy, beautiful or reasonable" but because of rampant real estate speculation.[9] Despite harsh words for the modernists, Hegemann passed onto Hudnut an approach to "civic design" that would have much in common with Sert's approach to "urban design." Hudnut and Sert both regarded city design as a synthetic endeavor, and they believed that this endeavor should celebrate even the commonplace in daily life. Finally, both had set out to bring art back into the process of city planning or design.

SHARED GROUND

As Richard Marshall argues in this volume, "synthesis" played a signal part in Sert's urban design program, at a time when disciplines vigilantly guarded their boundaries. In a "period of a cult to the individual and the genius," Sert wrote, "with all due respect to genius, it is not to them that we owe our best cities."[10] Synthesis also lay at the crux of Hudnut's notion of civic design. From Hegemann, Hudnut had learned to regard civic design as a synthetic endeavor. Hegemann had been a broadly educated man—versed in political science, economics, art history, philosophy, and sociology—and for him civic design drew from all these as well as from other fields, including architecture and landscape architecture. Hudnut's founding of the GSD, the decisions he made as dean there, and his prolific writings on the city all underscored the importance of uniting disparate fields to confront the issue of city design. In one telling but (partly) tongue-in-cheek article, "What a Planner Has to Know" (1946), Hudnut recounted imaginary conversations with the chairs of the "seven score departments" at Harvard ("we live here in separate cells like doves in their dove-

cot") in which he asked what courses of study they considered indispensable to the education of those designing the postwar city. What he had in mind in asking this question, Hudnut said, was to gauge the "range and depth of understanding" that would allow city designers to contribute in a significant way to the "forward march of humanity." The result of Hudnut's query: 120 courses of study were deemed essential and 75 others desirable. If done right, educating students for the practice of city design would take thirty-three years.[11]

Hudnut and Sert not only believed that a number of fields must join in the process of urban design, they both held that cities must be designed "for the people and with the people," in Sert's words. As Sert made clear to those in attendance at the first Urban Design Conference, to bring an "element of life into the city," urban designers must celebrate the "informal" and the "intimate," the commonplace aspects of daily life, rather than the formal and monumental. By reorganizing our "everyday life," which meant to him dwellings, recreation centers, workplaces, streets, and highways, Sert had arrived at the scheme of organization for the CIAM city he put forth in his 1942 book. As for the sources of this informality and intimacy, Sert explained, "we shall have to find in man and his needs and spiritual aspirations, the measure and guide for our designs."[12]

Unlike Sert, who came of age in the modernist era, Hudnut had learned in school to regard the city as "an arrangement of streets which afford building sites to an architect," or as "an arrangement of spaces and structures which might assure the architect opportunities for the exploitation of his formal principles of pattern."[13] His work with Hegemann brought Hudnut to an entirely different point of view. He came to recognize that the seemingly mundane elements of urban form, those unspectacular places essential to the daily lives of ordinary citizens, all contributed significantly to the larger urban pattern. Moreover, Hudnut now believed that the city's physical pattern—of which streets, parks, waterfronts, and buildings were components—must grow out of the ever-changing "idea pattern" that governs the lives of its citizens.[14] By idea pattern, Hudnut meant the shared values, habits, customs, and symbols of the people who live in a place.

Hudnut made the "everyday" central to his vision of civic design in one other way: by urging people to participate in the process of shaping cities through politics.[15] He exhorted readers in articles he published on urban design in popular magazines—*Mademoiselle* and *House and Garden,* among others—and by speaking to a range of audiences, including garden clubs and civic groups. While in theory Sert may have favored citizens' direct participation in the process of urban design, he saw only a limited role for it, given that few people had any training in visual literacy. He considered this form of illiteracy a serious failing of "general education"— a mantra of the postwar era.[16]

Hudnut also took his case for civic design to professionals in the fields of city planning and architecture. In 1944 he was one of the founders and the leading force of the American Society of Planners and Architects (ASPA), intended as a progressive alternative to the American Institute of Architects (AIA) and a U.S. alternative to CIAM.[17] ASPA had two purposes: to advance the cause of modern architec-

ture and to deepen the connection between planners and architects through a common professional organization. Although the latter cause remained closest to Hudnut's heart, it was the former that actually drew most members to the group. The eighty or so members included a number of well-known figures in the architectural world, among them Louis Kahn (who followed Hudnut as president), George Howe, G. Holmes Perkins, Hugh Stubbins, Alfred Barr, Catherine Bauer, William Wurster, Eero Saarinen, Paul Rudolph, Marcel Breuer, Serge Chermayeff, Sigfried Giedion, Philip Johnson, Lawrence Kocher, Pietro Belluschi, Richard Neutra, Walter Gropius (who kept a low profile, unusual for him), and Josep Lluís Sert. Since he was the primary organizer of the group, its first president, and the author of many of its documents, Hudnut assured that his issue, civic design, remained squarely on the docket. In its constitution and publications, ASPA emphasized the importance of architects and planners working together in shaping the modern city.[18] ASPA proved to be a short-lived society, however, effectively ceasing to exist by 1948. The reason, as Holmes Perkins remarked, was that "we succeeded so well that we didn't need it any more."[19] What Perkins meant was that by the time ASPA folded, many of its members were running thriving modern practices. The demise of the organization, however, signals Hudnut's failure to interest modern architects in the union of the architecture and planning fields in the cause of city design.

During their respective years at Harvard, Hudnut and Sert shared another important idea for the city and its future. Both maintained—albeit two decades apart—that the "scientific" aspect of city planning had been given too much weight, and that the time had come for art to play a major role in shaping urban form. Neither, of course, wanted to return to the art of the City Beautiful, with its fixed design principles, classical embellishments, and indifference to the living conditions of citizens. To the contrary, Sert and Hudnut both regarded the city as a living and growing organism that forever changed in form and in direct relationship to the people who lived there. Both believed that art must be an essential part of the shaping and assembling of spaces and forms for civic use. It was the art in city planning that gave expression to the "heart and content of society." [20] In his foreword to *Can Our Cities Survive?* and in many subsequent essays, Hudnut called for cities shaped not only by the science of planning but also by art, or, as he put it, "By those spiritual forces which throughout human history have left repeated imprints upon the human environment." [21]

Hudnut and Sert shared similar views on the place of urban design at the GSD and in the design fields more broadly. Neither regarded urban design as a neatly bounded discipline, distinct from architecture, city planning, or landscape architecture. Instead, both viewed it a field of activity in which architects, landscape architects, and city planners would all participate. They envisioned that each of these design disciplines would bring particular expertise to the collaborative process of shaping practical ideas and emotional ones into visible patterns in the city fabric. [22] As it happened, Sert had a much easier time than Hudnut in making this activity central to the mission of the GSD.

Several members of Sert's faculty, especially Jaqueline Tyrwhitt and Sigfried Giedion, helped assure that the issue of urban design moved quickly to the forefront at the GSD, an advantage Hudnut did not have. Deeply involved with CIAM by 1947, Tyrwhitt joined the group's postwar debates over reconstruction and played an active part in the subsequent discussion of the urban core, interests she brought to Harvard from 1955 to 1966. Tyrwhitt's view of the core seemed more akin to Hudnut's conception than to Sert's or Giedion's. Like Hudnut, she favored a small-scale, populist "gathering place of the people" at the core that encouraged democratic social interaction. Sert and Giedion instead stuck by the principles of the Athens Charter and the urban proposals of Le Corbusier as they argued for a grand symbolic space, a piazza, at the heart of the city. [23] Even if differences surfaced between these proponents of urban design, Sert, Giedion, Tyrwhitt, and others who passed through the GSD during the Sert era—Hideo Sasaki, Jerzy Soltan, and Wilhelm von Moltke important among them—promoted the common ground between the school's fields, for the sake of the city.

OBSTACLES

When he founded the GSD in 1936, Hudnut intended to make the activity of civic design a fundamental part of the curriculum. Before he could begin to do so, however, he had to battle some of the old-guard city planners on the faculty—including the head of the department of city and regional planning, Henry Hubbard. Hubbard, a founding figure in the field of city planning who had taught planning courses at Harvard since 1909, had a different idea from Hudnut's of how cities should be shaped and who should participate in that shaping. Hubbard considered city planning and design as distinct from architecture and landscape architecture—and he intended to keep it that way. For him, as for many of his contemporaries in the planning field, the design of cities was an art in which a specially trained practitioner brought a certain set of skills to bear on the urban landscape, including expertise in site planning, land subdividing, zoning, and transportation planning.

According to Hubbard, planners "coordinated" the uses and appearance of the city's whole physical environment. The job of architects was to create individual buildings. Hubbard intended to uphold these professional distinctions by educating planners in one way and architects in another. He tried to prevent Hudnut, whom he regarded as a neophyte in the planning field, from making changes in the way city design was taught. After the two butted heads for five years over the issue of civic design, Hubbard finally resigned his post in 1941. Hudnut wielded power at the GSD and had just canceled all planning courses for the school year for the second time in three years.[24]

Hudnut had wanted to establish a common first-year course of study almost from the start of his tenure at Harvard. With that core course, as he envisioned it, instructors would begin to teach the shared processes of civic design by introducing the basic techniques and principles of architecture, landscape architecture, and city planning. Given opposition from Hubbard and then the outbreak of World War II, which brought all university initiatives to a halt, Hudnut had to postpone his curricular plans. Finally, in 1946, Hudnut got his course in

place. Planning I, as he named it, revolved each year around a single collaborative project—often the design of an area near Boston. Students from the three GSD departments would begin the project by researching patterns of land use, traffic, recreation, commerce, housing, educational needs, and other aspects of urban life, and then set to work designing each urban element. At the end of the year they would submit a lengthy research report and a comprehensive plan. In carrying out these projects students came to appreciate the fact that social, economic, aesthetic, and technical factors were all parts of the civic or urban design process.[25]

Hudnut took to the classroom himself to advance the cause of civic design. Starting in 1942, he began teaching a series of courses on the history of civic design, a subject receiving almost no attention elsewhere in those years. Hudnut underscored the relationship between the physical design and the social and political order of major cities. He seemed to have a certain hold over his students, one of whom expressed that Hudnut's courses were "the most affecting single learning experience . . . for many of us." This same student, however, conceded that "beyond this course, [Hudnut's] was not an effective view in the school."[26] Sigfried Giedion would teach similar courses during the Sert era at the GSD, though Giedion would call them History of Urban Design.

Hudnut already had some experience with educating architects for the activity of "civic design" before teaching his history courses, before Planning I, and even before he came to Harvard. He had been dean of the Columbia School of Architecture between 1934 and 1936, and there he had created a

Figure 6.4 Design Fundamentals exercises on display, 1951, by Harvard University Graduate School of Design students

Town Planning Studio aimed at preparing students for their part in the inevitable rebuilding of cities when the Depression ended. This studio was central to Hudnut's accomplishments at Columbia, where he had become rather famous for having overthrown the Beaux-Arts educational system and for his embrace of European modern architecture. Hudnut hired regional planner and housing expert Henry Wright to lead the studio, along with his own mentor, Werner Hegemann, who was once again in the United States as a political refugee. Wright and Hegemann taught their students a variety of skills related to site planning, housing development, and community organization, and engaged them in planning issues in the Columbia neighborhood. On a more philosophical level, the two planners tried to get their students to understand the city as a vast composition of related buildings and spaces rather than as a landscape of frontages waiting for their constructions. City planning and architecture, students learned, were parts of a single design process—that is, civic design. Finally, Wright and Hegemann advanced the notion that as architects took part in the shaping of city form, their task included thoughtful efforts to improve the lives of individuals and communities living in the place.[27]

While he was still at Columbia, Hudnut had begun to lay out his ideas for establishing an Institute of Urbanism (to be housed at the university) where researchers from a range of disciplines would explore the built environment of New York City in its physical, design, administrative, political, social, and economic contexts. This was the first time Hudnut used the term "urbanism." He could easily have substituted "civic design" here, but he viewed the Institut d'urbanisme in Paris as his model.[28]

Though Hudnut had not been looking to leave his post at Columbia, Harvard's president, James B. Conant, lured him with the promise that he could rebuild not just the school of architecture but also the schools of city planning and landscape architecture. "Many factors" attracted Hudnut to Harvard, he later claimed, but "none was so urgent as the opportunity offered me to forge into one strong school [these] three weak schools."[29] Intending to build on what he had accomplished at Columbia, Hudnut went to Harvard to create a premier design school in which the activity of civic design would play a leading part.

Even after Hubbard had gone and the war had ended, however, Hudnut did not succeed in elevating civic design to the stature he had hoped. He needed to spend much time during his first few years at the GSD building up the individual departments of the new unified design school, sweeping out antiquated courses, teaching methods, and teachers (where possible), and hiring new faculty who could teach in a modern vein. And then there was Gropius.

Only a few years after Hudnut brought Gropius to teach at the GSD the two began a heated battle over the direction of the school. Gropius tried to build a curriculum that gave pride of place to Bauhaus principles; in particular, he wanted all GSD students to spend their first year in a Bauhaus-like preliminary course, Basic Design, modeled after

the famous *Vorkurs.* He considered this course, and not Planning I, as the "indispensable prerequisite" to further study in the GSD's three fields.[30] Basic Design embraced the two primary aims of Gropius's design philosophy—to foster individual creativity and to establish a "universal language of form" for all the arts, from graphic design to urban design.

Hudnut fundamentally disagreed with the aims and methods of Basic Design, and he knew that it would take students still further from the city design effort he championed. Gropius, however, got his way. In 1950, he persuaded President Conant to fund the course from his discretionary account on a two-year trial basis. When two years were up, Hudnut would have to evaluate the course—now named Design Fundamentals (fig. 6.4)—to determine whether he wanted to fund it from his GSD budget. In 1952, Hudnut decided not to fund it.[31]

To Hudnut's dismay, Design Fundamentals proved tremendously popular, even beyond the GSD. Only a few years after Gropius got his course, several universities added versions of it to their curricula, and by 1960 almost every school of architecture and planning taught the course.[32] That course (short-lived as it was at Harvard), Gropius himself, and his Bauhaus ideals became synonymous with the GSD.

To protest Hudnut's canceling the course, Gropius resigned from Harvard in 1952, the year before he and Hudnut were due to retire. As he departed Harvard, the national press praised Gropius roundly and even credited him with having been the sole director of the GSD, ignoring Hudnut's existence completely.[33] At the same time, the *Harvard Crimson* hailed Gropius as the GSD's "spiritual leader," claiming that "to the outside world he was the school; to much of the faculty, he, not Dean Joseph Hudnut, set the policy; and to the students, he was the ideal architect, the master mold into which they poured their talents."[34] Gropius remained a heroic figure at the GSD, with celebrations, symposia, lectures, and exhibitions held in his honor. Hudnut, in contrast, ended his association with the school abruptly after he retired in 1953. He taught his history of civic design courses at nearby MIT until the early 1960s while living away from Cambridge in a modest modern house in Dover, Massachusetts.

SERT'S ARRIVAL AT THE GSD

Hoping to avoid the power struggle that had marred the Hudnut-Gropius era, in 1954 Conant named Josep Lluís Sert to serve as both dean of the school and chair of its department of architecture. The *Crimson* weighed in on Sert's appointment, calling it a "clear-cut victory for those favoring the policies of Walter Gropius."[35] Sert and Gropius knew each other well, and the Spanish modernist had been on Gropius's short list of people he wanted to head the GSD. With one person in charge now, the school would put forth a single point of view, and it seemed as if it would be a viewpoint akin to Gropius's.

True to expectation, Sert quickly brought back and injected new life into Gropius's course, Design Fundamentals. Sert also hired a number of Gropius's allies to teach at the GSD, among them Sigfried Giedion, Naum Gabo, Serge Chermayeff, and Reginald Isaacs, Gropius's former student and future biographer. It seemed clear to everyone that the legacy of Walter Gropius would live on during the Sert years.

While Sert built on Gropius's legacy at Harvard, his tenure at the GSD also coincided with a period of grave crisis for the American city. Slums increased in number, environmental conditions and infrastructure deteriorated rapidly, and myriad unmet human needs seemed to multiply as those who could do so moved to the suburbs. The problems of the city Sert had addressed in *Can Our Cities Survive?* had worsened, and as head of the world's leading school of design, Sert was determined to act. He did so, first by establishing the Urban Design Conferences as a forum for discussion of the problems of the city, and then, in 1960, by creating the GSD's interdisciplinary program in urban design. The GSD would now turn out students well prepared to give shape to cities and towns. That program is still active and has served as the pilot for programs in place at many other universities. In this work Sert owed a debt to Hudnut's interdisciplinary and humanistic approach to city design and the foundation that he laid at Harvard.

NOTES

1. Walter Gropius, "Program of the Staatliche Bauhaus in Weimar," April 1919, reprinted in Hans M. Wingler, *The Bauhaus: Weimar, Dessau, Berlin, Chicago* (Cambridge, Mass.: MIT Press, 1976), 31.

2. Harvard University Archive, Urban Design Conference Announcement and Program, February 1956, Frances Loeb Library, Harvard University Graduate School of Design, Rare NAC 46 Harv 1956. Many thanks to Richard Marshall for sharing this and other related documents.

3. Ibid.

4. J. L. Sert in "Harvard Urban Design Conference," *Progressive Architecture* 37, no. 8 (August 1956): 97.

5. See Joseph Hudnut, "Housing and the Democratic Process," *Architectural Record* 93 (June 1943): 42–46; or Hudnut, "New Cities for Old," *Mademoiselle,* January 1945, 9.

6. Hudnut in J. L. Sert, *Can Our Cities Survive?* (Cambridge, Mass.: Harvard University Press, 1942), iv.

7. Joseph Hudnut, statement on Werner Hegemann, July 29, 1936, GSD Papers, UAV 322.7, sub. I, Harvard University Archives, hereafter cited as HUA. There is no mention in Hudnut's or Hegemann's papers of where their meeting took place. On the Hegemann/Hudnut relationship, see Jill Pearlman, "Joseph Hudnut and the Unlikely Origins of 'Post-modern' Urbanism," *Planning Perspectives* 15 (July 2000): 201–239.

8. Werner Hegemann and Elbert Peets, *The American Vitruvius: An Architect's Handbook of Civic Art* (1922; New York: Princeton Architectural Press, 1989).

9. See his remarks on Le Corbusier's "ghastly" skyscrapers: Werner Hegemann, *City Planning/Housing* (New York: Architectural Book Publishing, 1936), 274. See also Werner Hegemann, "Kritik des Grosstadt-Sanierungs-Planes Le Corbusiers," *Der Städtebau* 20 (1927): 69ff.

10. Josep Lluís Sert, opening remarks to the Urban Design Conference, April 9, 1956, Frances Loeb Library, Harvard University Graduate School of Design, Rare NAC 46 Harv 1956.

11. Joseph Hudnut, "What a Planner Has to Know," *American Society of Planning Officials Journal* (1946): 157–158.

12. Sert, "Harvard Urban Design Conference," 97.

13. Hudnut, statement on Hegemann.

14. Ibid.

15. Hudnut, "A 'Long-Haired' Reply to Moses," *New York Times Magazine,* July 22, 1944, pp. 16, 36–37, and Hudnut, "Pressure Planning," *Architectural Record* 95 (February 1944): 50–53.

16. Sert, "Harvard Urban Design Conference," 97.

17. Letter, Hudnut to G. Holmes Perkins, November 27, 1944, GSD Papers, Records of External Offices and Organizations, UAV 322.7, sub. X (HUA). ASPA records are housed in this collection.

18. Report of the President, ASPA, First Annual Meeting, January 27, 1945; "Constitution, The American Society of Planners and Architects," Special Collections, Frances Loeb Library, Harvard University Graduate School of Design.

19. G. Holmes Perkins, interview by author, December 31, 1990, Philadelphia.

20. Hudnut in Sert, *Can Our Cities Survive?* iv.

21. Ibid.

22. Letters, Hudnut to Frederic Delano, July 5, 1940, GSD Papers, UAV 322.138 (HUA), and Hudnut to John Coolidge, November 12, 1940, UAV 322.7, sub. I (HUA).

23. Ellen Shoshkes, "Jaqueline Tyrwhitt: A Founding Mother of Modern Urban Design," *Planning Perspectives* 21 (April 2006): 185–186; Eric Mumford, "The Emergence of Urban Design in the Breakup of CIAM," *Harvard Design Magazine* 24 (Spring/Summer 2006): 11–13.

24. "Professor H. V. Hubbard," *Harvard Alumni Bulletin* 42 (March 15, 1940); "School of Regional Planning to Close," *Harvard Crimson,* June 3, 1936; "Memorandum of Proposed Curriculum in Regional Planning," January 28, 1936; and letter, Hudnut to Conant, September 13, 1939, Conant Papers, Harvard University Archives, UAI 15.898. Also see the GSD's entry in *Official Register of Harvard University,* 1936–1941.

25. On Planning I, see the student pamphlet entitled *Harvard,* March 1949, Robert Weinberg Papers, Long Island University Library, Brooklyn Center;

G. Holmes Perkins, interview with
author.

26. Henry Cobb, quoted in "Alumni
Meet to Discuss Legacy of Hudnut/
Gropius Era," *HGSD News* 11
(November–December 1982): 6. Walter
Creese, a teaching fellow in civic
design, described the course in a letter
to the author, September 28, 1987.

27. On the Town Planning studio, see
letters, Hudnut to Nicholas Murray
Butler, November 19, 1934, and January
21, 1935; Hudnut to the president and
trustees of the Carnegie Corporation,
November 16, 1934, Central Files,
Columbia University; and "School of
Architecture, Report of the Dean,
1935," 183–184.

28. "New Dean, New Institute,"
Architectural Forum, June 1934, p. 36.

29. Letter, Hudnut to Delano, July 5,
1940.

30. "The Bauhaus in Dessau Curriculum
(1925)," reprinted in Wingler,
Bauhaus, 108.

31. "GSD Final Report, Committee for
the Revision of the Curricula," GSD
Papers, UAV 322.7, sub. II, IIa (HUA);
and "Hudnut Drops Design 1, Based
on Gropius Ideas," *Harvard Crimson,*
February 23, 1952, p. 1.

32. On Basic Design in 1954, see Shlomo
Sha'ag, "Architectural Education in
America," *Architectural Record* 115
(February 1954): 318, 320, 322, and
John Knox Shear, "How Should
Architecture Be Taught?" *Architectural
Record,* August 1954, pp. 302, 304, and
September 1954, pp. 292, 294.

33. "Retrospect in Boston," *Time* 59
(January 21, 1952): 58.

34. Michael Maccoby, "Design—A
School Without Direction," *Harvard
Crimson,* December 11, 1952, p. 3.

35. "Sert Proposes to Introduce New
Design I," *Harvard Crimson,* March
18, 1953.

Chapter 7

JOSEP LLUÍS SERT'S URBAN DESIGN LEGACY

RICHARD MARSHALL

The Conference laid a sound foundation for the fur-
ther development of a Program in Urban Design at
the Harvard Graduate School of Design. It dealt
effectively with the "forces that are shaping our cities
today" and with means of effectuating designs rather
than with the problem of how to design a city. Of
course, in the two days the breadth of the field could
not be adequately explored nor could any one aspect
be examined in depth. Dean Sert announced at the
close of the Conference that a further meeting would
be held in the autumn.

— Report of Faculty Committee on
the Urban Design Conference

Josep Lluís Sert became dean of the Graduate
School of Design in the fall of 1953. Almost immediately he set about developing a "common ground"
within the school, focusing on the problems of
design in the contemporary city. For Sert this common ground was a space of mediation in which
architecture, landscape architecture, and planning

would operate in the realm of urbanism. This
initiative started as a series of courses taught by Sert
and a selection of visiting professors, developed
through a series of Urban Design Conferences, and
led ultimately to the establishment of the urban
design program at the GSD. The Urban Design
Conferences brought together a collection of mid-
century urban thinkers and established the emerging
discourse to support new lines of academic and
professional endeavor.[1]

Although there is debate as to how successfully
Sert's vision was executed, his urban design legacy is
evident. Not only has the program he started continued uninterrupted to this day, but urban design programs at universities around the world have direct
and indirect connections to Sert and the Harvard
program. A review of professional practice uncovers
a tremendous scope of urban design services and
specialists, many of whom are graduates of the
Harvard urban design program. Yet the definition of
what urban design is, or is not, has always been
somewhat ambiguous. Sert's attempts to define the

terms on which urban design might be founded, through an extraordinary series of conferences held at the GSD, are worthy of exploration.

Throughout his professional life Sert was preoccupied with the development of ideas and themes related to the improvement of the human environment at a variety of scales. He believed that architecture was not a hermetic pursuit but one that should engage with a wide array of issues and creative practices. His vision for the potential of urban design was instrumental to how this field of activity evolved.

THE UNITED STATES IN THE 1950S

The intellectual underpinnings of urban design can be traced to an era of tremendous change in urban situations in and around U.S. cities. In a special edition of *Architectural Review* from December 1950 entitled "Man-Made America," one critique of the urban scene is captured well:

> The American way of life is concerned fundamentally with thinking bigger, going faster, rising higher, than the Old World; with improving on the Old World, that is to say merely quantitatively . . . far from creating a new kind of world it has merely raised to the power of "n" the potential of the old, lending to the virtues and vices of materialism a kind of giantism in which there is nothing new except the giantism, so that the new world is merely the old one drawn in caricature.[2]

In search of an emerging urban-mindedness, the editors of the *Architectural Review* asked:

> Where does the United States stand in this matter? Does it wish (as other communities in the world

today have shown they do) to be directly instrumental in molding its own environment, in such a way as to reflect a visual ideal—a concept of what constitutes order and propriety in the environment—or has the American community rejected a visual ideal, in favor of a *laissez-faire* environment—a universe of uncontrollable chaos sparsely inhabited by happy accidents?[3]

The editors at *Architectural Review* were not alone in their call for action in the urban realm. The American Institute of Architects considered inaugurating a national program to "consider the problem of relationship between buildings."[4] The time was ripe for thinking at a larger scale, and it was in this context that Sert began developing his vision for urban design at Harvard.

SERT'S EARLY THOUGHTS ON URBAN DESIGN

Evidence of an increasing concern for the plight of the city can be found in the early writings of Sert. *Can Our Cities Survive?* (1942) represents the bridge between Sert's old life in Europe and his new life in the United States. In 250 pages Sert lays out the CIAM conception of the problem with cities, breaking the city into a series of discrete categories—dwelling, recreation, work, transportation, and large-scale planning—and concludes with a call for a holistic view of the city.

It is here that we find evidence of Sert's early conception of urban design. Unlike other intellectual movements that dealt with the civic aspects of urban form, notably the City Beautiful movement, Sert was concerned with the ordinary elements of the urban situation. He wrote that "without a reorganization of our everyday life, which depends on the proper functioning of dwellings, recreation centers, work-places, and the streets and highways that are the connecting links, life in the city cannot produce benefits for the individual or for the community as a whole."[5] This interest in everyday life would set Sert's idea for urban design on a different trajectory from some of his contemporaries'. Sert dissociates his intentions from the tradition of "civic design," which he regarded as being concerned only with the creation of monumental civic centers, ignoring the living conditions of people in the neighborhoods around those centers.[6]

Can Our Cities Survive? does not use the term "urban design." But it is clear that in his argument for a better articulation of a "frame" that would allow for a greater possibility of social interaction, Sert is describing his early notion of the role that urban design should play. The professional responsible for solving these urban problems, according to Sert, was the town planner, whose task was to coordinate with other specialists—sociologists, economists, hygienists, teachers, agriculturalists, and others—in the preparation of regional plans and to lead the team of specialists in the preparation of master plans. The town planner would be responsible for "determining the location of those 'organs' which are the basic elements of urban life and of establishing their layouts."[7] The term "town planner" as Sert uses it, however, refers more to a state of mind than to a professional distinction, because those that referred to themselves as town planners were for the most part trained as architects. And indeed many of the attributes associated with the town planner in *Can Our Cities Survive?* bear an uncanny resemblance to those deemed necessary for the urban designer, as they were articulated a decade later in the urban design program curriculum.

Sert stressed that his conception of a town planner required a "complete knowledge of the means of procedure, widened by a constantly evolving world of technics."[8] This certainly suggests that the role required a broader and different kind of knowledge than that of the architect. Sert was clear that he was not asserting an increased professional role for the architect. He was not arguing for the creation of a superprofessional, a kind of genius architect able to deal with all of the complexities of the city. Rather, he was advocating for a new attitude where the town planner would become a coordinator, a kind of urban facilitator. This remained a consistent aspect of Sert's conception of urban design and one that others would rally around. Sert's town planner would require a new and different set of skills and knowledge but should not be empowered to be the ultimate urban authority: "It should not be left to the town planner alone to determine what human needs consist of and what conditions will satisfy those needs. The complexity of the human organism and of its material and spiritual aspirations requires the assistance of . . . [others] . . . to rehabilitate existing cities or shape new ones . . . the town planner should therefore join with these specialists in a labor of collaboration."[9]

In later writings Sert would elaborate upon this notion of facilitator and collaborator.[10] He thought that it had become increasingly apparent, especially after the CIAM Frankfurt Congress of 1929, that the study of modern architectural problems led to those of city planning, and that no clear line of separation could be drawn between the two. In many respects the primary concerns expressed in *Can Our Cities Survive?* shifted from singular architectural concerns to those of the entire city, and in so doing expanded the field of architectural enquiry such that "architecture and city planning were tied closer together than ever before, as many architects were faced with the problems of reconstruction and the development of new regions demanding the creation of new communities."[11] Put simply, architecture's purview was necessarily expanded by the demands of the postwar context to an understanding of the need for integration and coordination of all city planning activities to deal with the chaotic growth in cities all over the world.

Sert employs a hybrid term in an essay entitled "Centres of Community Life" that embodies much of what he aimed to accomplish in urban design. He uses "architect-planner" to describe a new kind of professional attitude that encompasses a broader kind of knowledge. The coupling of these terms is relevant in light of emerging separations between the interests of architects and those of planners, which would have tremendous consequences some decades later within the GSD. He clearly articulated what for him was the task for the architect-planner: "The architect-planner can only help to build the frame or container within which this community life could take place. We are aware of the need for such a life, for the expression of a real civic culture which we believe is greatly hampered today by the chaotic conditions of life in our cities. Naturally, the character and conditions of such awakened civic life do

not depend entirely on the existence of a favorable frame, but are tied to the political, social, and economic structure of every community."[12] These are the limitations of the architect-planner as Sert understood them. This issue recurs in much of Sert's writing and speaks to the unheroic posture that Sert saw as the domain of the urban designer, in opposition to the idea of the creative genius.

SERT AT HARVARD

In 1953 Sert was appointed professor of architecture and dean of the Graduate School of Design at Harvard University and chair of the department of architecture. The GSD's first dean, Joseph Hudnut, and the GSD's first chairman of architecture, Walter Gropius, had both retired, leaving Sert tremendous scope in which to define a new agenda within the school. Sert embraced this opportunity.

In 1954 Sert hired Sigfried Giedion to teach and started a series of initiatives that would culminate in the formation of the urban design program in 1960. The first time the term "urban design" appeared in the GSD curriculum was in 1954–55, introduced through Giedion's History of Urban Design class and a course simply called Urban Design taught by Sert, Hideo Sasaki, and Jean-Paul Carlhian. Giedion's course dealt with the culture of cities and the development of urban design as a "natural expression" of the needs, knowledge, means, and social conditions of each period, including the structure of the community: streets, squares, open spaces, the civic core (heart of the city), pedestrians, and traffic.

Urban Design was a course of lectures and seminars that dealt with the physical expression of city planning. The course was linked to a series of collaborative problems in the urban design studio and dealt most directly with issues of measure and scale—groups of buildings, open areas, roads, and their relationships—and the effect of the different functions of the city on the design of residential sectors; parks; industrial, commercial, and business sectors; the (civic) heart of the city; and transportation networks. Giedion's History class grew to become Space, Structure, and Urban Design and later split into two distinct courses, one for the urban design program and the other, Space and Structure, for the department of architecture. The Urban Design course was integrated with a class called The Human Scale in 1960 and served as the core of the new urban design program.

After several years of developing an emerging urban design curriculum at Harvard, Sert and the GSD faculty initiated a remarkable event. The postwar situation in American architecture had rallied many people to the problem of the city. Aware of this growing momentum, Sert organized a faculty committee consisting of Professors Wells Coates, Charles Eliot, William Goodman, Huson Jackson, and Jaqueline Tyrwhitt to prepare for an urban design symposium. Harvard had a legacy of such events. Hudnut and Gropius had previously organized the Conference on Urbanism in March 1942 to grapple with the task of rebuilding cities. Hudnut had organized a symposium in May 1949 entitled Debunk: A Critical Review of Accepted Planning Principles, which Sert, as president of CIAM, attended. The other gathering of note was a symposium in March 1951 entitled Debunk II—Metropolitan Planning,

which addressed planning in Boston. These conferences addressed at length planning's ability to deal with the problems of the city and involved a broad range of political, social, and economic issues. Taking this same format, the first Urban Design Conference was held at the GSD on April 9 and 10, 1956.

HARVARD URBAN DESIGN CONFERENCES

The aim of the first conference, as articulated by the faculty committee, was to define the essence of urban design. The intention was to gauge the broad acceptance of the emerging discourse and determine whether there was a set of readily agreeable principles around which it might cluster. The conference announcement invited participants to explore the "role of the planner, architect and landscape architect in the design and development of cities."[13] Among those in attendance were Robert Geddes, Pittsburgh Mayor David Lawrence, Edmund Bacon, Eduard Sekler, Josep Lluís Sert, Robert Little, William Muschenheim, Garrett Eckbo, Richard Neutra, Charles Eliot, Hideo Sasaki, Ladislas Segoe, Charles Abrams, Gyorgy Kepes, Lloyd Rodwin, Frederick Adams, Charles Haar, Jaqueline Tyrwhitt, Victor Gruen, Lewis Mumford, and Jane Jacobs (then an associate editor with *Architectural Forum*).

In the condensed report of the conference, edited by Tyrwhitt and published in *Progressive Architecture,* Sert spoke to the challenge that American cities were likely to face in the coming decades. "I should like to make a case for the city. We cannot deny that there is an American culture which is both civic and urban. . . . The younger generation in this country . . . has become aware that the uncontrolled sprawl of our communities only aggravates their problems, and that the solution lies in re-shaping the city as a whole."[14]

These remarks highlight a critique of contemporary planning, which in Sert's view had lost its capacity to deal with the challenges the city presented. Sert's ambition can be seen as both expanding architecture's purview to engage more with the city and rescuing the city from the social-science positivism endemic to planning at the time. Urban design was Sert's attempt to reengage architects in the making of city-scale propositions. After describing city planning as a "new science" concerned with careful research and analysis, he went on to say, "In late years the scientific phase has been more emphasized than the artistic one. . . . Urban Design is the part of city planning that deals with the physical form of the city. It is by nature three- or four-dimensional. This is the most creative phase of city planning and that in which imagination and artistic capacities can play a more important part."[15]

His opening remarks articulate another of his primary concerns—the development of a "common ground" within the professions: "Each of them [architecture, landscape architecture, road engineering, and city planning] [is] trying to establish a new set of principles and a new language of forms, but it also seems logical now that synthesis or reunion of progress in the different professions be brought together into urban design to get a total picture of our physical environment by integration of those efforts."[16]

Several key themes emerged from the conference. Based on the conference proceedings, there appears to have been equal concern for the idea of urban design from a variety of disciplinary backgrounds. Further, there seems to have been general agreement with the diagnosis that the city required a radical change and that the "professions" needed to be retooled to address these problems. Richard Neutra led a discussion panel, "Attitudes Towards Urban Design," in which he called for a renewed role for landscape architecture in the making of cities. In a similar way Sert addressed the idea that the best cities are "living organisms" that require a holistic approach. Reinforcing Sert's call for the development of common ground, the landscape architect Garrett Eckbo described what for him was the greatest issue to be addressed by the professions. He noted that the professions are "conditioned by our jobs to work within isolated fragments" and stressed the need to "work in terms of continuity of design, which does not have boundaries."[17] The participants agreed that urban design was less a discipline in its own right than a way of thinking and working that applied to all disciplines.

Another preoccupation of the conference was a discussion of "forces that are shaping cities today," which focused on the relative inability of the design professions to influence outcomes in the making of the city. Lloyd Rodwin (founder of the MIT-Harvard Joint Center for Urban Studies with Martin Meyerson and others in 1959) described the essential problem that "architects, planners and landscape architects rank among the least important of the forces." He asks who the "tastemakers in urban design" should be and "what evidence is there that these professions really do have much to contribute today to urban design? What are they doing now to justify the role they would like to have?"[18] Charles Abrams and Gyorgy Kepes, responding to Rodwin, affirmed the idea that professionals' knowledge about legal, political, and technical issues was essential to the making of cities.

Lewis Mumford and Jane Jacobs argued against the "folly of creating a physical structure at the price of destroying the intimate social structure of a community's life."[19] Here we see evidence of a degree of discord between an emerging "community" perspective and that advocating for "professional" agency in the design of cities. Hideo Sasaki, responding to Mumford and Jacobs, maintained that "since the visual aspect of a city is only that which is created, it is obvious that to a large degree the individuals mentioned [architects, planners, landscape architects] are the most responsible for the ultimate expression of the urban environment" and that there existed significant opportunities to improve the urban environment through design.[20] Sasaki was explicit about what he viewed as the chief faults in design and by implication what should be the foundation for new ways of thinking about design's agency in the city. He identified three issues that urban design should redress: eclecticism without meaning; monumentality without meaning, or lack of scale; lack of relationship with surroundings, or emphasis on the spectacular.[21]

The remainder of the conference involved a series of lectures followed by debate and a formal dinner discussion. Mayor Lawrence presented Pittsburgh as a case study; Edmund Bacon presented Philadelphia; Victor Gruen presented Fort Worth. Frederick Adams, the head of the department of city and regional planning at MIT, opened the discussion of "Problems of Implementation of Urban Designs," which considered how large-scale projects should be implemented. The conference was wrapped up by a general discussion titled "Is Urban Design Possible Today?"

In his closing comments Sert described an issue at the heart of his vision for urban design that would later prove to be of tremendous consequence for the urban design program and for the development of the intellectual foundation of urban design. He said that the conference indicated clear agreement between architects and landscape architects on the need for a new design role in the city. But in referring to the relationship between designers and planners, he stated, "When we come to the city planners and architects there may be a little conflict. There is a certain misgiving among architects, as someone has said here, that city planners do not know anything about the three-dimensional world we want to help shape. And the city planners think that architects know nothing about city planning. The result is when we come to the field of urban design, where both should meet and shake hands, there are many who are not prepared."

On November 26, 1956, Sert convened an Urban Design Round Table as a follow-up to the conference. In attendance were Bacon, Walter Bogner, Serge Chermayeff, Crieghton, Eliot, Fry, Walter Gropius, Gruen, Hosburgh, Reginald Isaacs, Huson Jackson, Kepes, Lopez, Lynch, Neutra, Mario Romañach, Sasaki, Sekler, Sert, and Tyrwhitt. The purpose of the meeting was to continue the momentum that the previous spring's conference had generated. In minutes of that meeting, Sert stated, "I think there are three main points that stand out. First of all can we establish a common ground for the participation of architect and planner in urban design, or physical planning if you want to call it that, as well as a series of other professions. If this possibility does not exist there is no hope. But if this common ground does exist then can we establish a basic program of what we want along broad lines which represent the general ideas of a whole past generation of people. . . . If we can frame this clearly we shall then have a program for action."

Sert's program of action was multifaceted. As the Report of the Faculty Committee on the Urban Design Conference states, the conference "laid a sound foundation for the further development of a Program in Urban Design at the Harvard Graduate School of Design."[22] In addition, it established the basis for twelve more Urban Design Conferences during the rest of the 1950s and through the 1960s.

The second Urban Design Conference (April 12 and 13, 1957) aimed to further refine the idea of urban design. The concepts agreed upon in the first conference were not discussed. In addition, the scope of the conference was reduced. It appears that Sert was concerned with the breadth of discussions at the first conference and sought greater focus and clarity in the second meeting. This reduction reflects again the growing discord between architectural and planning interests. Although economics, sociology, psychology, and other disciplines were recognized as having an impact on the contemporary form of the city, the field of urban design was intentionally reduced to the physical components only. Before the conference, the following statement was issued: "This conference is confined to a discussion of the *design section* of the planning process. This does not

mean this is considered more important than other essential sections—such as the establishment of relevant data or the means of implementation—which may fall more directly in the fields of sociology, economics or government."[23]

Six statements formed the basis for discussion. The first was an affirmation for the need for reurbanization, in opposition to suburbanization. The second was a call for the reestablishment of connections between people and nature, as well as among people. This call concerned a larger thread present in much of the conference discussions, a desire to reinforce a humanistic approach to city making in opposition to the abstraction wrought by modern planning "science." The third statement reinforced the growing dislocation between the preoccupations of planning and those of design, and further articulated the nature of the "conflict" to which Sert's closing comments at the first conference referred: "Even the best two-dimensional land-use or zoning plan cannot ensure a three-dimensional implementation that will achieve livability and beauty: therefore visual standards are as important a tool of planning."[24] Here we begin to see the emergence of a territorial claim that would separate planning from design in even more radical ways and ultimately define urban design at the GSD, based on the idea that "the essence of urban design is the inter-relation of a number of forces—visual, physical, social, economic, governmental, etc.—which all appear as causes and effects of design decisions."[25] Furthering this claim, the fourth issue was the idea that a design framework capable of coordinating between scales should be agreed on by architects, landscape architects, and city planners. Here the notion of common ground is posited, but there is also a positioning of the design professions in relation to territory controlled by planning. The fifth statement dealt with a desired separation between automobiles and pedestrians, and the sixth concerned the promotion of open space in the making of the city, reinforcing the need for thinking in terms of exterior spatial design.

DEVELOPMENT OF URBAN THINKING AT HARVARD

In April 1957 appeared the first issue of *Synthesis,* a journal published by GSD students to provide a platform for student views and work. This issue was devoted to urban design and included ten essays by students and faculty. Writers included Eckbo, Sasaki, Tyrwhitt, and Goodman. Richard Dober, working on a master's of city planning, described the current state of urban design as "the problem of the conscious, artistic design of the urban environment requiring a specialized training for which no curriculum has yet been established."[26] He wrote that urban design was the common meeting ground for the three design professions, and as a collaborative effort it was the "most productive problem at Harvard today." Yet in his reflections Dober freely admits the limitations of the collaborative idea at the GSD, describing "departmental introversion that too often encourages intellectual isolation." In Dober's opinion, the urban design problem was productive not in terms of its success but rather for introducing to the student a "macroscopic view of the totality to which he (she) will create and contribute a part." Dober's words highlight a struggle that was to emerge within the GSD in the 1960s—a problem that must have been recognized by Sert—of an increasing

separation between the three departments. Dober's words capture what may have been Sert's ultimate agenda with the introduction of urban design as a program within the school: "It is Harvard's recognition that if the pedagogical process itself cannot be changed, then the professional designer can be introduced to an over-all view in anticipation that such an introduction, no matter how frustrating, will stimulate his imagination to ameliorating the physical paradoxes with which he must work."[27] Tyrwhitt's essay, "Definitions of Urban Design," described how shortly before Christmas 1956 the editors of *Synthesis* had written to thirty-two distinguished architects, landscape architects, planners, sociologists, economists, lawyers, and prominent citizens asking their definition of urban design; her essay summarized the responses. Ten of those replying refused to commit themselves to a definition. Four "no's" were on account of being too busy (Paul Rudolph was in this class). Three "no's" were on grounds of impossibility. Robert Moses's response was short ("I am unable to comply with your request") as was Frank Lloyd Wright's ("I am not interested"). Le Corbusier's reply attempted to define the actual form that urban design should take:

> Urbanism is the most vital expression of a society. The task of urbanism is to organize the use of the land to suit the works of man, which fall into three categories:
>
> 1. The unit of agricultural production
> 2. The linear industrial city
> 3. The radio-concentric city of exchange (ideas, government, commerce)
>
> Urbanism is a science with three dimensions. Height is as important to it as the horizontal expanse.

Neutra wrote: "Giving shape to a community and moulding its activities is urban design. It deals with the dynamic features in space, but in time as well." Gropius offered: "Good urban design represents that consistent effort to create imaginatively the living spaces of our urban surroundings. In order to supersede today's soul-destroying robotization, the modern urban designer's exciting task is to satisfy all emotional and practical human needs by coordinating the dictates of nature, technique and economy into beautiful habitat." Giedion wrote poetically that for him, "Urban Design has to give visual form to the relationship between You and Me."

SUBSEQUENT URBAN DESIGN CONFERENCES

There was no conference in 1958; however, a series of panels met in April to prepare for the next Urban Design Conference. It was agreed that the goal of the third gathering should be to "arrive at certain principles which can guide the design of large scale residential developments of an urban character . . . both with the city complex and on the fringes of the metropolitan area."[28]

By the third conference, in April 1959, the principles of urban design seem to have been sufficiently developed so that the first case study of projects was attempted. The architectural component of the conference reinforced the separation from planning, but the diminution of landscape architecture's influence is also evident. This marks a fundamental shift from the previous two conferences and would set the tone for subsequent meetings. There was a definite attempt to deal with tangible design issues at this conference, and unlike the first two conferences,

abstract notions of the "forces" shaping cities—economic, social, and political—were left off the agenda. Indeed, in his opening comments Sert spoke explicitly to this, stating that "after the second [conference] many of us realized that, though these conferences proved interesting and stimulating, it would be useless to continue discussions on general topics as we were tending to become repetitious."

Sert spoke of his frustration with the emerging urban design discourse, describing the previous conference results as a "fog of amiable generalities."[29] In his opening comments, Sert offered one of the defining aspects of urban design: "This is a conference upon Urban Design and upon a special aspect of Urban Design—the residential sector. I think I have already said enough to show that it is not a general conference upon city planning."[30] These projects were examples of how Sert imagined urban design in practice; despite the idea of urban design as "common ground," urban design was starting to carve out a territorial claim that would have consequences for the position of the program within the school. The developing rift between planning and architecture was to eventually mean that planning would leave the GSD for a new home at the Kennedy School of Government—interested more in the abstract notions of the "forces" shaping cities than in the physical design of urban situations.

At the third conference, six projects were presented: Washington Square, Philadelphia, by I. M. Pei; Mill Creek, St. Louis, by I. M. Pei; Gratiot Redevelopment (Lafayette Park), Detroit, by Mies van der Rohe and Ludwig Hilberseimer; Lake Meadows, Chicago, by Skidmore, Owings and

Merrill; Don Mills, Toronto, by Macklin Hancock; and Vallingby, Stockholm, by the Stockholm Town Planning Office. Material on each project had been assembled in advance by a GSD alumnus, who then moderated a respective panel, assisted by current students. In most cases the architect of the project, the responsible developer, and the city planning director not only provided information but also took part in discussions. It is unclear why these projects were chosen above others; one can only surmise that in some way the projects represented physical manifestations of the "principles" outlined in the previous conferences. After a day of discussion, each of the six panels reported to a meeting of alumni and students, and an afternoon was spent in open discussion under the chairmanship of Robert Geddes, president of the Harvard GSD alumni association.

The six selected projects, as Geddes remarked, divided themselves fairly neatly into pairs. Vallingby and Don Mills were new towns. Lake Meadows and Gratiot were similar in terms of programs and sites. The Washington Square–Society Hill development and the Mill Creek development have similar links to their surroundings and share problems and programs. The format of the third conference proved successful and was repeated at several conferences, including the fifth one. The sixth conference changed scale and dealt with the issues of inter-city growth. The eighth conference refocused its attention on the core of the city, but by 1964 the social, political, and economic concerns outweighed any emphasis on form or aesthetics.

Overall, there was a tendency for the later conferences to become more abstract and general. The ninth and tenth conferences (1965 and 1966)

addressed design education. The tenth conference again raised the issue of urban design's definition. On a panel entitled "Changing Educational Requirements in Architecture and Urban Design," there was still significant debate about exactly what urban design was. Benjamin Thomson, chair of the department of architecture at the GSD, described urban design as "large-scale architecture." Roger Montgomery, professor of architecture at Washington University, called it "project-scale design." GSD Professors Chermayeff and Soltan stated in a joint declaration: "Architecture and Urban Design are but a single profession. DESIGN is at the heart of these efforts." Chermayeff and Soltan precisely articulated the emerging trajectory of urban design's development. Wilhelm von Moltke, chairman of the department of urban design, in a move away from architectural definitions, stated: "Urban Design is not architecture. The function of urban design, its purpose and objective, is to give form and order to the future. As with the master plan, urban design provides a master program and master form for urban growth. It is primarily a collaborative effort involving other professions."[31]

In line with growing social and political developments in the United States, there arose a growing critique that the conferences had little to do with the reality of city life. The twelfth conference, conducted in an atmosphere of grief surrounding the assassination of Senator Robert F. Kennedy, dealt with a report of the New Communities Project, a year-long research study supported by a grant from the U.S. Department of Housing and Urban Development to investigate plans for a compact city for more than two hundred thousand people. Principal investigators for the project were Sert, William Nash, chair of city and regional planning, Walter Isard, and George Pillorge.

The last of the Urban Design Conferences took place in 1970. The event was cosponsored by the GSD and the National Urban Coalition and took up the broad implications of mass-industrialized housing. This conference was strongly affected by significant changes in the GSD, as well as in American society at large. Maurice Kilbridge, a Harvard Business School professor, had replaced Sert as dean in 1969. The school was experiencing financial difficulties, and there was significant social turbulence within both the faculty and student body. An active student movement politicized the atmosphere of the conference. Discussions of the nature of urban design had given way to critiques of state and federal housing programs.

URBAN DESIGN PROGRAM AT HARVARD

Beginning in the academic year 1960–61, the GSD offered an advanced interdepartmental program in urban design, open only to selected candidates from among those who already held one of the school's first professional degrees (B. Arch., MLA, or MCP) or an equivalent qualification from another institution. The program, as it was initially developed, required a minimum of one year's study in residence and led to the degrees master of architecture in urban design, master of landscape architecture in urban design, or master of city planning in urban design. The fact that there were three urban design degrees is in itself significant and speaks to how urban design was imagined as a floating program in which students from the three disciplines would come together in the consideration of a holistic approach to the city. Urban design was conceived as an exten-

sion of one's own disciplinary education and not as its own discipline. These separate roles were reinforced within the course of study, with each discipline engaging in different activities.[32]

Although the three departments jointly offered courses within the urban design program, continuing Sert's ambition that it be the common ground within the school, the role of landscape architects within the program was small. The Urban Design Studio of 1960 was an intensive course with problems conducted conjunctively rather than collaboratively, to give all members of the class a shared experience in the three professional aspects of the work. The fall part of the course, led by Sert, dealt with new developments or new towns. The spring session, led by von Moltke, concerned the rebuilding of large-scale parts of the city. The studio used Boston as a laboratory, and the students' work addressed different parts of the city for new and redevelopment projects, with the Charles River, the Fenway, the North Shore, and Fort Point Channel among the sites of investigation. In addition, the studio included theoretical projects at the scale of some of Sert's pilot plans.

The 1962 GSD *Register* lists faculty who taught in the urban design program: Sert, Martin Meyerson, Sasaki, Soltan, Sekler, Tyrwhitt, Fumihiko Maki, François Vigier, and Shadrach Woods. These first faculty members shaped the origins of what urban design became at Harvard, and their influence informed what urban design was to become in universities throughout the United States and the rest of the world.

In its fifth year of existence at the GSD, the urban design program once again became the focus of a student publication. In an April 1965 issue of *Connection* were critical appraisals of the program by Perry Neubauer and Roy Mann. Neubauer is candid, writing: "The Urban Design Program has made considerable progress in the formulation of educational objectives and a curriculum of study; but it has not fully realized one of the concepts on which it was based: The integration of the three design disciplines of architecture, landscape architecture, and city planning. At the present time, in fact, the program seems to be setting up a fourth discipline with a definite architectural bias."[33]

ON COMMON GROUND

Although urban design was established as a field of activity rather than as a professional discipline, it quickly began to develop its own territory, both within the GSD and professionally. Neubauer's comments reflect the emergence of urban design as a "fourth discipline" at the design school. Although it was initially imagined as an extension of the core disciplines within the school, it became something quite separate. The Urban Design Conferences began as an undertaking to explore the common ground of the city. They bear testament, however, to the fragmentation of the professions and the emergence of troubled social times in the 1960s.

Once urban design arrived at Harvard, the department of city and regional planning went through a tremendous crisis. Symptomatic of larger trends affecting the planning profession's view of itself, the department increasingly moved away from a "physical" view of the city, alienating itself from the departments of architecture and landscape architecture. The divide became so wide that in 1984 the master of city planning degree program departed the GSD and moved to the Kennedy School of Government, although several key planning faculty, including Vigier and William Doebele, continued to teach planning within the urban design program.

With the master of city planning gone from the GSD and the department of city and regional planning decimated, the school established the department of urban planning and design and moved the urban design program under this new department. Urban design, the "fourth discipline," filled the void left by planning. The department of urban planning and design offered the degrees master of architecture in urban design and master of landscape architecture in urban design.[34]

URBAN DESIGN AS A COMMON UNDERTAKING

The Urban Design Conferences (particularly the first two) were remarkable unions of interested parties engaged in the making of cities. They created the momentum that Sert and his faculty needed to establish the urban design program at Harvard. They promoted recognition of a different field of design endeavor, one that required a particular set of perspectives and skills. Sert's conferences created a place for likeminded thinkers to gather and argue about what urban design was, who would carry it out, and what role it would have within the world at large. Although an accepted understanding of the territory of urban design was never fully reached, the conferences nevertheless established a foundation for the emergence of urban design and for agreement on the need to design the future of the city.

NOTES

1. Report of Faculty Committee on the Urban Design Conference, April 24, 1956. Harvard University Archives, UAV 433.7.4, sub. IIB, Box 19.

2. "Man-Made America," *Architectural Review* 108, no. 648 (December 1950): 341.

3. Ibid., 343.

4. Edmund Bacon, "A Talk Presented to the Second Invitation Harvard Conference on Urban Design, Cambridge, Massachusetts, April 12, 1957," *Second Urban Design Conference Announcement and Program* (Cambridge, Mass.: Harvard Graduate School of Design, 1957). Special Collections, Frances Loeb Library, Harvard University Graduate School of Design (hereafter Special Collections), Rare NAC 46 Harv 1957.

5. Josep Lluís Sert, *Can Our Cities Survive? An ABC of Urban Problems, Their Analysis, Their Solutions* (Cambridge, Mass.: Harvard University Press, 1942), 229.

6. See Josep Lluís Sert, Opening Remarks to the Urban Design Conference, April 9, 1956. Special Collections, Rare NAC 46 Harv 1956.

7. Ibid.

8. Sert, *Can Our Cities Survive?* 224.

9. Ibid., 234.

10. In a later essay titled "Centers of Community Life," written as the introduction to *CIAM 8: The Heart of the City* (1952), a book Sert wrote with Jaqueline Tyrwhitt and Ernesto Rogers, he reinforced and expanded on many of the issues developed in *Can Our Cities Survive?* See *CIAM 8: The Heart of the City* (New York: Pellegrini and Cudahy, 1952).

11. *CIAM 8: The Heart of the City*, 3.

12. Ibid., 11.

13. Sert, Opening Remarks to the Urban Design Conference.

14. Sert, Report of the Faculty Committee, 98.

15. Sert, Opening Remarks to the Urban Design Conference.

16. Ibid.

17. Sert, Report of Faculty Committee, 99.

18. Ibid.

19. Ibid., 103. Also see Lewis Mumford, Letter to Sert, December 28, 1940. Special Collections.

20. Ibid., 101.

21. Ibid., 102.

22. Ibid.

23. *Second Urban Design Conference Announcement and Program*.

24. Ibid.

25. Ibid.

26. Richard Dober, "The Collaborative Process and Urban Design at Harvard," in *Synthesis,* April 1957, p. 3.

27. Ibid.

28. *Third Urban Design Conference Program* (Cambridge, Mass.: Harvard University Graduate School of Design, [April 25, 1959]). Special Collections, Rare HT107.U712x 1959.

29. Ibid.

30. Ibid.

31. *Tenth Urban Design Conference Proceedings* (Cambridge, Mass.: Harvard University Graduate School of Design, 1966), 14. Special Collections, Rare NAC 46 Harv 1966.

32. An interview with Emeritus Professor Charles Harris at GSD, March 25, 2003. Hired by Hideo Sasaki to teach in the department of landscape architecture in 1958, Professor Harris was chair of the department of landscape architecture from 1968 to 1978.

33. Perry Neubauer, "Educating the Urban Designer," *Connection,* April 1965, p. 62.

34. The urban planning degree program was eventually reintroduced at the GSD in the mid-1990s.

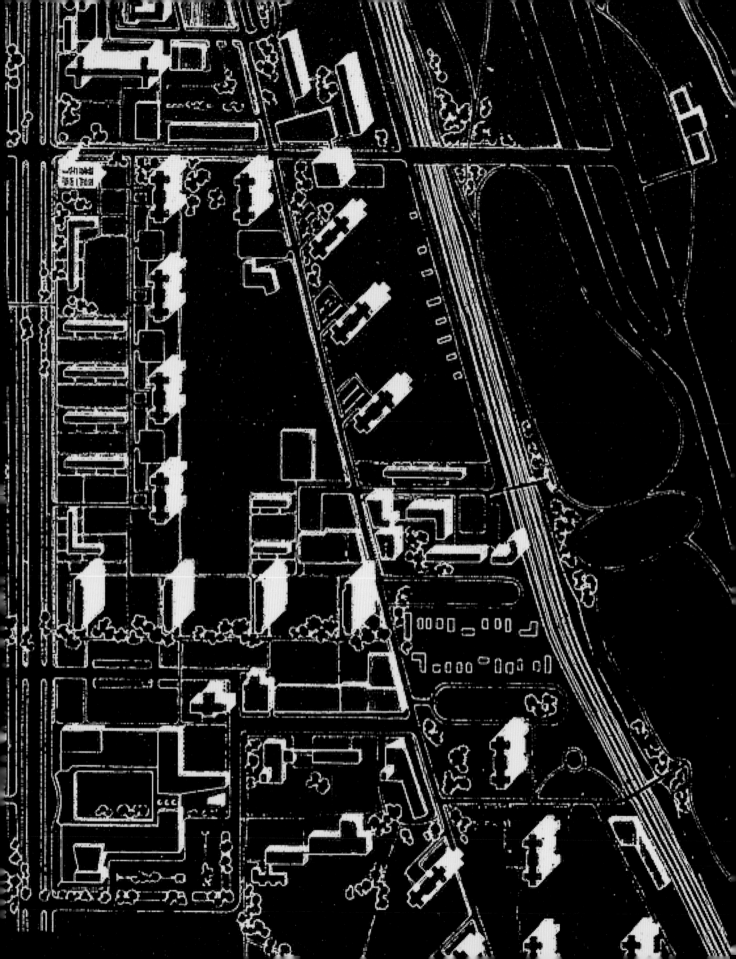

Chapter 8

FROM THE HEART OF THE CITY
TO HOLYOKE CENTER

CIAM Ideas in Sert's Definition of Urban Design

ERIC MUMFORD

In 1962, Denise Scott Brown wrote that the "strongest force to touch the destiny of cities in recent times is the centripetal movement of population to the regions around the great cities."[1] Yet during the previous decade architects and planners had embarked upon a massive effort to redesign the centers of American cities. Backed by large amounts of funding from the federal government, and commissioned by reform mayors, downtown businessmen, and civic activists, architects attempted to provide models for reorganizing metropolitan life on a new basis. The often disastrous outcomes of these efforts are now well known, and celebrated failures like Minoru Yamasaki's Pruitt-Igoe public housing project in St. Louis and similar projects across the country now dominate the historical view of the period, even as their physical presence is disappearing. The widespread view that destructive urban clearance and high-rise public housing were the main outcomes of the modern movement in the United States has tended to overshadow other important preoccupations of architects at this time.

High-rise housing on cleared sites was only one aspect of the new discipline called urban design, a term given widespread usage after the first Harvard Urban Design Conference in 1956.

Urban design took as its point of departure the necessity of cities and urban life to culture, and it was based on the idea that collaboration between architects, landscape architects, and planners could produce new forms of pedestrian urbanity in reorganized metropolitan environments, avoiding both the visual monotony of slightly earlier modernist housing and what was seen as the dullness of suburban life. Although little studied and usually rhetorically lumped together with earlier stages of the modern movement, the new discipline has had a significant and lasting effect on how architecture has been conceptualized. There are many unacknowledged continuities between the ideology of postwar urban design and later postmodern urbanism, as well as more recent efforts ranging from the New Urbanism to neo-avant-garde efforts to engage the overlaps between architecture and landscape design. In the

145

following text, part of a larger study on the subject, I examine how the discipline of urban design developed through built and unbuilt urban renewal efforts in Philadelphia and Boston and through professional training programs established at the University of Pennsylvania and Harvard, and examine some of the responses that it provoked.

Among the difficulties in reconstructing this theoretical basis is the decisive split between urban and suburban environments that occurred during the racial, social, and political upheavals of the later 1960s. This split, which may finally be healing, makes it difficult now to understand the interconnectedness of the urbanistic approaches taken by architects in the 1950s, when the problems of center cities and suburbs were seen as being more similar than they would later appear. This was an era when what would later be seen as a naïve faith in urban racial integration was held by most architects and urban planners. Questions of who can legitimately speak for whom and charges of professional elitism vis-à-vis urban dwellers were only beginning to be raised in the early 1960s, and planners such as Charles Abrams could still confidently offer themselves at the first Harvard Urban Design Conference as spokesmen for the racially disadvantaged. Another difficulty is the relatively small amount of theoretical writing by architects engaged in urban design at the time. Key figures like Josep Lluís Sert and Edmund N. Bacon tended to write for general audiences, advocating the idea of planning and stressing the need to redesign central cities in general but not revealing much about the detailed premises upon which such activities were to be based.

These premises came in part from the Patrick Geddes–inspired regionalism advocated by Lewis Mumford and the Regional Planning Association of America (RPAA) in the 1920s. At the Harvard GSD under Walter Gropius and Joseph Hudnut, the intellectual antecedent of both the Penn and later Harvard programs, these ideas about metropolitan interconnectedness began to be addressed through collaborative design studios for the redesign of American cities that combined architecture, planning, and landscape architecture. By later standards these efforts were often remarkably indifferent to the real economic and racial inequalities that were an essential part of American society at that time, and they tended to view metropolitan physical reorganization and architectural design as the cure for a wide range of social problems. Nevertheless, they provided some of the basis from which urban design would later develop.

These interdisciplinary efforts were related to the ideology of CIAM, whose influential combining of collectivist social action with specific design approaches underlay much of what followed. Both Gropius and Hudnut were members of both the New York CIAM group set up by Sert and Sigfried Giedion in 1944, along with (briefly) Wallace K. Harrison, William Wurster, and some twenty other CIAM members, most of them émigrés, as well as members of ASPA (American Society of Planners and Architects), a related group to which Sert, Serge Chermayeff, and Marcel Breuer also belonged. After Gropius's and Hudnut's initial alliance at the GSD had devolved into a long-running power struggle by the late 1940s, leading to the resignation of Gropius in 1952 and Hudnut's retirement by the summer of 1953, the appointment of CIAM president Josep Lluís

Sert as dean in 1953 signaled the continuation of Gropius's and CIAM's legacy. Sert's first appointments reflected important continuities from the Gropius era. Reginald Isaacs, director of planning for the South Side Planning Board in Chicago, frequent GSD visitor and close Gropius associate, was appointed to the Charles Dyer Norton Chair of Regional Planning.[2] Isaacs then suggested that Sert rehire Hideo Sasaki,[3] a young landscape architecture professor who had returned to the University of Illinois after resigning with other GSD faculty in 1952 in a show of support for Gropius over Hudnut.[4] Sert's appointments to the GSD indicated an increase in CIAM influence just as the organization had more or less ceased its efforts to influence urban development in the United States. Not everyone viewed this positively, and when Sert was appointed in 1953, some students carried sarcastic protest banners reading "Congrès International Admiration Mutuel." Although Sert himself does not appear to have made much effort to change Gropius's American policy of not emphasizing his links to CIAM, a number of Sert's new appointees were indeed CIAM members, including Chermayeff, director of the Chicago Institute of Design from 1946–51.[5]

Sert also continued the CIAM emphasis on the continuity of design from the smallest household object to the design of metropolitan regions, and he added to this the concern for the "synthesis of the arts" at the "heart of the city" that he had helped introduce into CIAM after the war. He brought in the CIAM organizer Jaqueline Tyrwhitt, trained as a garden designer in England in the 1920s before becoming involved with planning education at the University of London and with the MARS (Modern Architecture Research) Group after the war. Indicating the higher value he placed on history, Sert also attempted to bring in Sigfried Giedion, the Swiss art historian and CIAM secretary-general. Giedion, by then in his late sixties, preferred to remain a frequent visitor. Instead, a young Austrian CIAM member then studying at Harvard on a Fulbright scholarship, Eduard Sekler (1920–), was hired at Giedion's recommendation to reintroduce history to the school.[6] Along with the recently retired but still professionally active Gropius, a CIAM vice-president, this core of important CIAM members—Sert, Gropius, Tyrwhitt, and Giedion—began to reshape the Harvard Graduate School of Design with a strong focus on urbanism.[7] In contrast to Isaacs, who differed with Sert over the role of architects in the collaborative synthesis between architecture, planning, and landscape architecture, Sert was insistent that architects have the directing role in urban design, which would eventually put him at odds with Sasaki as well.[8]

These changes went along with the appointment of a new Harvard president, Nathan Marsh Pusey, a conservative Christian educator recruited from Lawrence College in Appleton, Wisconsin. Pusey had successfully instituted a new general education curriculum there in the 1930s, doubled the school's modest endowment, brought in outstanding teachers, and was known for his outspoken religious convictions. Appleton was also the home of Senator Joseph McCarthy, and Pusey's opposition to McCarthyism and general good reputation there seem to have made him a politically shrewd appointment for Harvard at this time.[9] Pusey enthusiastically supported Sert, the GSD, and efforts to intro-

Fig. 8.1 Cover, "Two Cities: Planning in North and South America," *Museum of Modern Art Bulletin*, June 1947

duce modern architecture at a time of expanded federal support to the university. Although Harvard
continued to build neo-Georgian dormitories and
other buildings at the business school and at the
Radcliffe campus through the 1950s, Hudnut and
Gropius had begun to push the Harvard administration toward modern architecture. Sert would continue this direction, although in the first years of his
deanship most of the modern architecture on campus continued to be done by the firm of Shepley,
Bulfinch Richardson & Abbott (SBRA), successors
to the same Boston firm that had done much of the
campus's earlier neo-Georgian buildings.[10]

As a practitioner, Sert was still designing town
plans for government planning agencies in Venezuela
and Cuba when he became dean. His interest in
urbanism had grown out of his experiences as a
young CIAM member in Barcelona in the 1930s, and
it continued to develop in the series of urban projects he designed for Latin America between 1944
and 1958 with his partners in Town Planning
Associates. Beginning with the Brazilian Motor City
project, exhibited along with Gropius's plan for the
South Side of Chicago at the Museum of Modern
Art in 1947 (fig. 8.1), Sert proposed pedestrian civic
centers that would function as "cores" for new
industrial cities.[11] These spaces, which combined
municipal auditoriums, offices, retail outlets, and
recreational facilities into figural compositions of
solid built volumes, bounded open spaces, and
extensive landscaping, were a new element in CIAM,
one perhaps programmatically inspired by Lewis
Mumford's negative reaction to the lack of attention
to civic centers in Sert's first presentation of CIAM in
the United States, *Can Our Cities Survive?*

Figure 8.2 Le Corbusier, Saint-Dié civic center project model, 1945,
as illustrated in Sigfried Giedion, *Architecture, You and Me*

Architecturally they were an original combination
of constructivist and Corbusian architectural monumentality, though with a more extensive adherence
to both landscape elements and to the typology
of the traditional Latin American plaza.[12] They also
showed some influence of both the Brazilian
Ministry of Education and Health and the civic
center projects of Eliel and Eero Saarinen at this
time. Along with Le Corbusier's contemporaneous
project for the rebuilding of the war-destroyed
French town Saint-Dié (fig. 8.2), which toured the
United States in the fall of 1945, this new focus on
the civic core and the related idea of the synthesis
of the arts began to resonate within CIAM after Sert
became CIAM president in 1947.

In his opening address at CIAM 8 four years later,
titled "Centres of Community Life," Sert invoked
the Spanish philosopher José Ortega y Gasset in
emphasizing that the traditional Mediterranean town
square was a deliberate human construction, a place

where "nature" was bounded out and a human civil space created. Sert believed that this space could be a place for democratic assembly, where citizens would discuss and demonstrate, and that it should not be a commercial space full of advertising.[13] He specifically cited the Piazza del Duomo in Milan as an example (see fig. 3.9), and he exhibited his and Paul Lester Wiener's civic centers for Lima and Chimbote, Peru, as modern versions of the concept. Although generally critical of the "outmoded" city patterns of 1940s Latin America, in another text Sert and Wiener praised the "good pedestrian promenades or 'paseos,' public squares serving as meeting places surrounded by arcades of sheltering shops or cafes from sun and rain."[14] For Sert the task of the "architect-planner" was to "build the frame or container within which . . . community life could take place," adding that such civic centers would consolidate governments, which permit a "free and democratic exchange of ideas leading toward the government of the majority." The design of these civic centers should separate pedestrians and automobiles, with "necessary parking facilities" located on the perimeter, and he insisted that "landscaping must play a very important role" in their design.

It was also in these Latin American projects that Sert began to explore the typology of the courtyard house. This modern revisitation of an ancient type made its first appearance in the master plan for Chimbote and was then deployed by Sert as an alternative to Corbusian high-rise slabs in many Latin American projects. The implications of the concept for urbanism were explained by Sert in a 1953 article, "Can Patios Make Cities?" Sert emphasized that the use of the enclosed courtyard (patio) at various

scale levels gave an "underlying coherence" to each city plan. These scales ranged from the house to the neighborhood to individual public buildings to the monumental city center composed of a "series of gigantic piazzas (or big patios) that form places of outdoor assembly for all citizens." The article contrasted the "typical American residential street of today," a series of single-family houses on individual lots on curving streets, with Sert's approach, which used less space, provided more private outdoor areas, would have shortened utility lines, and would create a coherent urban design. The community patios Sert proposed would always be "walled in" spaces, based on the idea that by feeling that they were in an "outdoor room," people would "associate with others more freely than they would in an 'unframed' park area," such as the central green spaces at the planned community of Radburn, New Jersey.[15] It contrasted this approach with the less formal "village green" at Clarence Stein's Baldwin Hills Village (1941), low-rise multifamily apartments in Los Angeles, which had been hailed as a model for postwar housing by Catherine Bauer and was widely imitated in the immediate postwar years.[16]

Within CIAM itself, however, Sert's influence was waning after 1953. In May of that year the decision had been made by the CIAM council to hand over the group to the "younger generation." This effort led to the formation of Team 10, originally a group of CIAM "youth members" charged with organizing the tenth CIAM Congress, scheduled for Algiers in 1955 and held in Dubrovnik in 1956. For them, Sert's focus on "'human scale' as the architecture *summum bonum* was derided," although Team 10 retained the late-CIAM emphasis on pedestrian urbanity, and, in its own way, similar ideas about the timeless nature of basic human dimensions in the built environment.[17] Sert continued to preside over the organization until it dissolved in 1957, and he, along with Gropius, Giedion, and Tyrwhitt, was reluctant to accept the Team 10 decision to stop using the name CIAM in 1959. At CIAM 10, the second on the theme of "Human Habitat," Sert opened his talk by stating that the goal of the event was to address the "future structure of the human habitat." After a brief history of previous CIAM Congresses, he praised the transformed CIAM grids "prepared under the guidance of group X" as "remarkable documents." He did not discuss their challenge to the Athens Charter, however, and instead stressed the importance of CIAM for "students in every country." He mentioned that "some organization of university groups that could exchange ideas and work on problems now being determined by the congress" was being put in place, and he called for a change in the CIAM council, which "may bring a different CIAM, a new CIAM."[18]

Around the same time, Sert inaugurated a series of annual Urban Design Conferences at Harvard, which he would continue to preside over until his retirement in 1969. In these conferences CIAM members and concepts were still present, but the emphasis was on current North American planning efforts rather than the European focus of CIAM. The first of these conferences, held in April 1956, brought together a wide range of American planners, architects, landscape architects, and artists, and included at least six CIAM members, Sert, Tyrwhitt, Chermayeff, Richard Neutra (1892–1970), and William Muschenheim (1902–1989), all in the United States, and MARS member Wells Coates (1895–1958),

who taught at GSD in 1955–56 and then moved to Vancouver, Canada, where he died in 1958. The second Urban Design Conference, held a year later, acknowledged the growing importance of Team 10 by including Jacob Bakema of Holland; the only other speakers from CIAM were Neutra and Chermayeff. The third Urban Design Conference (1959) included Chermayeff and the young Polish Corbusian Team 10 member Jerzy Soltan (1913–2005), who had joined the GSD faculty in 1958, along with two tangential CIAM members active in Philadelphia, Oscar Stonorov and the 1951 GSD graduate Robert Geddes, who had been part of the Philadelphia CIAM group that had sent a board analyzing Levittown, Pennsylvania, to CIAM 9. Former CIAM members made occasional appearances at the remaining conferences, including Giedion, but with the exception of Shadrach Woods's anguished Eighth Walter Gropius lecture at the twelfth Urban Design Conference in 1968, Team 10 had little to do with these events.[19]

Instead, the Urban Design Conferences focused on the role of planners versus architects and on the discussion of actual urban design projects in such U.S. cities as Philadelphia, Detroit, and Boston. At the first conference, the cluster of interventions administered by Edmund N. Bacon (1910–) in postwar Philadelphia were a major part of the presentations.[20] These had grown out of the efforts of George Howe, Stonorov, and Louis Kahn to create a new civic American modernism in that city, and they were supported by the reform Democratic administrations that began to redevelop it after 1946. At the first Harvard Urban Design Conference, Bacon, by then director of the Philadelphia City Planning

Commission, presented some of the major Philadelphia urban renewal projects then under way. He stated that he had found that Louis Kahn's housing project for the Mill Creek area (1952), with its "backbone of connecting walkways," offered a good model for creating a design system that could help to coordinate various smaller projects by different architects (fig. 8.3). The Kahn project also introduced the principle of connecting greenways focused on "significant existing symbols such as churches, schools and clubs." According to Bacon the "sequence of sensations" of that movement through these greenways formed the basis for all later urban design efforts in Philadelphia. Bacon's remarks were also illustrated with a plan for the Old City Redevelopment area around Independence Hall by the firm of Harbeson Hough Livingston & Larson (the successor firm of Paul Cret), which also used pedestrian greenways to connect historic buildings.[21]

Bacon's presentation of Philadelphia at the first Harvard Urban Design Conference was followed by Victor Gruen's on his plan to pedestrianize the entire center of downtown Fort Worth, Texas (fig. 8.4). After his emigration from Austria in 1938, Gruen (1903–1980) had worked on exhibits for the 1939 New York World's Fair and established a practice as a store designer, first in New York and then in Los Angeles. In the mid-1940s he became associated with Morris Ketchum, a shopping center pioneer and proponent of an influential plan to pedestrianize downtown Rye, New York, in the mid-1940s. While Gruen is often seen as the inventor of the shopping center concept, in fact the type was a preoccupation of a number of postwar American architects, including Louis Kahn, whose first Yale studio in the fall of 1947 was for the design of a suburban shopping center, and of G. Holmes Perkins, a Gropius protégé and later dean of the University of Pennsylvania School of Architecture, who directed a GSD collaborative studio on the topic in 1950.[22] Contemporaneous with Gruen's first full built realization of the shopping center concept at Northland

Figure 8.3 Louis Kahn, Anne Tyng, Kenneth Day, and Louis McAllister, Mill Creek project for Philadelphia Public Housing Authority, 1952, Kahn drawing of pedestrian street from *Architectural Forum* (April 1952).

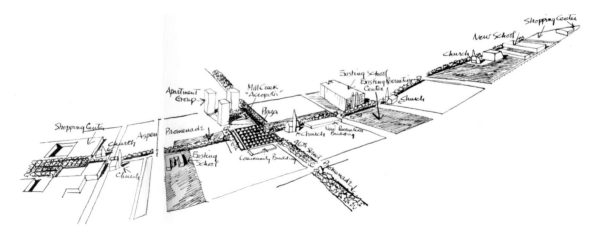

Figure 8.4 Plan of redesigned pedestrian downtown of Fort Worth, Texas. Victor Gruen Associates, *A Greater Ft. Worth Tomorrow* (1956).

near Detroit was former GSD faculty member I. M. Pei's Roosevelt Field Shopping Center on Long Island near New York City (1954), developed by William Zeckendorf; it was one of a number of early shopping malls from the time.[23] Like these other architects, Gruen also saw the shopping center in terms similar to Sert's, as the focal point for new "shopping towns" outside the city limits of older cities.

Gruen's Southdale Center (1956) in Edina, outside of Minneapolis, was the first enclosed shopping center in the world. For Gruen, the purpose of the

shopping center was to provide "crystallization points for suburbia's community life." His models were not only earlier American shopping centers, such as the Country Club Plaza in Kansas City, but also Greek agoras and medieval market towns. In a series of 1955 speeches, Gruen began to show his scheme for the proposed complete pedestrianization of "City X," whose identity as Fort Worth was revealed only with considerable press coverage a month before the first Harvard Urban Design Conference.[24] At the conference Gruen described how he had been approached by the president of the largest utility company in Fort Worth about saving the company's sizable investment in downtown. Gruen calculated that there would be a tremendous increase in automobile traffic there over the next fifteen years, which led him to propose massive parking facilities at the entrances to the downtown from the new system of expressways being built at its edges. He proposed six garages for sixty thousand cars, directly accessible from the freeways, which would be connected by moving sidewalks for a two-minute trip to the center of downtown. No cars would be permitted downtown, but truck deliveries would be made from an underground service loop, whose construction would require only the demolition of a few low-rise structures, leaving all the major downtown buildings intact.[25] New areas of landscaping for pedestrian plazas would allow for a "steady surprise of new features—of new space experiences."[26] The reaction to Gruen's plan was not published, but he was one of a smaller number of speakers invited back to the second Urban Design Conference held the following year, suggesting that at this point his views and Sert's were not so far apart, perhaps at least until his unpopular scheme for the redevelopment of Boston's West End was completed in 1960.

Sert's initiatives in urban design at Harvard were paralleled and in some cases preceded by related efforts at the University of Pennsylvania. Under Perkins, various efforts were made to teach collaborative studios that combined architects, planners, and landscape architects, with faculty that included Robert Geddes, Louis Kahn, and Ian McHarg. It was in this context that a group of planners around David A. Crane, a Harvard-trained planner who

had studied architecture at Georgia Tech and who had been an assistant to Kevin Lynch and Gyorgy Kepes on their "Perceptual Form of the City" research at MIT, began to develop a critical stance toward architects in urban design. Their efforts would bear fruit in Crane's studio on the critical redesign of Chandigarh,[27] and in sociologist Herbert Gans's studies of urban residents displaced by the clearance of Boston's West End (*The Urban Villagers,* 1962) and of the residents of Levittown, New Jersey (*The Levittowners,* 1967). Students influenced by this critical direction, arguably one of the sources for much contemporary thinking about urbanism, included Denise Scott Brown, who studied in the planning program at Penn from 1958 to 1960 and then taught there, initially as Crane's assistant, from 1961 to 1965, as well as Paul Davidoff, who received his doctorate from the program in 1956 and taught there in the early 1960s. For this disparate group of Penn faculty, the "architect in planning, the 'civic designer,' was everyone's villain," as Scott Brown would later put it.[28]

Sert was certainly aware of these efforts at Penn, and his creation of a new master of urban design program, announced in the spring of 1960, may have been in part a response to the creation of Penn's civic (later urban) design program in 1956. Like the Penn program, the Harvard urban design program was intended to be a one-year interdisciplinary program for those already holding a professional degree in architecture, landscape architecture, or city planning. Two faculty members in the new program had previously taught at Penn, Martin Meyerson (1922–) and Wilhelm von Moltke (1911–1987). Meyerson had taught at Penn from 1952 to 1957, after having taught

in Rexford Guy Tugwell's short-lived planning pro-
gram at the University of Chicago in the late 1940s
and having worked with Reginald Isaacs on the
South Side Redevelopment. In Chicago he was the
director of development for the Chicago Housing
Authority under the controversial integrationist
administration of Elizabeth Wood, which ended in
1952. He came to Harvard in 1957 as the Frank
Backus Williams Professor of City and Regional
Planning and founded and directed the MIT-
Harvard Joint Center for Urban Studies. Von
Moltke, chief urban designer for the Philadelphia
City Planning Commission and a visiting critic at
Penn from 1954 to 1960, was brought in 1964 to
direct the Harvard urban design program, just after
Meyerson left to become dean of the College of
Environmental Design at Berkeley.[29]

In addition to these Penn and Philadelphia planning connections, the links to CIAM in the Harvard
urban design program were quite direct, although
CIAM no longer really existed after the group's 1959
Congress in Otterlo. By 1962 architects teaching studios in the Harvard urban design program were
Sert, Soltan, and a former Sert student, Fumihiko
Maki (1928–), who arrived as an associate professor
in the program after having taught for six years at
Washington University in St. Louis (fig. 8.5).[30] Maki
had designed the art building there, Steinberg Hall,
and was also a Graham Foundation Traveling Fellow
in 1957–58, an appointment he had obtained with
Giedion's assistance.[31] Planners teaching in the program were Tyrwhitt, who seems to have taken a
coordinating role until moving to Greece to work full
time as the editor of *Ekistics* with Constantinos
Doxiadis in 1965; and François (Frank) Vigier, for-

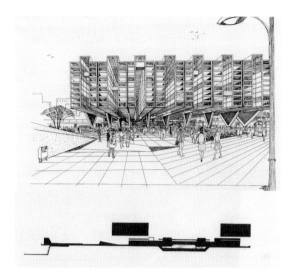

Figure 8.5 Fumihiko Maki, proposed MTA exchange station
by Jan Wampler. F. Maki, *Movement Systems in the City,* 1966.

merly of Sert's Cambridge office. Landscape architecture was taught by Hideo Sasaki, who had
worked with Sert on the Baghdad Embassy and
on Holyoke Center, and history seminars were by
Sekler, with Giedion as a regular visitor.

In 1962 Tyrwhitt described the program at the
annual ACSA (Association of Collegiate Schools of
Architecture) Cranbrook Teacher Seminar organized by David Crane, who was by then chief of
urban design for the Boston Redevelopment
Authority. Tyrwhitt stated that the program was
based on the belief that urban design was about
shaping the environment both to produce a "personal sensation of delight" in a "really lovely environment" and to arouse feelings of "mutual respon-
siveness and mutual interest in the environment"
among those who used it. She emphasized that
"such a feeling of social responsibility" could arise
only where there was a "very clear distinction

between privacy and communality." The program thus aimed to design for "order and hierarchy," which she saw as the "basis of civilization itself." It saw itself as operating on two scales, "the conceptual system and the visual scene." The first was a not necessarily visually apparent environmental order, such as the mile-square grid of the Detroit area, while the second "is directly concerned with what is physically visible at the human scale." The one-year urban design studio was structured such that there were two studio problems given, "one more or less a downtown renewal scale, the other tackling some new development in an open area." In 1961 the urban studio problem was the Charles River basin, using the "plans already prepared in the local planning offices of the bordering cities and universities." The second studio problem was titled "Intercity," and it focused on design interventions in a suburban development corridor. In addition to the studio, the program also required seminars on Factors that Shape the City and on the Shaping of Urban Space, with the latter taught by Sekler and Giedion.[32] The Charles River basin projects included Sert's plans for Harvard and Boston Universities, which might be seen as demonstrations, in the somewhat unusual Boston context, of the translation of some late-CIAM preoccupations with urban space into the American city. Sert had begun working as a consultant to the Harvard Planning Office in 1957 and served as chairman of the Cambridge Planning Board at the same time, before resigning early in 1958. In 1960 he produced a document entitled *Harvard University 1960: An Inventory for Planning*. It opened with quotes from Lewis Mumford, Giedion, and Charles Abrams that situated this effort within the intellec-

tual context of planning at the time. The Mumford quote emphasized the importance of the Geddes-like "survey of actual resources" and the need to plan "with a knowledge of existing conditions and opportunities." The Giedion quote from *Space, Time and Architecture* stressed the need for a universal outlook linking past and future, while the Abrams quote introduced a more topical critical element by invoking the "mysteriously attractive chaos of cities" and the possibility that some physical goals might have to be modified to preserve democratic values.[33] Most of the *Inventory for Planning* document itself used a series of maps, tables, and short descriptive texts to present the current situation of the Cambridge campus, beginning at the regional scale and working down to specific architectural proposals. Particular problems identified were "those of housing, traffic and parking."[34] The report concluded with a proposal for a system of pedestrian green spaces woven through the existing urban fabric to link the three existing "yards" of the campus. Widely spaced high-rise buildings and peripheral parking structures would accommodate the university's rapid expansion within this framework, in contrast to the tabula rasa planning at IIT (Illinois Institute of Technology) and most other campuses at this time.

The first chance to demonstrate this new approach had already come in 1957, when Sert, with new associates Huson Jackson (1913–2006) and Ronald Gourley (1919–1999), received the commission to design a new health and administrative center for the university adjacent to both Harvard Yard and Harvard Square (see pp. 218 and 219).[35] Circulation, one of the CIAM "four functions," determined the organization of Holyoke Center. Although a common image of modern architecture is the isolated object building surrounded by acres of useless open space, in fact for Le Corbusier and CIAM this open space was to be carefully designed with both landscape and circulation elements. Le Corbusier defined the essence of circulation as the conflict between pedestrians and cars, which at the Harvard campus Sert attempted to address with new pedestrian routes. As the first major element of his new planning strategy for the campus, the center was intended to create a pedestrian link between the classrooms of the Old Yard and the dormitories of the South Yard. The orchestration of movement elements—"stairs, elevator shafts, access corridors and their links"[36]—became the focus of the design, which Sert later described as a "tentacular building."[37]

Although larger than almost any other building in Cambridge at the time, Holyoke Center was conceptualized not as a sculptural object but as the prototype for a contextual urban design process. The entire building reads in the cityscape as a series of events, from the two-story bank and plaza adjacent to the Harvard Square subway station through the pedestrian arcade (which was not made into a shopping street until the 1990s) to the low-rise clinic element and garden by Sasaki on Mount Auburn Street. The H-plan upper stories for university medical and administrative offices were set back from the narrow side streets, such that their ten-story bulk was not overwhelming. Sert calculated the setback of the north arm of the H so that it would appear from the Yard to be no taller than the four-story building it replaced. Further unusual sensitivity to an existing urban environment was expressed by including street-oriented shops and services along the two side

streets, and by almost concealing the necessary garage entrances and exits between them.

Instead of a single object, Holyoke Center is a series of complex interlocking parts that include a wide range of functions. It expanded gradually toward the Yard as construction progressed from 1961 to its completion in 1967, suggesting that it was part of an ongoing process rather than a single static object. Its external expression—similar to the Sert firm's nearly contemporaneous New England Gas and Electric Association headquarters, also in Cambridge (1961)—was controversial from the beginning, however. Its elevations of exposed concrete, clear and translucent glass panels, and precast concrete brise-soleils prompted objections from a campus community accustomed to red brick. Sert had consulted with the building's users to determine the arrangement of the clear and translucent two-foot, two-inch–wide (south elevation) and three-foot, seven-inch–wide (north elevation) panels, although the actual proportioning of the façades used Corbusian regulating lines based on Golden Section ratios. An additional visual coding system was provided by multicolored horizontal bars across the clear glass windows, "orange for windows one module wide, red for two, yellow for three,"[38] a strategy that Sert admitted was mainly to "enliven the vast grey concrete surfaces," which he said that he had learned "from my friends Fernand Léger and Joan Miró."[39]

Sert envisioned Holyoke Center as a key element in a series of built events that would strengthen the pedestrian and open-space network of Harvard's quasi-urban campus while still providing the large amounts of new square footage required. The other new campus buildings designed within Sert's planning framework, including Le Corbusier's Carpenter Center for the Visual Arts (1959–63, with the Sert firm as associate architects), were all set within the loose Sert planning framework.[40] All responded to real or imaginary patterns of campus pedestrian circulation, and most were designed with considerable attention to their older, low-rise surroundings.

Although in this era of Mies, Louis Kahn, and Philip Johnson, Sert was not considered one of the major form-makers of postwar American architecture, he and his firm received several other important commissions at this time, notably at the new Boston University campus (1960–66) on the opposite side of the Charles.[41] At BU, Sert responded to the difficult context of the existing Art Deco–Gothic buildings by Cram and Ferguson ranged along high-speed Commonwealth Avenue. By opening the campus to the river he created a central plaza and then provided space for the law and education schools in a seventeen-story tower. Between this tower and the stepped main library adjoining the student center are several plazas. As at Holyoke Center, Sert accommodated a complex program in a series of structures whose forms are designed in relation to each other, and in relation to carefully composed landscape elements. As in Sert's earlier plans for Latin American new towns, much of the campus design is about the public movement infrastructure of access roads, walks, plazas, corridors, and elevator cores that link the new buildings to each other and to their surroundings. Unlike the nearly contemporary work of Team 10 members Georges Candilis and Shadrach Woods, however, in Sert's work there is still a strong element of Corbusian formalism.

To what extent these built projects were influential on the Harvard urban design program itself remains to be determined. In her 1962 description of the program Tyrwhitt mentioned several projects that had influenced it, but she did not refer to the Sert projects. Their design certainly reflected Sert's efforts to adapt CIAM principles to the campus contexts of the Charles River basin. From CIAM came the emphasis on the building as a tool or piece of equipment to facilitate what are defined as desirable social goals, which in this case included an expanded sense of functionality that included not only light, air, view, and green space but also pedestrian interconnectivity and the idea of the civic core. Also from the more Corbusian part of CIAM came the use of the Modulor proportioning system, which attempted to use an idealized human male type as a basis for a "human scale" set of measurements based on standardized dimensions, as well as the inclusion of works of art by Miró, Mirko Basaldella, and others. As in most of the work of the modern movement at this time, there was also a real or intended use of prefabricated structural elements and a deliberate avoidance of "softer," more traditional materials, such as wood or stone.

In these projects one can see more clearly the strengths and limitations of Sert's approach to urbanism after CIAM. These projects still have something of an authoritarian, elitist element, perhaps inherent in any built productions by wealthy and prestigious institutions. President Pusey, determined to modernize the Harvard campus, welcomed Sert's interventions, apparently without concern about negative popular opinions. Both the clients and architects of 1960 were still largely convinced that modern architecture would be accepted in the future. Within that understanding, Sert said he wanted to avoid creating mere "prestige squares" of the type usually put in front of office buildings, where the "fountains and planting [are] merely decorative." At Forbes Plaza, on the Massachusetts Avenue side of Holyoke Center, his stated goal was to create "an oasis in the middle of noisy crossroads . . . a place for people to rest, to meet and to gather together in a human environment." He saw this as having a resistant dimension: "There is a worldwide need to establish a charter of 'urban rights,'" necessary because "the younger generations do not want to be dictated to . . . they ask for and need places to meet and to exchange views on their own."[42]

This intention of course took on an ironic dimension in the atmosphere of the later 1960s, in which the GSD became a focal point of campus unrest.[43] Although Sert continued to use late-CIAM concepts based on the importance of pedestrian vitality and the use of landscape elements at the core in his firm's work at Roosevelt Island and elsewhere until his death in 1983, the expectation that these concepts would be implemented under the direction of architects using their own definitions of visual and social value came under increasing challenge. In his keynote address at the 1968 Urban Design Conference, the last to be organized by Sert,[44] John Kenneth Galbraith defended architects as society's "arbiters of taste," since "beauty, no more than measles or syphilis, is to be entrusted to the uninstructed intellect."[45] This position was understood by a critical student as a defense of the "need for artistic license in the architectural handling of new 'forms.'" The student, Richard Joos, writing in the GSD stu-

dent journal *Connection,* took issue with the fact that the conference had not been canceled or modified after the recent assassinations of the Reverend Martin Luther King, Jr., and Senator Robert Kennedy, and he "found it ironical that the conference should be held in a theater [the Loeb Drama Center] on a stage, like a play." Joos suggested that "academia, like the business community and the architectural profession, seems to have lost contact, through its scholarly approach, with the people. In this sense perhaps only the advertising industry has been able to make any useful contact—through marketing analysis and other techniques." He argued that the basic question was, "Is community planning for the people or with the people?" raising the issue of popular participation and legitimation that would eventually undermine the whole basis of urban design as it had developed under Sert's leadership after CIAM.[46]

In CIAM's early history its members did not doubt that CIAM was planning both for and with the people, since in Germany and elsewhere it had successfully linked techniques of architectural design and presentation to a set of formal solutions to real housing needs. The group's later history in the United States, on the other hand, reveals the growing gulf between popular tastes and desires and CIAM's formal techniques and solutions. Sert attempted to bridge this gulf by making his buildings more responsive to existing urban conditions, imagining that in the future the CIAM approach would become generally accepted.[47] The new radical social critiques of architecture and planning that emerged in the later 1960s, some from within the GSD itself, made this acceptance impossible, since they questioned the master planner or master architect's legitimacy to act "for the people" and instead suggested that his only legitimacy came from closeness to undemocratic and unrepresentative sources of power.

Shadrach Woods' Eighth Gropius Lecture, also given at the 1968 Urban Design Conference, was an effort to ruminate on, if not actually solve, this dilemma. He argued that "urbanism as we know it in Europe and North America is a stupendous hoax." "Our predecessors," he said, rightly presented themselves "as being exemplary of social consciousness in their time." In America, however, their area of concern became "essentially esthetic, that is, an abstraction of the total scene." Evoking projections that predicted a world population of seven billion in forty years, he suggested that the "present reality, as far as we can seize it, seems to constitute an accusation of our civilization." Given the present "dangerously inequitable" distribution of wealth, he proposed that "for we here, for whom the whole world is a city, urbanism is not only the organizing of a certain physical environment . . . it is also the efficient and equitable allocation, distribution, use, replenishment, and substitution of the world city's wealth." Woods then related his recent experiences in Paris in May 1968, where for him "one of the most interesting aspects of this urban event was the deadly influence of allegorical urbanism on the students' movement." Locked out of the Sorbonne, "that temple of class, that symbol of an elite, their movement was coherent and powerful." But "when the students got off the streets and back into the system, where they belonged, the bourgeois power structure was reassured."

For Woods, "the urbanism of our concern, every-

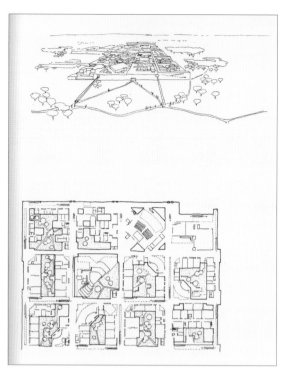

Figure 8.6 Shadrach Woods, Joachim Pfeufer, and Maurice Hogan, new facilities, University College, Dublin, 1964. Perspective and partial plan.

day urbanism, is continually preoccupied with change, that is, with continually adapting the physical mileu to the evolving needs of a changing society" (fig. 8.6). It springs from a dynamic idea, more of an intention than an act, of "constantly organizing the environment without ever getting it completely, definitively organized." These urban organizations "should be capable of growing and changing," and this requires "systems, structuring devices, which present possibilities for adaptation and change. We usually rely on simple geometries, stems and webs, since these are easiest to adapt and to deform as the need arises." His definition of the task of the architect-urbanist was to take "those quantifiable data which are collected by the technocrats, put these into context with the imponderables" and then collate the whole set to "make a temporary equilibrium of development policy." Woods insisted that the architect-urbanist, unlike the new kind of systems planner that emerged around this time, was still concerned with ordering the "city of man," articulating its public and private domains. It was from this stance that Woods attempted to broaden "urbanistic attitudes to include the rest of the world" as part of a "coherent and equitable system."[48]

Woods, then, can be seen as still operating within the CIAM paradigm of master planning, but attempting at the same time to take into account several of the critical positions that had emerged in the 1960s. Like his fellow Team 10 members, he made reference to the need for provisionally organizing the urban environment in ways that could be continually changed and modified over time, ideas that of course had been carried much further, at a polemical level, by Archigram and the Situationist International. He

also attempted to address attacks on planning being made by advocacy planners, suggesting that architects had to somehow work for the revolutionary global masses and not for those currently in power. Neither of these responses seemed especially convincing, and in fact Woods himself does not seem to have been able to produce work after this point that could demonstrate how any paradigm of the urban designer could adequately respond to the political situation as he conceptualized it. What did remain from the earliest period of CIAM in the position he set out in this talk was the emphasis on the maximum effect for the minimum of means, now recast within a global framework. This now appears as the most compelling part of what was one of the final statements of CIAM.

NOTES

1. Denise Scott Brown, "Between Three Stools: A Personal View of Urban Design and Pedagogy," in Ann Ferebee, ed., *Education for Urban Design* (New York: Institute for Urban Design, 1982), 132.

2. Reginald R. Isaacs, *Walter Gropius: An Illustrated Biography* (Boston: Little, Brown, 1991), 271. Isaacs, who had graduated from the GSD in 1939 and studied with Chicago sociologist Louis Wirth in the late 1940s, was director of the Michael Reese Hospital planning staff from 1945 to 1953. He was a key figure in the South Side Planning Board's efforts to clear and reconfigure the large area between East

21st and 47th Streets, which included the Illinois Institute of Technology, Reese, and other institutions, as well as several Chicago Housing Authority projects. Isaacs taught a large-scale collaborative studio that focused on this area at GSD in 1950–51, which was the subject of a June 1951 exhibition in Chicago.

3. Hideo Sasaki, born near Fresno, California, had received his MLA from the GSD in 1948. He had studied at UCLA and Berkeley before being interned in a camp in Poston, Arizona, during the war on account of his Japanese ancestry. He received a BFA at the University of Illinois in 1946,

and then worked at Skidmore, Owings, & Merrill (SOM) in both New York and Chicago and taught at the University of Illinois in 1948–49. In 1949 he won a competition for a combined office building and war memorial sponsored by the U.S. Junior Chamber of Commerce in Tulsa, Oklahoma, with partners J. Edward Luders, James V. Edsall, and Harry A. Morris. (Melanie Simo, *The Offices of Hideo Sasaki: A Corporate History* [Berkeley, Calif.: Spacemaker, 2001], 10–12.)

4. Anthony Alofsin, *The Struggle for Modernism: Architecture, Landscape Architecture, and City Planning at Harvard* (New York: W. W. Norton,

2002), 235–236. According to an *Architectural Forum* news item (May 1953, pp. 43, 46), many GSD faculty, including the modern architect Hugh Stubbins, said they resigned rather than be part of a Sert-led program that had "such a strong flavor of international modern design." None of the TAC (The Architects Collaborative) faculty members hired by Gropius who had been let go by Hudnut in 1951 were rehired by Sert. One other returnee was Naum Gabo, a visiting artist in 1948–49 who had worked with Herbert Read in England during the war and had moved to the United States in 1946 (Alofsin, *Struggle for Modernism,* 250). Despite Sert's continued support and interest in publishing his lectures, Gabo found the students unreceptive to his ideas, and he was unwilling to continue teaching after one year. (Martin Hammer and Christina Lodder, *Constructing Modernity: The Art and Career of Naum Gabo* [New Haven: Yale University Press, 2000], 351.) Herbert Read himself gave the Charles Eliot Norton lectures in 1953–54, which were then published as the book *Icon and Idea: The Function of Art in the Development of Human Consciousness* (Cambridge, Mass.: Harvard University Press, 1955).

5. Chermayeff was appointed director of the Institute of Design after the death of its founder, László Moholy-Nagy. He left in 1951 after it was merged with IIT, and he then practiced in Boston with Heywood Cutting and taught design

studio at MIT before coming to Harvard. (Richard Plunz, *Design and Public Good: Selected Writings, 1930–1980, by Serge Chermayeff* [Cambridge, Mass.: MIT Press, 1982], 316.)

6. Giedion wrote to Sert about the latter's appointment as dean, "I agree with you: it is our chance." To teach history Giedion tentatively suggested G. E. Kidder Smith, "who has no real historical background," and Sekler, who "has a certain knowledge and speaks our vocabulary." He objected to Sert's intention to invite Marcus Whiffen, whom he felt lacked a "solid historical background *and*—what is most important—does not possess our vocabulary." (Letter, Giedion to Sert, August 30, 1954, Folder E-6, Josep Lluís Sert Collection, Frances Loeb Library, Harvard University Graduate School of Design [JLS].)

7. Gropius, Sert, and Giedion (who also belonged to the Swiss CIAM group) were members of the New York CIAM group after 1943. Tyrwhitt was an English MARS Group member; Sekler was a member of Austrian CIAM, and Jerzy Soltan, hired by Sert in 1958, had been an associate of Le Corbusier since 1946 and was also a Polish CIAM member. In 1961 Sert mentioned to Giedion that he would have liked to have brought in Swiss CIAM member Werner M. Moser as acting chairman of the department of architecture, if he "had been younger and free." (Sert to Giedion, November 14, 1961, Folder E8, JLS.)

8. Isaacs records that in his first speech

as dean, Sert described planning as a "province of architecture," and insisted that only an architect could be a city planner (Isaacs, *Gropius,* 271). This is probably an overstatement of Sert's position.

9. Richard Norton Smith, *The Harvard Century: The Making of a University to a Nation* (New York: Simon and Schuster, 1986), 197–201.

10. Under the name Coolidge Shepley Bulfinch & Abbott, the firm had designed most of the residential South Yard between 1913 and 1930. In 1946, under Henry R. Shepley's direction, it designed the "Scandinavian modern" Lamont Library, which included the Woodbury Poetry reading room by Alvar Aalto. This was followed by Gropius and TAC's Harvard Graduate Center dormitories (1948) and the Shepley firm's Allston Burr lecture hall (1951, demolished), built for undergraduate instruction in science on the present site of Stirling and Wilford's Sackler Museum. The first modern River Houses were also by the Shepley firm, Quincy House (1957, Jean-Paul Carlhian, design associate) and Leverett Towers (1957, Harry Shepley, designer).

11. "Two Cities: Planning in North and South America," *Museum of Modern Art Bulletin* 14, no. 3 (June 1947).

12. On Sert's work in Latin America, see Xavier Costa, ed., *Sert: arquitecto en nueva york* (Barcelona: Museu d'Art Contemporani de Barcelona, 1997).

13. J. L. Sert, "Centres of Community Life," in J. Tyrwhitt, J. L. Sert, and

E. N. Rogers, *CIAM 8: The Heart of the City* (New York: Pellegrini and Cudahy, 1952), 3–16.

14. Paul Lester Wiener and José Luis Sert, *Urbanisme en Amerique du Sud/ Town Planning in South America* (Paris: l'Architecture d'aujourd'hui, 1951), 33.

15. "Can Patios Make Cities?" *Architectural Forum* 99 (August 1953): 124–130.

16. In this article, "patio civic centers" were illustrated with a plan of Harvard Yard and Sert and Wiener's projects for civic centers at the Cidade dos Motores, Brazil; Chimbote, Peru; Medellín, Colombia; and Quinta Palatino, a Havana subdivision. "Patio buildings" were illustrated with models of their church for Puerto Ordaz, Venezuela; the plan of a school for Pomona, Venezuela; and a model of their Santa Cruz clinic project for Maracaibo, Venezuela.

17. Scott Brown, "Between Three Stools," 133.

18. Sert, Opening Talk, CIAM 10, Dubrovnik, August 6, 1956 (CIAM 42-X-14/19).

19. Shadrach Woods, "Eighth Gropius Lecture: The Incompatible Butterfly," *12th Urban Design Conference, New Communities: One Alternative* (Cambridge, Mass.: Harvard Graduate School of Design, 1968), 13–22.

20. On Bacon, see Alexander Garvin, "Philadelphia's Planner: A Conversation with Edmund Bacon," *Journal of Planning History* 1, no. 1 (February 2002): 58–78.

21. Edmund N. Bacon, *Progressive Architecture* 37 (August 1956): 108–109. Peter S. Reed suggests that Kahn's July 1950 model of a continuous, open-to-the-sky pedestrian concourse in part of his scheme for the Triangle area is the probable source of the Bacon and Kling Penn Center plan of 1952. (Peter S. Reed, "Toward Form: Louis I. Kahn's Urban Designs for Philadelphia, 1939–1962" [Ph.D. diss., University of Pennsylvania, 1989], 86–87.) Bacon later stated that he had hired Kahn to work on models for the Penn Center, but found him difficult to work with and replaced him with Kling (Garvin, 72–73). Bacon said in the film produced for the 1960 Philadelphia AIA convention, *Form, Design and the City,* that he chose Kling for the Penn Center based on his work on the design of Lankenau Hospital in Overbrook, Pennsylvania (1953).

22. David Brownlee, in David Brownlee and David DeLong, *Louis I. Kahn: In the Realm of Architecture* (New York: Rizzoli, 1993), 47; "A Shopping Center," in "Walter Gropius et son école/Walter Gropius—The Spread of an Idea," *l'Architecture d'aujourd'hui* 28 (February 1950). Holmes Perkins, then the Charles Dyer Norton Professor of Regional Planning, taught this collaborative studio with Bremer Pond of Landscape Architecture and Walter Bogner of Architecture.

23. Roosevelt Field shopping center was designed by Zeckendorf's in-house architectural team. Led by Pei, it included Henry Cobb, a former GSD student of Pei's, and Ulrich Franzen, another GSD graduate. (Carter Wiseman, *I. M. Pei: A Profile in American Architecture* [New York: Harry N. Abrams, 2001], 52–53; "Roosevelt Field Shopping Center, a Webb & Knapp project," *Progressive Architecture* 36 [September 1955]: 91–97.)

24. Howard Gillette, Jr., "The Evolution of the Planned Shopping Center in Suburb and City," *American Planning Association Journal,* Autumn 1985, 451–456. Richard Longstreth, *City Center to Regional Mall: Architecture, the Automobile and Retailing in Los Angeles, 1920–1950* (Cambridge, Mass.: MIT Press, 1997) emphasizes the many similar directions to Gruen's in the 1940s, including Ketchum, Gina, & Sharp's unbuilt North Shore Center in Beverly, Mass. (1947), and similar Shopper's World in Framingham, Mass. (1948, demolished 1994), the first built postwar shopping center, and many other related projects at this time.

25. Victor Gruen, "Urban Design of Today—Fort Worth," *Progressive Architecture* 37 (August 1956): 110–111.

26. Ibid., 111.

27. David A. Crane, "Chandigarh Reconsidered," *AIA Journal* 33 (May 1960): 32–39.

28. Scott Brown, "Between Three Stools," 136.

29. Wilhelm Viggo von Moltke received his diploma at the Technische Hochschule in Berlin in 1937, and he worked for Tecton member Anthony Chitty in London and in Sweden before attending the Harvard GSD from

1940 to 1942. While there he worked summers for Alvar Aalto, Hugh Stubbins, and Howe, Stonorov & Kahn. He served in the U.S. Army from 1943 to 1948 and was a member of the postwar American military government in Germany. He then worked for Marcel Breuer, SOM-NY, and Eero Saarinen, and was involved in Saarinen's unbuilt North Campus Master Plan at the University of Michigan (1951). He was chief of the division of land planning and later chief designer for the Philadelphia City Planning Commission under Bacon from 1953 to 1961, and was a visiting critic in the department of architecture at Penn from 1954 to 1960. (Wilhelm V. von Moltke, "Urban Design Intent: Three Case Studies" [unpublished memoir, 1981], 1, 5, 6.)

30. Fumihiko Maki received his B.Arch. from the University of Tokyo in 1952, and then two M.Archs., Cranbrook (1953) and Harvard (1954). He worked for SOM in New York under Gordon Bunshaft in 1954–55 and for Sert's new Cambridge office from 1955 to 1958. He began teaching at Washington University in St. Louis in 1956, where he was also an associate in the Campus Planning Office until 1958 under the direction of a former dean, the architectural historian Buford Pickens. After receiving a Graham Foundation fellowship with Giedion's assistance for 1958–60, and completing the Steinberg Hall commission for the university (with Russell, Mullgardt, Schwarz & Van Hoefen, associated architects), he

was then associate professor at WU from 1960 to 1962. He was an associate professor at GSD from 1962 to 1965, before establishing his office in Tokyo in 1965. He remained a visiting critic at GSD until 1967.

31. Letter, Maki to Giedion, May 1, 1958, Sigfried Giedion Archive, GTA (Institute for the History and Theory ofArchitecture) archives, ETH (Eidgenössische Technische Hochschule), Zurich.

32. Memo by Tyrwhitt on the proposed urban design program, n.d., c. 1960, Harvard University, Graduate School of Design (Tyrwhitt Collection, Royal Institute of British Architects [RIBA] Library). Tyrwhitt listed nine sources as major references for the program: Frederick Gibberd, *Town Design* (1959); Sigfried Giedion, *Space, Time, and Architecture* (1954), esp. chapters 2, 7, 8, 9; Kevin Lynch, "The Form of Cities," *Scientific American* 190, no. 4 (April 1954): 55–63 and *The Image of the City* (1960); Lewis Mumford, *The Culture of Cities* (1938); Steen Eiler Rasmussen, *Towns and Buildings* (1951); Camillo Sitte, *The Art of Building Cities* (1945 trans.); Christopher Tunnard and Henry Hope Reed, *American Skyline* (1955); and Tyrwhitt, Sert, and Rogers, *CIAM 8: The Heart of the City* (1952).

33. Charles Abrams (1902–1970), a New York lawyer and housing activist, had organized the Institute for Urban Studies at the New School for Social Research in New York in 1939, whose invited speakers included Lewis Mumford, Clarence Stein, and

Tyrwhitt. (Jaqueline Tyrwhitt, "Working with Charles Abrams," in O. H. Koenigsberger, S. Groak, and B. Bernstein, eds., *The Work of Charles Abrams: Housing and Urban Renewal in the USA and the Third World* [Oxford: Pergamon, 1980], 35–36.) Abrams taught at Penn in the 1950s and was appointed chairman of the New York State Commission Against Discrimination in 1955. At the first Harvard Urban Design Conference he had spoken vigorously about the plight of darker-skinned urban migrants to the suburbanizing American cities of the 1950s. (Charles Abrams, *Progressive Architecture* 37 [August 1956]: 100–101.)

34. Harvard University Planning Office, *Harvard University 1960: An Inventory for Planning* (Cambridge, Mass.: Harvard University, 1960), n.p.

35. Huson Jackson had worked for Charles Eames in St. Louis in the 1930s, and he received his M.Arch. in 1939 from GSD. He practiced in Boston in 1940–42, and in New York after 1944, and taught at Columbia and Pratt before Sert brought him to GSD in 1953. Ronald Gourley had received his M.Arch. from the GSD in 1948 and then taught at MIT before Sert brought him to Harvard, also in 1953. He was later the dean of the University of Arizona School of Architecture from 1970 to 1980. (Obituary, *Harvard Magazine*, July–August 2000, p. 96.)

36. Josep Lluís Sert, "Changing Views on the Urban Environment," *RIBA Journal* 70, no. 5 (May 1963): 194.

37. Donald Canty, "Harvard Completes a Course in Urban Design," *Architectural Forum* 126 (January–February 1967): 76; see also Andrea Oppenheimer Dean, "The Urbane and Varied Buildings of Sert, Jackson and Associates," *AIA Journal* 66 (May 1977): 50–57.

38. Canty, "Harvard Completes a Course in Urban Design," 75.

39. Sert, "Changing Views," 192.

40. Fumihiko Maki, one of Sert's first GSD students, presented some of these buildings to a Japanese audience in "Modern Buildings at Harvard," *Apuraochi [Approach]* (Osaka), Summer 1964, pp. 2–5. Maki's article illustrated TAC's Hoffman Center, Yamasaki's psychology building, Sert's Holyoke Center and Peabody Terrace dormitories, and the Carpenter Center.

41. The Sert firm also designed a new campus for Guelph University in Ontario (1965). Unbuilt urban design commissions of the Sert office at this time include projects for the central business district in Worcester, Massachusetts; the redesign of South Station in Boston; one neighborhood of Interama, a proposed "permanent Latin American trade fair" on an island in Miami; and coastal vacation villages on Mediterranean and Caribbean islands (Jaume Freixa, *Josep Lluís Sert: Works and Projects,* 2nd ed. [Barcelona: Gustavo Gili, 1992], 94–99, 108–111).

42. Josep Lluís Sert, Interview—Holyoke Center Plaza, circa 1965 (Folder D39, JLS).

43. Morton and Phyllis Keller, *Making Harvard Modern: The Rise of America's University* (New York: Oxford University Press, 2001), 269. Isaacs, Vigier, and Vigier's associate in planning William Wray Nash in particular were criticized as an "aesthetics-obsessed Old Guard," out of touch with the radical implications of urban design in an era of social upheaval.

44. This conference was devoted to the presentation of a HUD-funded study of a new town design by students under the title "New Communities: One Alternative." The last Urban Design Conference was the next one, the thirteenth, held in 1970 by Sert's successor as dean, former Harvard Business School professor Maurice Kilbridge.

45. Harvard Graduate School of Design, *12th Urban Design Conference, New Communities: One Alternative, Proceedings, June 7 and 8, 1968* (Cambridge, Mass.: Harvard Graduate School of Design, 1968), 9.

46. Richard Joos, "An Irrelevant Show: The Urban Design Conference," *Connection* 5, no. 4 (Summer 1968): 42–43.

47. Constantine (Dinos) Michaelides, a former student and employee and later dean of the Washington University School of Architecture, recalls Sert saying in his office in about 1958 that the artistic revolution of the modern movement was like the Renaissance, the kind of change that occurs only every five hundred years or so. (Interview with Constantine Michaelides, St. Louis, June 21, 2003.)

48. Shadrach Woods, "The Incompatible Butterfly," in Harvard Graduate School of Design, *12th Urban Design Conference,* 13–22.

Chapter 9

FROM THE GROUND UP

Hideo Sasaki's Contributions to Urban Design

CAMMIE MCATEE

In his introductory comments to the first Urban Design Conference held at Harvard in April 1956, Josep Lluís Sert, dean of the Graduate School of Design, remarked upon the significant shifts all fields of design were undergoing and the potential for them to come together to unite under the rubric of urban design: "With the new approach to architecture, landscape architecture, road engineering and city planning, accepted formulas had to be thrown overboard. It is logical that the changes in all these fields have developed independently, each group trying to establish a new set of principles and a new language of forms. It now seems equally logical that the progress in the different professions be brought closer together, so that a synthesis can be achieved in urban design. I do believe that now, after many years of individual, isolated work, we are logically coming to an era of synthesis."[1]

The boundaries between architecture, planning, and landscape had become blurred. It was now possible to imagine broader frameworks for tackling the complex problems facing designers in the postwar

period. Among the conference participants, who included architects, planners, developers, city administrators, social theorists, and activists, the landscape architect Hideo Sasaki stands out for his contributions to the redefinition of the territory that would be claimed for urban design. In 1956, Sasaki was in the early stages of a reform that would profoundly change the way landscape architecture and planning were taught and practiced in the United States. By the early 1960s, Sasaki would bring together the elements of Sert's synthesis, arguably more fully than Sert himself would manage to do.

Sasaki is well known for the design of several iconic modern landscapes in the United States, including those created for the Upjohn Corporation headquarters, Kalamazoo, Michigan (Skidmore Owings & Merrill; 1957–61), John Deere & Company headquarters, Moline, Illinois (Eero Saarinen & Associates; 1956–63), and the First Church of Christ, Scientist, Boston (I. M. Pei; 1964–75) (figs. 9.1 and 9.2). However, much of Sasaki's work evades easy assimilation within the canon of modern land-

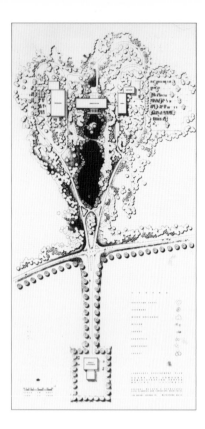

Figure 9.1 Landscape plan for John Deere & Company headquarters, Moline, Illinois, 1958. Sasaki, Walker & Associates, landscape architects; Eero Saarinen & Associates, architects.

scape architecture.[2] Sasaki, as many of his colleagues have noted, was not a "plant man." And despite being highly respected as a designer, he was much less interested in creating the distinct formal landscapes that characterize the work of his slightly older colleagues Thomas Church, Dan Kiley, Garrett Eckbo, James Rose, and Lawrence Halprin, who brought high modernism to landscape architecture during the 1940s and 1950s. As his office evolved in the 1950s, Sasaki increasingly turned his attention away from formal design, leaving that aspect of his practice to such associates as Peter Walker and Stuart Dawson, to concentrate on new avenues of research and activity in land planning and design. Sasaki did not consider himself a landscape architect, seeing limitation in such a narrow designation

for the scope of activity he envisioned.[3] The term land designer or land planner, suggesting an integration of planning and landscape architecture, more appropriately describes the professional role that Sasaki felt was critical to the broadening field of land development and design.

In this essay I examine the development of Sasaki's vision for a land-based integrated design as seen through the collaborative model he pursued in the 1950s in the landscape curriculum at Harvard and in his professional practice. Almost without interruption, Sasaki taught at the GSD from 1950 to 1970, and he was chair of the department of landscape architecture from 1958 to 1968. To give form to his vision Sasaki drew on many forces, chief among them the evolving discourse on collaborative design introduced to the curriculum by Dean Joseph Hudnut in the 1930s. This approach was reinterpreted by leaders within the school, first by Walter Gropius in the late 1930s and the 1940s, and in the 1950s and 1960s by Sert as dean and G. Holmes Perkins and Reginald R. Isaacs as successive chairs of the department of regional planning (and in the case of Isaacs, briefly of the department of landscape architecture).[4] Establishing a dialectic between education and practice was critical to Sasaki's efforts to transform the profession. During Sasaki's tenure at Harvard, his office in the Boston suburb of Watertown operated in tandem with the landscape architecture program at the GSD. The collaborative model he promoted in the studio was reflected in his practice, which evolved into a multidisciplinary firm comprising landscape architects, planners, architects, and civil engineers, with later additions of graphic, interior, and systems designs.

I will first consider the development of Sasaki's educational model within the context of the GSD. In doing so, I return to ground covered by Melanie Simo and Peter Walker in their writings on Sasaki's contributions to landscape architectural education and on the development of his practice.[5] What I intend to achieve, however, is a more focused examination of how Sasaki used the discourse on collaboration to establish new parameters for the field of landscape architecture, which in turn would redefine the landscape architect's participation in what Sert called urban design. The last part of the essay enters less charted scholarly waters. The limited writing on Sasaki's production has primarily focused on the landscapes he created for corporate headquarters.[6] I instead consider areas of design that Sasaki believed more fully engaged the expertise of the land-based specialist. Campus planning was one such area that enabled Sasaki to assert a new role for the land planner/designer.

RECONCEIVING LANDSCAPE ARCHITECTURE

As early as 1950, when Sasaki was still a junior faculty member at the University of Illinois, he took an extremely challenging stance on the future direction of landscape architecture. In a brief text published in *Landscape Architecture* in July 1950, Sasaki outlined an empirical methodology of "research, analysis, and synthesis," emphasizing the role of "critical thinking."[7] Carl Steinitz, a planner who taught with Sasaki in the 1960s, has observed that this article introduced the themes that Sasaki would develop for the rest of his career.[8] Before analyzing this early text it will be helpful to look at Sasaki's formation and professional experience to that point in time.

Figure 9.2 View of lake from John Deere & Company headquarters building, 1964. Sasaki, Walker & Associates, landscape architects; Eero Saarinen & Associates, architects. Photograph by Ezra Stoller.

By all accounts it was Sasaki's interest in multidisciplinary study that brought him into the world of architecture and design. In 1939 during his first year at the University of California at Los Angeles, a fellow student told him about city planning, a field of study offered at Berkeley within the department of agriculture.[9] Sasaki was immediately taken by the interdisciplinary nature of planning.[10] He enrolled at Berkeley the following year but soon discovered that he was more interested in design than in administra-

Figure 9.3a Cover, *Landscape Architecture*, 1951

gram's progressive director, to update the curriculum, the traditional subjects of landscape architecture—parks, subdivisions, and estate design—remained the core problems.[12] Unsatisfied by the scope of the program, Sasaki also followed classes given by the planner Karl B. Lohmann. Sasaki completed his degree in landscape architecture in 1946 and then accepted a scholarship offered by Harvard.

Sasaki's decision to do graduate work at Harvard was taken with the expectation that he would finally be immersed in modern design. This was a reasonable assumption: three of the postwar period's leading landscape architects—Eckbo, Kiley, and Rose—had all attended Harvard's program, and the presence of the former–MARS Group member and landscape architect Christopher Tunnard, a faculty member between 1938 and 1942, similarly suggested that landscape architecture had gone "modern" at Harvard.[13] Tunnard, author of *The Garden in the Modern Landscape* (1938), a book that was as close to being a modern manifesto for landscape architecture as existed, promoted an attitude that reflected the rationalism of science and the belief that landscape architecture could play a major role in larger planning issues.[14] During his tenure, however, Tunnard had not taught in the landscape program, then still under the chairmanship of the dogmatic traditionalist Bremer Pond, working instead with Walter Gropius, Martin Wagner, and Hugh Stubbins on an architecture studio.[15] He also gave a course on site planning, which included the work of the Tennessee Valley Authority, and on residential densities.[16]

It was instead in a much-outdated program, still largely based on the design of classically inspired gardens, that Sasaki found himself in the fall of 1946.

tion, which seemed to occupy the planning students. His further investigation of either field was halted in 1942 when, as a Japanese American, Sasaki was forced to move inland from the West Coast, and it was not until near the end of the war that he could resume his studies in landscape architecture. In the interim, he took night classes at Roosevelt College in Chicago, majoring in psychology.[11] In 1944 he accepted a scholarship to study landscape architecture at the University of Illinois at Urbana-Champaign. Despite the efforts of Stanley White, the pro-

Tensions between Pond and Gropius were pushing the landscape students to the periphery of the school. They were not considered by faculty members in the other departments to be full participants in the collaborative projects that students in all three programs were required to do.[17] With their instructors maintaining that modernism had nothing to do with trees, it was all but impossible for the landscape students to bridge the divide between the departments and the two approaches.[18] Arriving almost ten years after Kiley, Eckbo, and Rose had left the GSD,

Sasaki found himself just as frustrated as they had been with the program's direction. Although Sasaki succeeded in designing distinctly modern landscapes, as his model for a "flexible garden" demonstrates (fig. 9.3), it was the collaboration he saw in the architecture studios and the stimulating conversations he shared with the architecture students that had the greatest impact on his work and approach to design.[19] Gropius's inspiring call for teamwork infused the school, touching even the isolated landscape students.

Figure 9.3b Hideo Sasaki, model for a flexible garden (c. 1946–48)

Sasaki took these approaches and values with him, as well as what would prove to be useful connections with several architecture students, among them I. M. Pei, Hugh Stubbins, and Paul Rudolph. Upon graduating from Harvard in 1948, Sasaki moved to New York to work for Skidmore, Owings & Merrill. Site planning rather than the traditional domain of landscape architecture occupied him there. He worked under Fred W. Kraft, a landscape architect who directed the firm's planning department, on the plan for Oak Ridge, Tennessee, the town of fifty thousand built for the Manhattan Project (1942–51).[20] Sasaki also assisted on the planning of Amuay, a community for workers in Venezuela commissioned by Creole Oil (a subsidiary of Standard Oil). In 1950 he was invited by White to return to the University of Illinois to be an instructor. While he was interested in teaching, Sasaki also recognized the need to maintain a presence in practice, and he worked during the summer for SOM's Chicago office and for Perkins & Will, a firm specializing in educational buildings. He also collaborated with other young practitioners, among them J. Edward Luders, a Cranbrook graduate with whom he partnered for a series of projects, including one of his first built works, a war memorial for a Junior Chamber of Commerce in Tulsa, Oklahoma (1949–52).[21] Sasaki and Luders, who worked for Robert F. Swanson in Bloomfield Hills, Michigan, would team up for other projects, including Swanson's commissions for the city plan of Champaign-Urbana, Illinois (1949–52), and a master plan for Wilmette, Illinois (1950). Years later Sasaki and Luders submitted an entry into the 1960 competition for the Franklin Delano Roosevelt Memorial, for which they received honorable mention.

In developing his teaching methods, Sasaki innovated techniques to give students as modern a basis for landscape design as possible. Drawing from the strong formal training he received at Harvard and ideas he had picked up about conceptual design, likely among them those developed by Walter Peterhans for the Visual Training course at Illinois Institute of Technology, Sasaki invented his own version of the Bauhaus *Vorkurs*, encouraging students to work with their hands, to cut shapes out of fabric, and to make abstract arrangements that would help them develop a sense of proportion.[22] He also worked at removing the boundaries between the various departments, inviting professors from both architecture and art to participate in discussions of his students' work. Sasaki took an active role in the Landscape Exchange Program, a national competition system paralleling that of the New York Beaux-Arts architecture program.[23] Not only did Sasaki prepare programs and criticize submissions, he also made significant changes to the overall program, eliminating the *esquisse* and initiating a design method based on an analytic process that required students to submit diagrams rather than sketches. In shifting the means of graphic representation from the beautifully rendered drawing to the rigorous scientific diagram, Sasaki sought to separate the subject from its object of knowledge, as Hyungmin Pai has characterized the "discourse of the modern diagram" in architectural practice.[24] Such radical teaching methods established Sasaki as a progressive educator.

It was the cumulative effect of his professional and teaching experience that led Sasaki to write his 1950 "manifesto" for the reform of landscape architecture education. While in many respects the two-

and-a-half-page text represented a "catching up" to changes that had begun to be implemented in architecture schools twenty years earlier, Sasaki's recasting of the field of landscape architecture was nothing less than a bombshell. He opened by directly addressing the shifting territory of landscape design and site and regional planning, and pointedly argued that the discipline needed to redefine itself or lose its relevance for society. While this was not the first time calls for such radical change had come from within the ranks—in 1944 the venerable Gilmore Clarke had supported a motion to rename the American Society of Landscape Architects the American Society of Land Planners—Sasaki's proposed reforms cut to the very heart of the profession. He succinctly laid out what was at stake: the profession could either adopt new approaches that would contribute to the "betterment of human environment," or it could stay the present course and risk becoming a "subordinate field of superficial embellishment."[25]

This text holds the seeds of Sasaki's redefinition of landscape architecture as land planning insofar as it emphasizes project and site planning, and regional planning as logically falling within the purview of landscape architecture. On the one hand, as Melanie Simo has noted, Sasaki was making a reasonable proposal to recapture ground lost to the profession in the interwar years, exemplified by the multidisciplinary practice of Frederick Law Olmsted. On the other hand, as Sasaki forcefully argued, land planning was integral to urban redevelopment projects, public and private housing, schools, and recreational planning. The problems posed by these areas of design required new approaches that were "bold enough to question and re-evaluate many of [landscape archi-

tecture's] precepts, and to change them for new ones if necessary to compete successfully with the other disciplines in the field of environmental planning." What was necessary was a tripartite "critical thought process" based on research: *verbal,* reading and discussing books on landscape architecture, art, and architecture, as well as on sociology and philosophy that would "help in understanding basic problems of environmental planning"; *visual,* looking at photographs, sketches, and work executed in the field, with special emphasis on the "vernacular—grain elevators, high tension lines, cultivated fields"; and *experimental,* exploring the "aesthetic possibilities of materials, construction methods, and spatial relationships." Research was followed by "analysis," which involved making relational diagrams of requirements and functions. The final step in the process was "synthesis," which Sasaki defined as the articulation of "all the factors into a design form, which distinguishes a designer from an engineer or a technician." Sasaki also commented on the trend within landscape architecture toward contemporary art and architecture movements, of which he approved, but he saw no reason why efforts to modernize the field should stop there. There would always be a similarity between architectural and landscape architectural expression, he reasoned, but landscape would distinguish itself through its own response to materials, methods, and functions. The article closed with a list of experiments leading to "new forms in environmental planning," among them contour plowing, freeway traffic routes, Radburn, and the greenbelt towns. In a rephrasing of "form follows function," Sasaki wrote, "New concepts applied frankly to solving problems of functions create new forms."

Figure 9.4a Detail view, model for the rehabilitation and conservation of Chicago's South Side (spring 1951). Collaborative project led by Reginald Isaacs, Harvard GSD.

These ideas appeared in print in 1950 just as Sasaki was preparing to leave the University of Illinois to return to Harvard at the invitation of G. Holmes Perkins, chair of the department of city and regional planning. The timing seemed propitious for introducing change to the landscape program: Pond had stepped down as chair and would retire the following year. And while it would seem that reforms would have been welcome after so many years of conflict, Sasaki instead encountered resistance from faculty in other departments at his attempt to develop collaborations that would go beyond the traditional field boundaries. As Simo has again observed, the idea of the master-builder at the top of the design hierarchy was difficult to topple in a school that still privileged architecture above the other disciplines. Sasaki did succeed in forging productive connections with Perkins, and he set joint problems for the planning and landscape students that had the former group working on site analysis. In the 1951–52 school year students were assigned to develop a residential area for one of the greenbelt towns.[26] Another problem focused on an ecological report for the New Town of Sudbury, Massachusetts.

For the first time since the collaborative studios were established during the war, landscape students were perceived as bringing something substantial to the design table.

The GSD went through a series of upheavals in the early 1950s—the retirements of Pond (1951), Gropius (1952), and Hudnut (1953), and the departure of G. Holmes Perkins for the University of Pennsylvania (1951)—that effectively suspended plans to overhaul the landscape program. In 1952 Sasaki, along with many of his colleagues, quit in protest of Gropius's forced retirement. He returned to the University of Illinois, where he helped establish a four-year undergraduate program in planning. It was during this period that Sasaki forged the first in what would be a series of intellectually satisfying collaborations. Through his involvement in the research arm of ACTION (American Council To Improve Our Neighborhoods), a group seeking community renewal, Sasaki resumed his acquaintance with Reginald R. Isaacs, then director of planning for the Michael Reese Hospital project in Chicago (1945–53).[27] Isaacs held a degree in architecture from the University of Minnesota (1935), a graduate degree in architecture from Harvard (1939), and had gone on to study sociology and planning with Louis Wirth and Rexford Guy Tugwell at the University of Chicago (1947–50). In addition to the hospital project and his involvement with the Chicago Plan Commission and Federal Housing Authority, Isaacs led city conservation studies in Minneapolis and Syracuse. His experience as well as his contributions to the discourse of city planning, among them his controversial 1948 article "Neighborhood Theory: An Analysis of Its

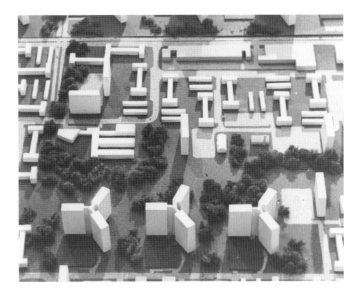

Figure 9.4b Detail views of model.

Adequacy," established him as a leader in the field of urban renewal.[28] It was likely in the context of a collaborative studio led by Isaacs as a guest lecturer at the GSD in the spring semester of 1951—a "Community Appraisal Study: A Program for Rehabilitation and Conservation in Chicago's South Side," involving students and faculty from all three departments and twelve invited experts—that Sasaki and Isaacs met (fig. 9.4).[29] What drew the men together was their shared interest in rethinking the bases of planning and commitment to urban renewal. Inspired by Isaacs's work, Sasaki assigned one of his city projects to his students at Illinois.

TOWARD URBAN DESIGN

Even before his appointment in 1953 as the new dean of the GSD was made public, Sert began searching for candidates to fill the chairs of the architecture department and the newly established joint department of city and regional planning and landscape architecture. After almost two years of discussion, the university decided to merge the two into a single department. Before retiring, Gropius had advised university president James B. Conant on the need to unify the two departments. He argued that the training of planners had veered too far from physical design and that the territory recently claimed by landscape architecture—namely site planning, topography, and road design— belonged to physical planning. He concluded that the two fields had become so indistinguishable that their autonomy need no longer be maintained.[30] He also insisted that the director of the school be the chair of the department of architecture, "since architecture is historically the mother art of design from

which all the others have branched out later." Choosing the person to fill the joint chair was an especially sensitive matter; not only was the future teaching of each discipline compromised by financial issues, the many years of friction between the three departments had left rifts between the direction of the school, alumni, and current students. Sert's handling of this appointment would be one of the first tests of his leadership.

Sert solicited Gropius for potential candidates. In late February 1953, Gropius put forward Charles Eames, a "born artist" and progressive thinker, for the chair of architecture, and Isaacs for planning and landscape, characterizing him as "a very able experienced planner, a courageous social fighter, [with] an unusually strong working capacity [who] has shown to be most loyal to our cause."[31] Two years earlier Gropius had recommended Isaacs to Sert for membership in CIAM, citing his "realistic work" and "opinions" as being compatible with those of the organization.[32] He also mentioned Isaacs's 1951 guest studio at the school, which had "got the students going full blast." Having met Isaacs only briefly, Sert inquired about Isaacs's position on planning. The phrasing of his question is revealing of both the problem of planning's identity at Harvard and Sert's own aspirations for establishing urban design as a discipline: "How close do you think he is to our views in planning? Does he see planning as an architect, in three dimensions, or is he mainly interested in the economic, social and administrative problems. It is not that I do not recognize the interest of the latter, but as you know, with the limited funds that the school has at its disposal, we should, I think, insist on teaching physical planning only and getting outside help to cover all other related subjects."[33]

Assured by Isaacs's formation as an architect and his many years of collaboration with Gropius on the Michael Reese Hospital, Sert appointed Isaacs as the first chair of what would be named the department of city planning and landscape architecture.[34]

Isaacs's contributions to the GSD and the early development of the urban design program have never been taken into consideration. Although tensions between Isaacs and Sert would develop, Isaacs began his tenure as chair fully committed to Sert's deanship and to what he believed was Sert's project of more deeply integrating the three disciplines. One of his first steps toward building the new program was to appoint a junior faculty member to assist in the merger of the departments. Rather than thinking in disciplinary terms, Isaacs recognized the importance of bringing in a strong designer to contribute to Sert's overall program. He presented Sert with three candidates for the position—Sasaki, Kevin Lynch, and David Crane—stressing the interdisciplinary training and experience of Sasaki and Crane.[35] Isaacs stated his preference for Sasaki, citing his knowledge of the joint fields of landscape architecture and planning, his openness to collaboration, and the high esteem in which he was held. Moreover, through his involvement in the University of Illinois's planning program Sasaki had demonstrated his ability to cross traditional academic as well as professional boundaries. While Isaacs's motivations in asking Sasaki to return to Harvard are clear, Sasaki's interest in the position seems somewhat surprising in light of his recent efforts to set up a planning program at Illinois and his awareness of the problems facing the GSD. But in a letter to Isaacs

he did not hesitate to accept: "There is no question but that I would choose to work with you, Sert, and the others at Harvard."[36]

Before leaving Chicago for Cambridge, Isaacs regularly met with Sasaki to plan the program for the merged departments.[37] They agreed to move slowly, maintaining as many of the former courses as the budget permitted. While master's degrees in landscape architecture, city planning, and regional planning would continue to be granted, Isaacs nevertheless wanted to make a strong statement in the name of the new department, suggesting it be called the department of city and landscape planning. (Although this title was used in internal documents in the summer of 1953, it does not appear in the official school register.) A subtler indication of their goal to fully integrate planning and landscape architecture was Sasaki's appointment as assistant professor of regional planning.

Both educators saw the collaborative studios as the best means of bringing significant change to how planning and landscape architecture were understood by architects and by students in the other two disciplines. Isaacs's plans for the joint program were announced in September and October 1953. Cognizant of the previous marginalization of the landscape students at the school, Isaacs emphasized the place of land design within the larger field of planning. The training of landscape architects would be geared toward developing both a "high competence in broad-scale aspects of the design of outdoor space and the land underlying it," and a "concern for specific form that characterizes the profession."[38] A full-year course titled Environmental Design was also inaugurated. The course description gives insight into not only Isaacs's and Sasaki's goals but also the effort to further establish an inter-disciplinary approach:

> Architecture, city planning and landscape architec-ture will be studied as part of the *human habitat* in the totality of environmental design. This course will enable each student to gain personal experience and insight as to what our environment is and should be. It will lead him to understand the need to design for a better physical environment—one that will take man as its measure, both as an individual and as a member of the community.
>
> In giving the students the *basic human approach*

to those problems, this course will enable architects, landscape architects and city planners to understand the relationship of their mutual problems and will prepare them for future teamwork.[39]

The text then went on to emphasize the intercon-nectedness of the three professions and the need for students to develop "a sensitive approach to the wholeness of the designer's problem." The course description appeared the following year in the gen-eral introduction to the GSD, and Environmental Design became the heading for the joint first-year course that all students were required to take.[40] The two parts of the course were also structured to follow

Figure 9.5 Model for the urban renewal of the downtown core of Springfield, Massachusetts (project; 1955–56). Collaborative project led by Reginald Isaacs, Harvard GSD.

"programming and research" and "organization and design," an analytical approach that shares much with Sasaki's 1950 definition of a "critical thought process" for landscape architecture.

While Isaacs's discourse on collaboration fell within the purview of urban design in the early years of Sert's tenure, his conceptualization of the role of the landscape architect in that collaboration elicited the first negative response to his unified program. Speaking to the American Society of Landscape Architects in July 1954, Isaacs presented his ideas for an overhaul of training in landscape and its integration within the collaborative model of urban design:

> Urban design is receiving increasing attention by architects and city planners—yet to me it is the province of the landscape architect. What do I mean by urban design. . . . It is the physical expression of the culture of cities. . . . It is the design of its streets, squares, open spaces and civic core for pedestrians and traffic. It is my belief that landscape architecture students are the best equipped, from outlook and academic training, to become urban designers. I have found in my experience that landscape architects are the least afraid of space—the best able to handle the design of volume and space to create a satisfying environment. [41]

Expressed in somewhat watered-down CIAM language, Sert's ideals for urban design are evident in Isaacs's model. However, the view that the landscape architect was the professional best positioned to "bridge the gap between Planners and Architects" drew an irritated response from Gropius: "I am not quite in agreement with your plans. First, I suppose you remember my conception of landscape architec-

ture which, for me, is only a part of the larger field of architecture. I cannot at all see that the landscape architect is 'the best able to handle the design of volume and space.' At least I have never met one, whereas there are quite a few architects who have that capacity on account of a long and detailed training. This, so far, has never been given to landscape architects." [42]

Isaacs's answer carefully sidestepped the issue. Although trained as an architect and dedicated to Gropius's ideal of teamwork, Isaacs clearly had reservations about the bias favoring the architect. He consistently argued for equality between the three professions, seemingly unaware that this position conflicted with that of Gropius and of Sert. [43] The similarity between the ideas articulated in his address to the ASLA and those expressed by Sasaki in 1950 also indicates that Sasaki's "critical thinking" had a significant impact on Isaacs and thus on how planning and landscape architecture were taught at the school. It is equally clear that both Isaacs and Sasaki believed that the architect-centered model could be, if not toppled, considerably nuanced, and they worked toward this end in the collaborative studios.

In the fall of 1954 Isaacs initiated a seminar titled the Collaborative Process. Its goal was to establish equality between the three disciplines in the design process. Isaacs presented on planning, Sasaki on landscape architecture/land planning, and Chester Nagel and Norman Fletcher—associates in Gropius's firm TAC—on architecture. Isaacs also invited speakers to address the extension of the planning process into the community, the structure of community politics, and policy issues. As often as possible the collaborative studios were based on real projects to give the students a deep sense of involvement. Among them was an urban renewal project for the city of Springfield, Massachusetts (1955–56), which grew out of Isaacs's commission for a study on the expansion of Springfield College. In the spring term of 1955 students were assigned to study the Connecticut River valley and the Springfield metropolitan area. The following year they were asked to redesign a middle-aged residential area within the city. This phase of work was to be "developed within the concepts of urban renewal."[44] The project attracted the attention of the editor of *Architectural Forum*, Douglas Haskell, who featured the students' work in the July 1956 issue, a high point in the history of the collaborative studios (fig. 9.5).[45] In 1957 the students were assigned the replanning of the central area of Lowell, Massachusetts, and in 1960 the redevelopment of Boston's Parker Hill–Fenway area, a project that Isaacs, Sasaki, and Nagel had begun studying two years earlier.[46] Led by Sert, Huson Jackson, Isaacs, Norman T. Newton, and Sasaki, with three guests—the planner Karl L. Falk and the architects Mario Romañach and Jerzy Soltan—the students were divided into two groups to prepare a "utopian" project for 1960 and a "realism" project based on expectations of the area's further deterioration by the year 1970. While clearly defined roles were specified for the architecture and planning students, no special instructions were given to the landscape architects, who were expected to work all the more closely with the architects and planners to ensure integration or synthesis of all contributions. Their primary contribution lies in the preliminary research component, which required a survey and visual inventory, followed by an analysis of the functional requirements and the "visual struc-

ture of the area." This last reference reflects Sasaki's interest in Gyorgy Kepes and Kevin Lynch's work on the "Perceptual Form of the City" at MIT.[47]

The formal union of planning and landscape architecture at the GSD was short-lived. In 1955 the programs were reestablished as autonomous departments, with Isaacs as chair of city and regional planning and Walter Chambers as chair of landscape architecture.[48] With the return to the previous order, Sasaki moved back under the umbrella of landscape architecture. Although rooted in a legal technicality that stipulated that landscape architecture remain autonomous in order to receive funding from an endowment, the failure to fully integrate the programs was symbolic of the difficulties Sert faced. While Sert may have initially believed that urban design could evolve out of a synthesis of the three disciplines, his efforts to establish urban design as a discipline at the GSD, which began as early as 1954 and culminated six years later in the institution of a new master's degree, suggest that he understood urban design as going far beyond collaboration or teamwork, at least as they were defined by Isaacs.[49]

Although Sasaki's participation in Sert's project is not as easily tracked as that of Isaacs, he was deeply committed to the effort to make urban design a field of study at the GSD. As Eric Mumford has noted, Sasaki collaborated with Sert and Jean-Paul Carlhian on the first GSD Urban Design Seminar in spring 1955.[50] Rather than representing the landscape architect's viewpoint, Sasaki likely contributed in the capacity of a land planner, emphasizing the analysis of geography and climate, as well as the relationship between buildings, open areas, and roads. Recognized by Sert as being sufficiently "urbanminded," he participated in the panel discussion

"Forces That Are Shaping Our Cities Today,"
chaired by Isaacs in the 1956 Urban Design Conference. The following year he gave a presentation on
Japanese architecture in The Human Scale, the first
of Sigfried Giedion's graduate seminars in the urban
design program.[51] Like Isaacs, Sasaki was critical of
the inherent bias toward architecture within urban
design. In 1955 he published a short article titled
"Urban Renewal and Landscape Architecture."
It reflected Sasaki's activities with ACTION and his
work with Isaacs in Chicago, which he discusses
in some detail. It was only in the conclusion of the
text that Sasaki put forward his vision of the city:

> To achieve a full measure of livability, a city should
> provide its occupants with a wide range of intensity
> of activities, with comparative ease and freedom to
> move from one level to another. The city is a complex
> of diversified parts composed of the expression, and
> dedicated to the satisfaction, of a variety of interests
> and needs; its physical form should articulate these
> divergences, yet be related so that the inhabitant can
> always sense the whole while he circulates and lives
> within its various parts. To this end, the landscape
> architect can contribute his skills and, together with
> others, may create a good environment, not only in
> terms of economic functioning, but as a visually satis-
> fying expression, which in some respect is the mea-
> sure of cultural achievement of a civilization.[52]

In his presentation in the Urban Design Conference,
Sasaki expressed further concerns about bringing
wholeness to the city.[53] Amplifying his earlier comments on how a city should grow, he identified
"design feeling" or "visual satisfaction" as the most
sensitive element in the overall urban environment
and charged designers with the responsibility of

Figure 9.6 Plan for the U.S. Embassy, Baghdad
(c. 1955). Sasaki, Novak & Associates, landscape
architects; Josep Lluís Sert, architect.

bringing cohesion. He came out in favor of policy and participatory planning rather than ambitious architectural plans: "Indeed, it would take a wise oracle or a powerful despot to determine what a 'city' should be for all its inhabitants. Only the combined will of the city's inhabitants should determine this. . . . A series of wise decisions in policies and in design may create a more meaningful environment than some enormous artifact of super modernism conceived by a draftsman hell-bent to become a 'designer' of the urban environment."[54]

Sasaki then drew up a list of what he saw as the three major faults in urban interventions: "eclecticism without meaning," "monumentality without meaning or lack of scale," and "lack of relationship with surroundings, or emphasis on the spectacular."[55] The emphasis on wholeness—all the parts submitting to a greater unity—would define his professional practice.

Although Sasaki and Isaacs continued to have

Figure 9.7 IBM's Thomas J. Watson Research Center, Yorktown, New York (1957–61). Sasaki, Walker & Associates, landscape architects; Eero Saarinen & Associates, architects. Photograph by Wayne Andrews.

common projects, their previous closeness seems to have declined as the urban design program increasingly took center stage at the school, eventually eclipsing Isaacs's efforts within the collaborative studios. Sasaki's appointment to the urban design faculty in the early 1960s may also have had an impact on their relationship, because Isaacs was not invited to take a formal role.[56] By this time, however, Sasaki had more pressing concerns. Named by Sert in 1958 as chair of the department of landscape architecture, Sasaki had to contend with the department's financial difficulties, faculty problems, and student shortages. To resolve these woes Sasaki encouraged associates in his practice to teach part time in the landscape program. While in retrospect this may appear a closed system, the contributions of his office members to the teaching program proved invaluable to the development of the program. A symbiotic relationship between theory and practice evolved, bringing a higher degree of reality to the classroom and providing the practitioners with a laboratory to develop new ideas that would find their way into built form.

A LAND-BASED PRACTICE

Hideo Sasaki largely established his firm in the mid-1950s through collaborations with architects associated with the GSD. Sert invited Sasaki to design the landscapes for the U.S. Embassy, Baghdad (1955–60), and the presidential palace of Cuba, Havana (project; 1957). For the embassy Sasaki worked from Sert's on-site notes and sketches to produce a richly textured design for a series of canals, pools, walkways, terraces, courts, and gardens (fig. 9.6).[57] Harvard was also the source for several important

commissions: in addition to the landscapes for Sert's Peabody Terrace (1962–64) and Holyoke Center (1960–66), Sasaki's firm designed the grounds of Shepley, Bulfinch, Richardson & Abbott's Quincy House (1957–59) and Leverett House (1958–60). While the design for Quincy House stands out as the first modern landscape in the Boston area, it was followed by an even bolder design for Leverett House in which a patterned grid of slate and marble slabs challenges rather than softens the strong geometrical expression of the façades of the two towers. Sasaki was also a frequent collaborator on Eero Saarinen's projects, among them his contribution of a Japanese garden at IBM's Thomas J. Watson Research Center, Yorktown, New York (1957–61). Here grassy mounds punctuated an expanse of white stones to contrast with the masonry and glass-clad building (fig. 9.7).

Despite the critical praise these and other projects received, in Sasaki's eyes their potential was limited by the conventional nature of the professional collaboration: the landscape architect worked in a subordinate role to the architect to create landscape elements that would complement or bring contrast to an architectural design. More often than not the architect already had an idea in mind that he wanted the landscape architect to refine. For Sasaki this situation brought landscape architecture dangerously close to being "superficial embellishment." As his efforts in education revealed, what Sasaki was looking for was a deeper engagement of all the professionals in the overall siting, planning, construction, and finishing of a project.

The first significant opportunity to realize this model of design came through campus planning. By

1962, nearly all of the two thousand existing institutions in the United States had plans for expansion, and more than two hundred new campuses were being planned or were under construction.[58] It was within this context that modern architecture flourished in the United States, as exemplified by such buildings and complexes as Saarinen's Ezra Stiles and Morse Colleges at Yale University and Law School at the University of Chicago, and Rudolph's Jewett Arts Center, Wellesley. The master plans into which these and other achievements were inserted and integrated are much less known. Despite Sasaki's intense involvement in a context that is recognized as one of the most important areas of postwar design in the United States, the firm's contributions to campus design have received little attention.[59]

Sasaki was introduced to campus planning early in his career. Although undocumented, his work for Perkins & Will likely involved projects for educational institutions, the staple of the firm's practice. In 1954 he collaborated on Isaacs's commission for a ten-year campus plan for Springfield College (project; 1954–59).[60] Soon after accepting the project, Isaacs recommended TAC as architects and Sasaki as site planner and landscape architect. Their development proposal for the campus rationalized the distribution of buildings and services and eliminated car traffic from the central campus. Although the concept of pedestrian urban "cores" came from CIAM via Sert, Sasaki's application of this idea to American campus planning was a significant innovation.

The Springfield project encouraged Isaacs to formalize the collaboration between himself, Sasaki, and TAC. Invited by the city of Tallahassee, Florida, to consult on their urban renewal plans, Isaacs rec-ommended TAC for the commission of a civic center (project; 1956). On Isaacs's advice, Gropius in turn engaged Sasaki for the landscape component. A similar scenario was played out in the proposed civic center for Columbus, Ohio (1956).[61]

While Isaacs was frustrated by the failure to realize these projects, the maintenance of disciplinary distinctions and boundaries in their conception was unlikely to have been entirely satisfying for Sasaki. A very different working relationship was necessary to further his goals. In 1956, Pietro Belluschi, dean of MIT's School of Architecture, asked Sasaki to participate in plans for the expansion of the MIT campus. The two men had met soon after Sasaki's return to Harvard in 1953. Invited to review the landscape students' work and to attend a national conference organized by the landscape and planning department, Belluschi was impressed by Sasaki's open approach to large-scale problems. He involved Sasaki in his own projects, among them Temple Adath Israel, Merion, Pennsylvania (1956–59), and Bennington College Library, Bennington, Vermont (Belluschi and Carl Koch; 1957–59), and had a desk in Sasaki's Watertown office. In Belluschi's collaborative model the landscape architect/planner played a central role in the definition of the development site and continued to be involved in the interpretation of the architectural design. A close relationship, one that Sasaki recognized as a "true" collaboration, developed between them. Their intellectual partnership was such that Belluschi has also been credited with putting into words the ideals he shared with Sasaki, who after the mid-1950s was less actively publishing his views.[62] The collaboration put Sasaki's practice in a position to go beyond the confines of projects

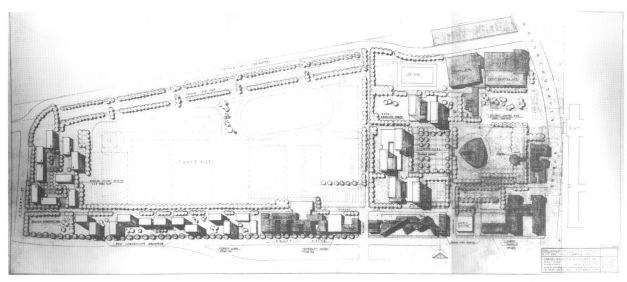

Figure 9.8 Plan study for the expansion of West Campus, MIT (October 9, 1959, rev. 1959). Sasaki, Walker & Associates, site planners and landscape architects.

orchestrated by architects.

As he would often do in his consulting work, in his role as chairman of MIT's Long Range Planning Committee, and as design advisor to the vice president of operations, Philip A. Stoddard, Belluschi proposed commissioning top architects, whose contributions he would personally coordinate.[63] He then suggested that Sasaki be invited to participate on the committee in two capacities: as a design consultant on the campus plan, and as a design reviewer. No other opportunity to date had so much potential for fulfilling Sasaki's ideals for the integration of architecture and landscape design and planning. Starting with MIT, campus planning became the center of Sasaki's practice.[64] Through this work the firm developed many of the planning typologies that have come to define the postwar educational campus.

Sasaki encountered the full range of problems facing educational institutions in the postwar period.

Housing shortages and the need for facilities to improve campus life topped the list of priorities, and significant growth in the fields of life and hard sciences required expanded laboratories, as well as classroom space. MIT wanted a plan that would both humanize the campus, long perceived as being industrial and severe in character, and harmonize new additions and buildings with the existing architecture. From 1956 until 1960, when the MIT Planning Office, under the direction of Robert Simha, took control of the master plan, Sasaki was largely responsible for preparing base studies for the expansion of the West Campus and for the redevelopment of the East Campus (as it was then configured) and northern areas of the campus.[65] And even after the Planning Office assumed the principal work Sasaki remained a member of the design review panel, and his firm carried out landscape projects on the campus well into the 1980s.[66]

Figure 9.9 Model for development of Eastman Court (1959). Sasaki, Walker & Associates, site planners and landscape architects.

Sasaki's plans of the late 1950s demonstrate that the firm played a lead role in proposing building types and groupings and in ensuring the assimilation of the work of other designers.

The first phase of Sasaki's work on the master plan focused on the West Campus. As early as 1957 Sasaki was preparing studies for the development of the open area between Eero Saarinen's Kresge Auditorium and Chapel and the playing field, and for the redevelopment of land along Memorial Drive and Audrey Street.[67] An October 9, 1959, revision of the plan addressed the acute lack of student housing (fig. 9.8). Most of Sasaki's projections were realized: a women's dormitory was erected across from the hospital on Danforth Street (Stanley McCormick Hall by Anderson, Beckwith & Haible with Sasaki, Walker & Associates; 1962–63), fraternity housing was added within existing dormitory blocks (Conner Hall, a dining hall by Eduardo Catalano, was inserted in its place; 1960), further undergraduate housing was planned as a series of eleven-story

blocks (realized a decade later in a much truncated form as Frank S. MacGregor House, a mixed complex of tower and low-rise blocks by Belluschi with TAC; 1968–70), and married student housing was proposed as a cluster of four- and eight-story slabs (realized as Westgate Married Student Housing by Stubbins; 1959–62).[68]

Sasaki also proposed the addition of a housing complex of fourteen-story tower slabs mixed with two-story structures in the open area between the auditorium and playing field, as shown in the October 1959 drawing. Another drawing, dated June 16, 1959, shows an alternative scheme for a series of six fifteen-story tower slabs laid out along the eastern edge of the playing field as a screening device for the inner campus. In this proposal the married student housing is reduced to two slab buildings at the extreme western edge of the campus, the student center is conceived as two flanking structures to the north and south of the auditorium and chapel, and four large parking areas are placed along Vassar Street. Another configuration presented in the 1960 campus model shows that the towers in the central area were also intended to balance the academic ones projected for the north and east campus (during this episode in the development of the campus, only I. M. Pei's Earth Science tower was realized) and the slightly lower residential towers marking the end of the western extreme of the campus. Each scheme focused on the need to increase the density of the West Campus, to clearly demarcate the boundaries of the playing field, and to visually and physically reinforce the auditorium's position as a focal point. As the situation stood then and remains to a lesser degree today, Saarinen's auditorium and chapel float within an open field, unanchored to the other buildings.

While Sasaki's projections for Kresge Plaza were not realized, he was largely responsible for the form of Stubbins's married students' housing complex on the extreme western edge of the campus. Sasaki was also directly involved in planning the development of the eastern part of the campus in an area adjacent to the Main Campus. Known as Eastman Court, the area was bounded by Eastman Labs to the west, the Dorrance Building to the north, the Alumni Houses to the east, and Hayden Library to the south. It was within this large opening in the fabric of Welles Bosworth's 1916 plan that MIT realized its first high-rise academic building, the Cecil and Ida Green Building for Earth and Planetary Sciences designed by I. M. Pei between 1959 and 1964.[69] Another two buildings by Pei—the Camille Edouard Dreyfus Chemistry Building (1967–70) to the west and the Ralph Landau Building for Chemical Engineering (1973–76) to the northeast—along with Beckwith, Haible & Anderson's Uncas A. and Helen F. Whitaker Building (1963–65) to the northwest, all low-rise slabs, were woven into Bosworth's sophisticated connection system, with bridges tying the new buildings to the existing framework.[70]

These forms grew out of studies for the long-range development potential for the Eastman Court area carried out by Sasaki's office in 1957. The most developed concept appears in a model for the overall area in which three low slab structures—shown in black—are arranged around a slightly off-center pinwheel of interconnected buildings (fig. 9.9). Although in the end the scheme was not adopted in favor of introducing a high-rise building, Sasaki's

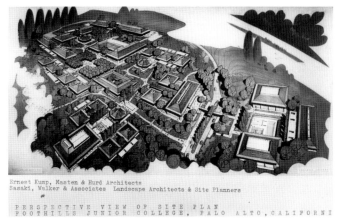

Figure 9.10 Bird's-eye perspective for Foothill College, Los Altos, California (c. 1959). Sasaki, Walker & Associates, landscape architects; Ernest J. Kump, architect.

plan reflects a close consideration of the existing relationships between buildings, proposing a continuation of the MIT tradition with the new buildings linking into the Eastman Labs, Killian Hall, and the Dorrance Building. The plan also created a series of courtyards, which again sensitively replicated patterns of the campus fabric. Later additions show that Sasaki's ideas for extending the wing of the Dorrance Building to the east and inserting a new wing into the large courtyard were largely followed.[71] This scheme reveals the attention paid to the existing arrangement—all designed to avoid what Sasaki had referred to in the 1956 Urban Design Conference as the three main faults of contemporary work.

On the opposite end of the spectrum from the partnership with Belluschi was Sasaki's work with the architect Ernest J. Kump on the plan and landscape for Foothill College, a new institution located in the Los Altos Hills on the San Francisco Peninsula (1957–62).[72] The project went far toward establishing the firm's credentials for handling large-scale land design problems. The main challenge at Foothill College was the creation of a strong identity for a nonresidential commuter campus, a new building typology for higher education. One of the chief contributions of the project to later developments was the definition of the campus as a strictly pedestrian zone, an idea Sasaki had first tried out in the plan for Springfield College. The result was an immediately copied idiom for campus design: the academic village.

By 1959, when Sasaki was asked to work on the landscape, Kump had already defined the groupings of low buildings in a manner consistent with that of his previous cluster schools. However, the tight compression of the low-rise buildings diminished the flow of interior and exterior spaces. Working with Peter Walker, Sasaki took the groupings and spread them over the two hills that made up the entire site, connecting the academic buildings and the physical education complex by a bridge (fig. 9.10). The land was graded a staggering thirty feet down—a previously unheard of amount—with flatter areas sculpted into mounds and curving paths. The pictorial impression of the campus was that of an acropolis. Despite the considerable movement of land, the natural outlines of the hill and outcroppings of rock were maintained and most of the trees preserved, revealing Sasaki's concern for environmental conservation. Although the car was central to the overall concept for the campus, it was relegated to the valley areas, which were planted with pear trees recalling previous land use. In terms of the formal landscape design, Sasaki and Walker worked closely with the architectural character of deep redwood shingled roofs defined by Kump. The court-yards connecting the building clusters became outdoor classrooms through planted terraces and sunken brick courts.

Even as the planning of Foothill College deepened the firm's expertise in site design and planning, it is clear that the collaborative dimension of the project left much to be desired from Sasaki's point of view. Although the firm was credited as an associate, reviewers consistently failed to recognize the critical role played by the siting and landscape, giving Kump the highest praise as the designer of the entire project. Once again landscape architects were seen as merely complementing the architectural scheme rather than providing the specialized expertise that harmonized the architecture with the site. Sasaki was more interested in further developing the model established with Belluschi at MIT rather than what remained limited collaborations with star architects.

Sasaki's reputation nevertheless grew as a result of the firm's associations with Sert, Saarinen, Pei, Stubbins, SOM, and Hellmuth Obata & Kassabaum, and through its work at MIT. A lengthy article on the firm accompanied by a substantial portfolio of its work appeared in *Progressive Architecture* in 1960.[73] The firm's profile also rose as a result of the writings of Richard Dober, a planner who joined the firm in 1956 and worked closely on the MIT projects. He published a series of articles on campus design (1960–61), which led to a book that was based on the expertise the firm had gained (1963).[74]

ACHIEVING SYNTHESIS

Sasaki continued to build on the model he had developed with Belluschi at MIT for subsequent university projects. He further developed his vision for growth, first establishing a strong site plan and then encouraging overseers to engage a design consultant to select architects and review their proposals to ensure the integration of new buildings into the existing campus. The third component was a landscape program that would fill in the areas not being developed for buildings. These ideas were brought together in Sasaki's master plans for the University of Colorado at Boulder, commissioned in July 1960, and the University of Massachusetts at Amherst, begun in 1961. By involving several architects, Sasaki designed campuses that have a varied yet integrated architectural expression, an approach that stands in striking contrast with the celebrated campuses designed by single architects and firms, among them Edward Durrell Stone's State University of New York, Albany (1962–69), and Rudolph's University of Massachusetts at Dartmouth (with Desmond & Lord; 1965–72).

As the firm grew in the 1960s, architecture and civil engineering were added to its expertise, and Sasaki began to take on some of the architectural work offered by the university commissions. Sasaki was extremely sympathetic to Belluschi's contextual approach to modern architecture, which, as the architect's biographer Meredith Clausen astutely points out, reflected a discomfort with originality that often led Belluschi "to use existing forms, sometimes those of his contemporaries, sometimes those of the past, never simply copying but always refining and adapting them to changed circumstances of time and place."[75] As early as 1950, Sasaki had similarly articulated a concern for place, even suggesting that inspiration could come from the vernacular. It was from this very context-aware position that Sasaki's

firm approached its first architectural projects. In 1960 the firm hired Kenneth DeMay, a Harvard graduate, as its first architect.[76] Initially working closely with Belluschi, DeMay was responsible for several well-received buildings that reflected an analysis of both the site and existing forms, as seen in the Student Residences at the University of Rhode Island, Kingston (1962–64), and the Engineering Sciences Center at the University of Colorado at Boulder (1962–65).[77] For the latter project, DeMay worked with Belluschi and the local firm of Architectural Associates Colorado to produce a design for a vast building complex that reflected both the forms and materials of the Tuscan style set in 1919 by the university's original architects, Day & Klauder, and the rugged natural backdrop of the Rocky Mountains (fig. 9.11).[78]

CONCLUSION

By the mid-1960s, little more than a decade after he first returned to Cambridge to teach and practice, Sasaki had brought landscape architecture into the discourse of postwar architecture and had so profoundly changed its profile within that discourse that it was possible to reconsider what the discipline constituted. Along the way, he established a multidisciplinary model for practice, which stood as an alternative to that of the architect-centered collaboration exemplified by Walter Gropius and TAC. Sasaki also resisted Sert's model; although Sert had publicly differed with Gropius's view of architecture as the mother of the arts, instead according that place to the city and thus to urban design, he too could only go so far in thinking past professional specialization. For Sert, the ideal conductor to lead

Figure 9.11 Engineering Sciences Center, University of Colorado at Boulder (1962-65). Sasaki, Dawson, DeMay Associates, with Pietro Belluschi and the Architectural Associates Colorado, architects.

the metaphorical orchestra of urban design was an architect, if one schooled in planning as well as architectural design.[79]

Sasaki's version of synthesis was perhaps simultaneously a natural outgrowth and an unexpected outcome of previous discourses on collaboration and the ongoing one on urban design at the GSD in the 1950s and 1960s. Deeply impressed by the ideals if not the practice of Gropius's teamwork, Sasaki reinvigorated the collaborative model, thinking beyond disciplinary distinctions to arrive at a deeper understanding of the complex problems of urban design. Looking back on his practice in later years, Sasaki said, "I wanted to bring the best and it did not matter where the best came from or what profes-

sion."[80] Through this open approach he defined a new paradigm for practice in which the landscape architect or land planner, no longer limited by a field specialization, could mediate between the concerns of the site and the decision-making process for architectural interventions. In many respects Sasaki's best work came out of contexts that required him to intervene within a strong existing framework. It was on the university campus, the most productive area of his practice during this period, that Sasaki came closest to achieving a "complete environment," as Sert termed it. Thinking and working from the ground up, Sasaki offered a vision of urban design that at once challenged and fulfilled Sert's 1956 call for the need to arrive at an "era of synthesis."

NOTES

I wish to thank Eric Mumford, who encouraged me to look into Hideo Sasaki's contributions to Harvard's urban design program as part of a graduate seminar he led as a visiting professor in the department of the history of art and architecture at Harvard University in spring 2004. I also thank him and Hashim Sarkis for offering the opportunity to further develop my paper for publication, and for their comments on drafts of the text. At Sasaki Associates I thank Tracy Finlayson and Terri Grey-Pearce, as well as Peter Hedlund, Richard F. Galehouse, and Perry Chapman. I would also like the thank former Deans Peter Rowe and Alan Altshuler of the Harvard Design School for access to the records of the landscape department; the MIT Institution Archives for permission to quote from letters and documents related to planning at MIT; Waverly Lowell of the Environmental Design Archives at the University of California, Berkeley; Neyran Turan for her help with photographs; and especially Mary Daniels, Special Collections at Frances Loeb Library, Harvard University GSD, for her many talents. As ever, Réjean Legault has been an enlightened reader of my work, offering insightful criticism along the way. The research for this essay was supported by a grant from the Social Sciences and Humanities Research Council of Canada.

1. Josep Lluís Sert, "Urban Design," *Progressive Architecture* 37, no. 8 (August 1956): 97.

2. In 1953, Hideo Sasaki founded his firm, Hideo Sasaki and Associates, in Cambridge and Watertown, Massachusetts. In 1955 he went into partnership with Paul Novak, the firm becoming known as Sasaki, Novak & Associates. In 1958, following Novak's departure for Chicago, Peter Walker became a principal, and the firm was renamed Sasaki, Walker & Associates. A second office with this name was opened by Walker in San Francisco (1959–60), briefly operating as Sasaki, Walker, Lackey (1963–65). From 1960 to 1962 there was a Toronto-based office, Sasaki, Strong & Associates. In 1964 the Watertown office changed its name to Sasaki, Dawson, DeMay Associates. In 1973, the San Francisco office severed ties with the Watertown office and became Sasaki, Walker, Roberts (dismantled in 1975). In 1975 the Watertown office changed its name to Sasaki Associates. For the history of the firm, see Melanie Simo, *The Offices of Hideo Sasaki: A Corporate History* (Berkeley: Spacemaker, 2001). In the present context, the firm will be referred to as Sasaki Associates.

3. "Interview with Richard F. Galehouse" (November 1988), 13. An excerpt from the interview was published in German (Galehouse, "Collaborative Design: Die amerikanische Tradition," *DBZ* 5 [1990]: 694–700). I am grateful to Mr. Galehouse for allowing me to quote from the unpublished portion of his interview.

4. On the evolution of the collaborative model at Harvard, see Anthony Alofsin, *The Struggle for Modernism: Architecture, Landscape Architecture, and City Planning at Harvard* (New York: W. W. Norton, 2002).

5. Both authors have written extensively on Sasaki and modern landscape architecture from their positions as historians and practitioners. See esp. Simo's *Offices of Hideo Sasaki* and *Sasaki Associates: Integrated Environments* (Washington, D.C.: Spacemaker, 1997); relevant chapters in Simo's and Peter Walker's *Invisible Gardens: The Search for Modernism in the American Landscape* (Cambridge, Mass.: MIT Press, 1994); and Walker's essay "The Practice of Landscape Architecture in the Postwar United States," in Marc Treib, ed., *Modern Landscape Architecture: A Critical Review* (Cambridge, Mass.: MIT Press, 1993), 250–259. Simo has also written on Sasaki as an educator: *The Coalescing of Different Forces and Ideas: A History of Landscape Architecture at Harvard, 1900–1999* (Cambridge, Mass.: Harvard University Graduate School of Design, 2000).

6. On Sasaki's corporate work, see Louise A. Mozingo's "The Corporate Estate in the USA, 1954–64: 'Thoroughly modern in concept, but . . . down to earth and rugged,'" *Studies in the History of Gardens & Designs Landscapes* 20, no. 1 (Spring 2000): 25–56; and Jeffrey Inaba's presentation in the GSD conference, "The Sasaki Years" (November 6, 1999), tape 2, Visual Resources, Frances Loeb Library, Harvard University Graduate

School of Design.

7. "Thoughts on Education in Landscape Architecture," *Landscape Architecture* 40, no. 4 (July 1950): 158–160.

8. Steinitz's comments were made in the context of the conference, "The Sasaki Years," and in a memorial service held at Sasaki Associates, Watertown, Mass., n.d. (videocassettes, Sasaki Associates).

9. A program in landscape design, known as the Division of Landscape Gardening and Floriculture, had been offered since 1913 by the department of agriculture. The name changed to the Division of Landscape Design in the 1940s. City planning was also offered by the department of agriculture until the creation of the College of Environmental Design in 1959. On the programs, see Michael Laurie, *Seventy-Five Years of Landscape Architecture at Berkeley, An Informal History* (Berkeley: Department of Landscape Architecture, 1992); and Verne A. Stadtman et al., comp. and ed., *The Centennial Record of the University of California* (Berkeley: University of California Printing Department, 1967), 89.

10. Galehouse interview, 1.

11. Sasaki's brief study of psychology, which may be significant for his perspective, is mentioned in William Mann's 1986 interview with Sasaki: "Creative Collaboration [excerpt from an interview by William A. Mann]," *Landscape Architecture* 91, no. 3 (March 2001): 70.

12. White was important to the later emergence of ecological design. On Sasaki's relationship with White, see Simo and Walker, *Invisible Gardens,* esp. 198–205.

13. In his interview with Mann, Sasaki mentioned the importance of the articles Eckbo, Kiley, Rose, and Tunnard were then publishing in *Pencil Points.*

14. Tunnard, *The Garden in the Modern Landscape* (London: Architectural Press, 1938). On Tunnard, see Lance M. Neckar, "Strident Modernism/Ambivalent Reconsiderations: Christopher Tunnard's *Garden in the Modern Landscape*," *Journal of Garden History* 10, no. 4 (1990): 237–246; and "Christopher Tunnard: The Garden in the Modern Landscape," in *Modern Landscape Architecture: A Critical Review,* 144–159.

15. On Pond at the GSD, see Simo, *Coalescing of Different Forces and Ideas;* and Alofsin, *Struggle for Modernism.* For a concise overview of Pond's training and career, see Mary Daniels's entry in Philip Pregill and Nancy Volkman, eds., *Landscapes in History: Design and Planning in the Eastern and Western Traditions,* 2nd ed. (New York: John Wiley and Sons, 1999), 300–302.

16. See the record of one of these projects jointly led by Gropius, Norman T. Newton, Stubbins, Tunnard, and Wagner, "Housing Problem: Problem 5 for the 2c classes and the 2d class [GSD]," 1941. Special Collections, Frances Loeb Library, Harvard University Graduate School of Design

(hereafter Special Collections). Newton represented landscape architecture.

17. These changes are described in an article by Norman T. Newton, "Professional Training of Landscape Architecture at Harvard," *Landscape Architecture* 39, no. 4 (July 1949): 181–183.

18. Garrett Eckbo recalled the reaction of the landscape faculty upon the news that Gropius was coming to Harvard: "They told us carefully that . . . Trees are not made in factories. Therefore you don't have to worry about modern design" ("Landscape Architecture: The Profession in California, 1935–1940, and TELESIS," an oral history conducted in 1991 by Suzanne B. Riess, Regional Oral History Office, Bancroft Library, University of California, Berkeley, 1993, 15).

19. Sasaki's student project was included in Lester Collins and Thomas Gillespie, eds., *Landscape Architecture* (Cambridge, Mass.: President and Fellows of Harvard College, 1951), 1. A built project by Sasaki—a communal shelter for a housing subdivision, Stoddard Acres in Monticello, Illinois—also appears in the catalogue (7).

20. George A. Sanderson, "America's No. 1 Defense Community: Oak Ridge, Tennessee," *Progressive Architecture* 32, no. 6 (June 1951): 63–84. Sasaki worked with Kraft again; in an interview he mentions master plans for Bloomfield Hills, Michigan (Galehouse interview, 4).

21. The project was featured in *Progressive Architecture* 33, no. 10

(October 1952): 79–84.

22. On Sasaki's teaching at the University of Illinois see his interview with Mann (74).

23. Sasaki used the exchange program to identify the most promising students who he then attempted to recruit, a technique that he would aggressively employ at Harvard.

24. The appearance of the diagram in landscape architecture underscores the modernization process as discussed by Hyungmin Pai in his *The Portfolio and the Diagram: Architecture, Discourse, and Modernity in America* (Cambridge, Mass.: MIT Press, 2002).

25. Sasaki, "Thoughts on Education in Landscape Architecture," 158.

26. Curricular Records, Department of Landscape Architecture Records, box 1, Harvard University Archives (UAV 322.148).

27. Sasaki discusses his involvement with ACTION in his interview with Galehouse (4–5). Through Isaacs, Sasaki became involved with the Michael Reese Hospital in 1955. Sasaki presented his analysis of the hospital project at the fifth Urban Design Conference, *The Institution as a Generator of Urban Form* (April 1961), recorded in a typed pamphlet.

28. Isaacs, "The Neighborhood Theory: An Analysis of Its Adequacy," *Journal of the American Institute of Planners* 14, no. 2 (Spring 1948): 15–23. An indefatigable proponent of urban renewal, Isaacs lectured on the subject throughout the 1940s in church basements, chambers of commerce, and men's

and women's clubs in Chicago, Milwaukee, Syracuse, New York, and Trenton, New Jersey.

29. The program for the community appraisal study is held in the department of landscape architecture's curricular records.

30. Letter, Gropius to Conant, October 22, 1951, copy, "Research—Harvard University, 1951—Memos, Reports, Correspondence," box 8, Reginald R. Isaacs Papers, Archives of American Art, Smithsonian Institution (hereafter Isaacs Papers). The letter also shows that Gropius was well aware of the potential legal problems of unifying the two programs.

31. Letter, Gropius to Sert, February 23, 1953, copy, "Research—Sert—Correspondence, 1950–51," box 11, Isaacs Papers. Sert chose to take on the position of chair of the architecture department himself.

32. Gropius also put forward Louis Wirth and Catherine Bauer (letter, Gropius to Sert, March 26, 1951, copy, "Research Material—Sert—Correspondence 1950–51," box 11, Isaacs Papers.

33. Letter, Sert to Gropius, March 2, 1953. Gropius responded four days later, affirming Isaacs's commitment to physical planning and adding, "I believe he would be a strong and very good man and a real support to you" ("Research—Sert—Correspondence, 1950–51," box 11, Isaacs Papers). Alofsin chronicles the changes in how planning was conceived under the chairmanship of John Merriman Gaus,

who emphasized the role of policy and public administration, and Perkins, who balanced the program between physical planning and studies in government, geography, economics, business, and sociology (*Struggle for Modernism,* 174, 200–202).

34. In March 1953 Sert appointed Isaacs as Charles Dyer Norton Professor of Regional Planning and Chairman of the combined department of planning and landscape architecture (later city planning and landscape architecture), an untenured position. This situation contributed to later tensions between Isaacs and Sert.

35. Isaacs first approached his friend and colleague Martin Meyerson to join him at Harvard. Meyerson declined, citing prior commitments to the University of Pennsylvania, and encouraged Isaacs to instead think in terms of a "design-oriented second person" (letter, Meyerson to Isaacs, April 11, 1953, "Research—Harvard University, Jan.–April 1953—Correspondence," box 8, Isaacs Papers). Isaacs's list of candidates also includes Max Locke, John Cordwell, James Webb, Robert Burlingham, David Longmais, Cecil Elliot, Jay Gould, and Daniel Stanton; another six that were unavailable: Meyerson, Sidney Williams, Hans Blumenfeld, Jaqueline Tyrwhitt, Simon Eisner, Israel Stollman; and six that Isaacs was unable to recommend: David Geer, Arthur McVoy, Willo von Moltke, George Raymond, James Drought, and Pearson Stewart (Isaacs to Sert, May 7, 1953, typescript, file

"Research—Harvard University, May 1953—Correspondence," box 8, Isaacs Papers).

36. Isaacs offered the position to Sasaki on May 6, 1953 (letter, Sasaki to Isaacs, May 6, 1953, "Research—Harvard University, May 1953—Correspondence," box 8, Isaacs Papers).

37. In a letter to Sert, Isaacs refers to semiweekly conferences with Sasaki on "Harvard problems" (August 5, 1953, "Research—Harvard University, 1954–55—Correspondence," box 8, Isaacs Papers).

38. Untitled announcement, GSD, September 1953, Special Collections.

39. "Description of Courses," Curriculum in Landscape Architecture, September 1953, n.p. [1], and "Description of Courses," Curriculum in City and Regional Planning, October 1953, n.p. [1]; both Special Collections.

40. *Official Register of Harvard University* 51, no. 11 (May 19, 1954): 8–9, 11, 13, 16.

41. "To Train Landscape Architects in Urban Design," *American City* 69 (September 1954): 123. Isaacs's comments were also reported in *Planning and Civic Comment* 20, no. 4 (December 1954): 33–34.

42. Letters between Isaacs and Gropius, May 17, 1954, and July 21, 1954, "Correspondence—Gropius—1954," box 2, Isaacs Papers.

43. In later years Isaacs attempted to summarize his contributions to the school. In these incomplete and undated texts he differentiates between "teamwork," the term Gropius used, and "collaboration," which Isaacs claimed Gropius achieved in the collaborative studios of the late 1930s and 1940s. He avoids discussing Sert's contributions ("The Collaborative Process," n.d., typescript, "Teaching Files—Methods of Planning—Lecture Notes," box 4, Isaacs Papers).

44. Curricular Records, Department of Landscape Architecture, Harvard University Archives.

45. "How to Start City Renewal," *Architectural Forum* 105, no. 1 (July 1956): 144–146.

46. Arch, 2–4ab, "Collaborative 1960: Parker Hill Redevelopment Area," February 23, 1960, Special Collections. In 1958 Isaacs, Sasaki, and Nagel produced a preliminary report on the sector, and seven years later the Boston Redevelopment Authority brought out a general neighborhood renewal plan (copies of both held in Frances Loeb Library).

47. Besides other connections, Sasaki and Lynch both worked on the Government Center project.

48. It was 1955 rather than 1956 (as reported in Alofsin's history of the school) that the two departments were reestablished (Course Register, Harvard Graduate School of Design, July 1955).

49. In his concluding remarks as chair of the panel discussion, "Forces That Are Shaping Our Cities Today," in the first Urban Design Conference, Isaacs arrived at the conclusion: "Urban Design cannot be the work of a single professional but the work of collaboration" (April 10, 1956, "Writings/Lectures," box 3, Isaacs Papers). On the establishment of the Urban Design program at Harvard, see Alofsin, 251–260; Eric Mumford, "The Emergence of Urban Design in the Breakup of CIAM," in *Harvard Design Magazine* no. 24 (Spring/Summer 2006): 10–20; and Mumford's essay, this volume. Isaacs was also involved in early efforts to establish an Urban Design Studio and Seminar; a memo to Sert in early 1956 outlines various options, including a possible master's degree in urban design (Isaacs to Sert, February 2, 1956, "Research—Harvard University, 1956, 1959—Correspondence, Meeting Minutes," box 8, Isaacs Papers).

50. Mumford, "Emergence of Urban Design," 16.

51. Sasaki's contributions are recorded in "The Human Scale: Urban Design Seminar" (Cambridge, Mass.: School [of Design, Harvard, University], Spring 1957), copy at Frances Loeb Library.

52. Sasaki, "Urban Renewal and Landscape Architecture," *Landscape Architecture* 45, no. 2 (January 1955): 101.

53. The fullest record of Sasaki's presentation in the Urban Design Conference is his text "The City and the Landscape Architect," published in the Berkeley student journal *Space* (1956), 19–21.

54. Sasaki, "City and the Landscape Architect," 19.

55. Sasaki, "Urban Design," 101.

56. Richard Marshall has written about Sasaki's efforts to have the urban

design program placed under the umbrella of the department of landscape architecture in Chapter 7, this volume.

57. "Sert—Baghdad—Addenda—Notes and Sketches," between July 7 and 13, 1955, Josep Lluís Sert Collection, Frances Loeb Library, Harvard University Graduate School of Design Sert Archive. In addition to not being able to visit the site, Sasaki was constrained by the necessity to work around a large dike and to conserve the existing palm trees. Sasaki's description of the project is included in Jan C. Rowan, "Design of Exterior Spaces [Sasaki, Walker & Associates]," *Progressive Architecture* 41, no. 7 (July 1960): 123. On the embassy, see Sandy Isenstadt, "'Faith in a Better Future': Sert's American Embassy in Baghdad," *Journal of Architectural Education* 50, no. 9 (February 1997): 172–188.

58. Paul Venable Turner, *Campus: An American Planning Tradition* (Cambridge, Mass.: MIT Press, 1984), 249–250.

59. Turner does not consider Sasaki's work even though he examines one of the firm's most well-known projects, Foothill College, a collaboration with Ernest Kump. Stefan Muthesius does not correct this absence in his more recent study, although he discusses Richard Dober's contributions to the discourse on campus planning, an expertise Dober developed in Sasaki's office (*The Postwar University: Utopian Campus and College* [New Haven: Yale University Press], 2000).

60. On the Springfield College project, see files "Project file—Springfield College," and "Correspondence—Walter Gropius—1954," both box 2, Isaacs Papers.

61. Isaacs persevered in his efforts to formalize the relationship between the three; in a 1957 proposal for the development of the University of Illinois at Chicago, he suggested a limited partnership called SINTAC, comprising Sasaki, Isaacs, Sasaki's partner Paul Novak, and TAC. Project coordination would be handled by Isaacs, financial management and on-site supervision by Novak, and design by Sasaki and TAC (letter, Isaacs to H. W. Pearce, Superintendent of Buildings and Grounds, University of Illinois, Chicago, December 13, 1957, "Correspondence/by subject—with Walter Gropius—July—December 1957," box 2, Isaacs Papers). Sasaki's 1961 prospectus lists two other collaborative projects with Isaacs—Michael Reese Hospital Development Plans (1955–57), and Puerto Rico Medical Center in Santurce, San Juan, Puerto Rico (1958).

62. Simo, *Offices of Hideo Sasaki*, 32.

63. Belluschi played this role on the Fine Arts Commission, Washington, D.C. (to which Sasaki also was named), and on the Architectural Advisory Committee to the State Department's Office of Foreign Buildings Operations, among others. On Belluschi's involvement in the MIT campus, see Meredith Clausen, *Pietro Belluschi: Modern American Architect* (Cambridge, Mass.: MIT Press, 1994);

O. Robert Simha, *MIT Campus Planning, 1960–2000: An Annotated Chronology* (Cambridge, Mass.: MIT Press, 2001); and an extensive article on I. M. Pei's Earth Science Building, "New Landmark for M.I.T.," *Progressive Architecture* 46, no. 3 (March 1965): 156–162.

64. More than half of the firm's projects between 1953 and 1970 were based on planning studies and architectural work for universities and colleges.

65. Projects that directly involved Sasaki include MIT Landscape Development/Campus Landscape Project (1956); President's Garden (1957); East Campus Study (1957–58); Briggs Field Study and Athletic Facilities (1958–65); Earth Science Building (1959); Preliminary Parking Accommodation Study West Campus (1959); West Campus Site Accommodation Study (1959); Amherst Alley Landscape and Master Plan (1959–63); MIT Planning Report (1960); Social Science and Management Buildings (1960–62); Technology Square (1960–66); Student Center (1960–65); West Campus Undergraduate Residence Accommodation Study (1961); McCormick Hall II Undergraduate Women (1963); Burton-Conner Master's Residence (1963–67); Chemistry Building (1964); Educational Research Center, East Campus Proposal (1964); Eastgate I Married Housing (1964–67); Athletic Facilities—Study, Existing Site William Crocker (1964–66, 1970, 1975); Student Center Kresge Court and Student

Center Environs (1965, 1972); Life Sciences Building (1966); Massachusetts Avenue Crossing (1968–70); Campus Expansion (1975); miscellaneous landscape projects (n.d.) (Planning Office Records, Institute Archives, MIT).

66. Sasaki's involvement seems to have further declined when Belluschi stepped down as dean in 1965. There appears to have been tension between Sasaki's office and the Planning Office. In his history of the MIT campus plan, Simha plays down Sasaki's contributions to the overall planning (*MIT Campus Planning, 1960–2000*).

67. It seems probable that the mixed reception to Saarinen's two buildings (completed in 1955) motivated the MIT Corporation's commission of a long-term plan. Concerned about the break in the more or less unified campus, in 1959 Stoddard asked Saarinen to design the student center and to prepare a master plan for Kresge Plaza, as this area of the campus was known. Although initially reluctant to take on the planning aspect of the project, Saarinen eventually submitted two proposals. His student center was conceived as a long building screening the plaza to the north, with a corresponding library building to the south and a second student building to the west. This project also included a plan to build a bridge over Massachusetts Avenue, thus physically connecting the old and new campuses and alleviating the dangers posed by automobile traffic to pedestrians. Saarinen planned

to introduce a campanile at the northeastern edge of the plaza to mark the entrance to the new campus and to balance the geometric forms of the auditorium and chapel with the imposing façade of the classical building across Massachusetts Avenue. This plan was likely the source for Sasaki's second scheme, in which the student center is broken into two flanking buildings. This idea did not survive long: the 1960 master plan shows the student center as a single building on the northern edge of the plaza with no provision for a building on the southern side.

68. Information on buildings from Simha, *MIT Campus Planning, 1960–2000*, and from Planning Office records c. 1958–2000, MIT Institute Archives.

69. Bosworth laid out the campus as a system of largely four-story buildings linked on all levels, the result being "infinitely" long corridors. This overall system was maintained as the campus grew, although building heights changed. This history was recounted in a long article on the Green Building ("New Landmark for M.I.T."). On Bosworth's plan, see Mark Jarzombek, *Designing MIT: Bosworth's New Tech* (Boston: Northeastern University Press, 2004).

70. Sasaki, Dawson & DeMay Associates are listed by Simha as the Consulting Architects/Engineers for the Dreyfus and Whitaker Buildings (*MIT Campus Planning, 1960–2000*, 154–155).

71. The firm was also involved in the

landscaping, chief among the projects being the distinctive grove of sycamore trees and long, narrow benches placed on the north side of the tower, and the location in 1963 of a large sculpture by Alexander Calder to the southwest edge of the McDermott Courtyard.

72. On Foothill College, see esp. Peter Walker's recollections in "The Sasaki Years"; Allan Temko's enthusiastic review, "Colleges: Foothill's Campus is a Community in Itself," *Architectural Forum* 116, no. 2 (February 1962): 52–57; "A Dream in Redwood," *Progressive Architecture* 43, no. 9 (September 1962): 136–143; and two later critical reassessments: Robert Montgomery, "Most Popular Campus," *Progressive Architecture* 54, no. 6 (June 1973): 113–117; Michael Laurie, "Foothill Revisited," *Landscape Architecture* 57, no. 3 (April 1967): 182–184. In their studies of campus design, Turner and Muthesius also briefly mention the project.

73. Rowan, "Design of Exterior Spaces," 108–126.

74. Dober emerged as the firm's spokesperson in July 1960, when he published a short article that followed Rowan's profile (Dober, "Specialist's Services in Land Design," *Progressive Architecture* 41, no. 7 [July 1960]: 127–128). Among Dober's other early publications, see esp. "Form and Style in Campus Design," *Progressive Architecture* 41, no. 9 (September 1960): 122–133; "The New Idealism and the State of Environmental Design," *Design* (India), (September

1961): 102–110; and his first book, *Campus Planning* (New York: Reinhold, 1963). After leaving Sasaki's firm in 1962, Dober formed the partnership of Dober, Walquist & Harris, specializing in campus design.

75. Clausen, *Pietro Belluschi*, ix–x.

76. For DeMay's recollections, see "Hideo Sasaki 1919–2000," tape 2. DeMay may have first encountered Sasaki as a student in Sert, Giedion, Sasaki, and Sekler's spring 1957 urban design seminar "The Human Scale."

77. See Clausen for a list of Belluschi/Sasaki, Dawson & DeMay collaborations. To her list should be added Life Magazine House, Palo Alto, California (1958), and Bennington College Library, Bennington, Vermont (with Carl Koch, 1957–59).

78. In a highly complimentary review of the University of Colorado in *Architectural Forum*, John Dixon Hunt concluded, "The design consultants saw and grasped a greater opportunity to create a harmonious environment, and a visible continuity with the past. How many other universities can offer as much?" ("Colorado U: Respect for a Robust Environment," *Architectural Forum* 117, no. 4 [October 1962]: 62). See also Dober's presentation of the firm's approach to the project: "Colorado Transition: Style to Plan," *Landscape Architecture* 51, no. 3 (April 1961): 172–173. On the history of the Engineering Complex, see Siegfried Mandel and Margaret Shipley, *Proud Past—Bright Future: A History of the College of Engineering at the University of Colorado, 1893–1966* (Boulder: University of Colorado, College of Engineering, 1966).

79. See discussion between Ladislas Segoe, Sert, Robert Little, William Muschenheim, and Garrett Eckbo in "Urban Design," 99.

80. Galehouse interview, 13.

A CONVERSATION WITH JOSEP LLUÍS SERT

ROBERT CAMPBELL

This interview was conducted on December 29, 1980. The following is an edited version of the conversation.

SERT: I've always been interested in the relationship between architecture and the city. Whenever I had an opportunity of doing something that turned toward the aspects of the city, that could be a statement in shaping space not only in the building itself but outside the building, more than one building, that's what I became interested in. And of course I started very early working with CIAM, the International Congress of Modern Architecture, which I joined in 1929.

CAMPBELL: *That was the year you were in Paris, isn't it?*

SERT: Yes. But since Paris and Barcelona were very close, I was constantly working in my house in Barcelona and going to spend some months in Paris. Then I was in Frankfurt for CIAM 2, which was a big demonstration of the new build-

ing; Le Corbusier, Mies, and Gropius were all there. I met many of these people and saw the Weissenhofsiedlung in Stuttgart. All these people were very much on that same line; all dreamed that the transformation of cities was a much easier matter than it has turned out to be, although many of the things we then considered utopian have materialized. I have always been concerned with the city as a whole. After that I continued with my work with CIAM and in Barcelona, and it came to pass that in Spain there was the change from a monarchy to a republic and—

CAMPBELL: *Polite way of saying "civil war and fascist dictatorship."*

SERT: In Catalonia in the 1930s, there was a government—home rule, you could compare it with the Irish situation in many ways—and we all had great hopes and made great plans, so we did not stop at anything. We had the daring that many

199

young people have and should continue to have. That is partly perhaps due to ignorance of the complications of life. But we were not stopped at that moment by any idea of life being so complex, and things evolving not at a great speed, but slowly; it was a situation of great hope. When I started my studies in Barcelona right after the First World War, which finished in 1918, I was already very conscious of international politics. I was interested in all the happenings, although Spain remained neutral. But one thing came after the other, all these events, and we had the feeling that the big war was supposed to end all wars, as was usually said. It would be a period of total change, and we were aware of the role that technology could play. We had great conviction that the war was bringing changes in the whole world, and that those changes were applicable to the work we wanted to do. So that made us feel very hopeful that we were going to be part of this.

At that early stage, I was lucky to meet all these people who were fighting in the same direction. It was a small group who talked about CIAM at that time. People who signed the CIAM La Sarraz manifesto were twenty or something. When CIAM met then, the biggest conference must have been around two hundred. But it was a driving force, and especially a conviction about the coming together of changes in the world as a whole, and of the possibilities of the new technology. Then with the example—because I had lived in Paris for years—of all that was happening there in painting, sculpture, and the arts in general.

CAMPBELL: *How did you come to know so many artists who became famous?*

SERT: Well, that was purely by chance, I would say, because I happened to go to Paris . . . I worked with Le Corbusier, who knew Fernand Léger. I met Alexander Calder through Paul Nelson, an American architect. This whole thing was a chain, of course. Joan Miró, I met in Barcelona. And Miró went to Paris. I met Picasso thorough my uncle, José Maria Sert, a mural painter, who had known him all his life practically. I met Giacometti because we used to go to the Café de Flore near Les Deux Magots in Saint-Germain during the time I was building the Spanish Pavilion. Every evening these people used to gather there, so they were not very difficult people to meet.

CAMPBELL: *Was that a function of it being a smaller world of people who were interested in modernism?*

SERT: Yes. When one sees today these enormous museums of modern art and shows with modern art, this is practically the trend that dominates everything. Well, it was nothing like that at that time. There were a minority of people interested in these kinds of experiments. I got to meet Piet Mondrian at that time, also Georges Vantongerloo and the Dutch group. They had a little magazine [*De Stijl*], and they were getting it published with great effort, and they were starting all those other experiments. . . . But those were the early twenties, and that is when I first found the works of Le Corbusier, which I discovered in the little booksellers that still exist in the corner of the Faubourg Saint-Honoré and the rue Castiglione, the little Castiglione that leads into the Place Vendôme. And they had these little books displayed in the window . . .

CAMPBELL: *You hadn't heard of him until you happened on the books?*

SERT: No, I had not heard of him. I did not know anything about the man, but I saw these books, *Vers une architecture, La Peinture moderne, L'art décoratif d'aujourd'hui, Urbanisme,* etc., displayed there by the publisher, Crés. I looked through them and they interested me very much. So I bought them and brought them back to Barcelona; we were a group of unhappy people in a sort of Beaux-Arts school there.

This was actually 1926. And so then these books—I think they had been just published— it's through them that we went and talked to other people, friends we used to meet in the café, or after classes, as we usually do in these countries. I brought the books and we started discussing them; one passed the book on to the other one, and so we all read them and discussed them. We were looking for some kind of new orientation and opening, different from what the school was teaching us. Well, we found something there that intrigued us and influenced our lives and our work very much.

CAMPBELL: *What was it about those books that struck you?*

SERT: At that time they were unusual. I had not seen any of the Bauhaus publications, for instance, at that time. We were much more in contact in Barcelona with Paris than we were with Germany. Curiously enough, Madrid was more in contact with the Bauhaus, more influenced by Germany. I had a friend who had been their first Spanish delegate to CIAM, Fernando García Mercadal. He is still alive, older than I am, and he had worked in Germany. My background was entirely from Paris.

CAMPBELL: *And your education in Barcelona?*

SERT: My education in Barcelona was in a Beaux-Arts school, following the Beaux-Arts methods of training and working.

CAMPBELL: *Which are now coming back into vogue.*

SERT: And they are coming back into vogue. I had some remarkable professors; one of them was a very talented man who worked with Gaudí, the man who helped Gaudí with some of his designs, the ironwork in the Casa Mila House, the tile work in the Park Güell, things like that.

CAMPBELL: *How did you decide to become an architect?*

SERT: I started with painting. My interest in life had always been visual arts in general; my uncle had been a painter. I came naturally from painting to architecture; somebody decided, I suppose, that as a painter nobody makes a living. I think it was my uncle, José Maria Sert, the muralist, who said, "Why don't you become an architect?" I was interested in architecture; it was one of the visual arts, so I was attracted to it. I had been dreaming of going to Italy to see things. I had been seeing things in Paris and so on. And I then started to do sketches in the Arts Club in Barcelona and met many other painters there, and friends of the painters and writers. And we had a group in one big café there; we used to meet in the evenings. Cafés were very important.

We decided to form a group of architects to try to change the school, protesting against the methods of education. This was the middle '20s, and we knew nothing really. We had no information about the Bauhaus. But that was our start. After that we started publishing a magazine that appeared four issues a year, *A.C.* But we got it moving and got into an exchange with many other magazines, and through that we got magazines from Holland, *De Stijl.* We got the Bauhaus magazine, then we began to widen our views because in the library of the Barcelona School of Design there was certainly nothing like that.

CAMPBELL: *If I may go forward a bit, how did you get involved in the Spanish Pavilion?*

SERT: I was in Spain when the civil war started in 1936. I had done a considerable amount of work for the Catalan government, and I had close ties with it. They sent me to a peace conference in Brussels because they had no other good delegates to represent the government. I did not make much of a representative, but anyhow I was there. Then I came back to Paris. I had lived in Paris for many years before, off and on, so they asked me to work for the Spanish embassy as the cultural attaché. They were organizing exhibits of what was happening in Spain to make people understand that the government of Spain was in a dangerous situation. There had been a lot of terrible things done, but there were quite a few people who were civilized and

who ran the government of Spain. There were actually many of them, the most distinguished people in the country. We had an extraordinary government at that moment.

I began working and organizing their exhibits; we had a place on the Boulevard de la Madeleine where we organized these exhibits, one on Catalan art. The '37 exhibit was already being organized, the international exhibit, and Spain had no pavilion to represent what was happening there. It became a rather extraordinary pavilion, because a country in the midst of a civil war could not show much about what it was producing, as it was destroying more than it was producing. But they asked us to design this pavilion—a friend, architect Luis Lacasa, who worked mainly from Madrid, and myself from Barcelona. And we designed this pavilion with a very limited budget. What we really had there was the great chance of having the collaboration of people like Picasso, Miró, and Calder.

CAMPBELL: *How did you happen to leave and come to America not too long afterward? Of course the civil war ended the way it ended . . .*

SERT: I went several times to Spain to pick up material for the pavilion. We had people coming from Madrid with design posters, and helpers in the pavilion and the whole crew. And then the war came to a bad end for our side with Franco's victory. The whole group couldn't do much after that and were blacklisted by Franco and his people. I had seen Gropius not long before, probably in '36, in one of the CIAM conferences at La Sarraz. He said, you should come to

Figure 10.1 Josep Lluís Sert and Le Corbusier at CIAM 4

America, you should come to Harvard. He had talked to me about all that. So the time came, and I said, why don't we go to America? And we left and came here, and we arrived in June 1939. I came with the idea of staying here about six months and then perhaps going back to France because then, of course, there was no war there. My uncle knew General Lyautey in Morocco, and he said when you go there—you're interested in cities—you will have a lot of work. And I had many other contacts in Paris and England, as well as here. But I got here and then a few months after that, the war started in Europe. So I stayed on, and then a few years later this country was in the war.

I had started a book in France with friends from CIAM, an illustrated book on the Athens Charter, which was published here by Harvard

University Press as *Can Our Cities Survive?* But it originated in Europe as a summary of some of the work of CIAM on city planning, in the sense of urban design, city planning as seen by architects. I came here with what I had of the manuscript and illustrations and continued working. And sometime after that I started meeting people and I lectured. While I was in New York, we had a group of CIAM people. Some had been in Le Corbusier's office, like Ernest Weissman, who was later at the United Nations. The group had many people who were refugees from Europe. Every month that passed, they had more and more friends from Paris and Germany and everywhere. I knew quite a few people, James Johnson Sweeney very well, and Sandy Calder and other people from America.

CAMPBELL: *What kind of work did you do?*

SERT: I did some lecturing on CIAM work. I met Paul Lester Wiener, who had contacts in South America. He knew people in Brazil, some of the modern architects. CIAM also had delegates in South America; Oscar Niemeyer and Lúcio Costa were members. And they had worked with Le Corbusier and Jorge Ferrari-Hardoy and all these people. I started my work in South America shortly after the war, I think it was in '47 or '48. I went down to Brazil, where they had asked us to design a new city. It was supposed to assemble airplane motors. It never really came to pass because it was sort of a war baby. And then one thing led to another, and I got commissions from there, in Peru, and from Peru to Colombia, from Colombia to Venezuela, and Cuba, and so on.

CAMPBELL: *Most of these designs were never realized.*

SERT: It was a very interesting experiment. It was right after the war. And there was nothing much really, especially for outsiders, to do. It was an opportunity to test the CIAM idea. I was quickly convinced about how much things could change when you brought them from Germany to Brazil. Many of these ideas that CIAM had developed were rather elementary and required much more study and experimentation.

CAMPBELL: *There's been a great deal of criticism in recent years of the CIAM ideas about urban design and city planning on the grounds that they destroy the concept of enclosed urban space. The Krier brothers and many other people have made that point. I wonder how you'd comment on that.*

SERT: I think you have to judge CIAM with a little more knowledge. CIAM was composed of very different people. We were always discussing. For instance, the German groups from the beginning were rather shocked at Le Corbusier's Plan Voisin with his "redent blocks," as he called them, these meandering kinds of lines of his buildings, which were inspired by Versailles and the Cour de Louvre. The German CIAM members had a theory by which they thought that every building had a perfect orientation toward the sun or whatever it was. And the next building had to be parallel to the first, and the third one parallel to the second. But within CIAM we were opposed to this idea. We had aspirations about other things, and then there were fights. Curiously enough, even Le Corbusier, when he designed his Unité d'Habitation, finally came to the one block kind of thing. I designed the Casa Bloc project that we did in Barcelona with this GATCPAC group, which was just finished when the civil war started. It followed these kinds of meandering forms and had courtyards and duplex apartments. There you find a certain kind of rhythmic expression in the façades of the buildings.

We were also influenced by Mediterranean folk architecture. It was obvious that some of these buildings that came in the German and Scandinavian and Dutch magazines resembled buildings in the Mediterranean. They started by having flat roofs, which was the traditional thing there. And the poorer houses were all white like these new buildings. The new buildings happened to have bigger windows with more glass. And so we found that these things were much more revolutionary in the north than they were in our country. Folk architecture is published now in our magazines, as they become things to keep. But we thought that what was being done in the name of folk architecture was completely wrong. They took the wrong details and they ignored the volumetric expression and simplicity of means. So we were rather in a state of revolt at that time against the Gaudí things, for instance, although I later understood Gaudí much better and appreciate him very much; I wrote a book with James Sweeney on him.

CAMPBELL: *You spoke of your building in Barcelona as being an example of new architecture, although different in content. When did you begin to feel that something in modern architecture was too new?*

SERT: I began to feel that already in Europe. The Mediterranean group—the Italians, the French, the Spanish—we considered ourselves not in agreement with principles that the Germans followed so precisely. And then we differed also by having an idea of the city. Thinking of the city has been throughout my life an obsession; I could imagine what would happen when we had other rules. The Siedlungen were just an example; they were spotlessly clean and well landscaped and every road was paved. They had little shops that were separated from the building because you couldn't mix anything. They were impressive, but that was not all of the modern architecture in Europe. The architecture in Vienna, the housing in Vienna, wasn't like that. They had courts.

CAMPBELL: *You mean courtyards?*

SERT: In the buildings, yes, and many other things. These purist attitudes of some of the German group and many of the Dutch were not within our taste or like the things we did. The proof is that the first plans we did for Barcelona are not that. I got more feeling about the limitations of modern architecture as time went by, and I started writing *Can Our Cities Survive?* When I started lecturing and talking to other people in New York, I began to see more and more bad modern, always repeating the same pattern, and one was perfectly convinced that it would be really dull and sad to see whole cities develop on that limited formula. I stated that from the beginning to my students, as much as I like Mies and believe in the quality of his architecture, and the qualities of the man as a whole. I always told my students, it's all right that there is a Mondrian, and you find a few Mondrians and a few followers of Mondrian in the museum or in school, but imagine a whole museum the size of the Louvre all with Mondrian and his disciples—it would be a disaster. I always had these points of disagreement in trying to get people from the Chicago School, when they came to Harvard, to get out of that and see what we could do. But it was very difficult. We were trying to create a new vocabulary; a new vocabulary doesn't develop in twenty-four hours.

CAMPBELL: *In a lot of the work you did, it seemed to me that you were trying to ornament buildings again but couldn't accept the idea of applying ornament. And therefore by sorting out functions . . . for example, the window: in some of your work you sort the window into three parts—the part you see out of, the part the light comes in, and the part you open for air—so you have three kinds of windows, and you animate a façade by having many kinds of windows, perhaps coloring the vents. In a way you're reintroducing ornament.*

SERT: Yes, I was introducing ornament. I believe that ornament not only can but should be reintroduced. And I don't see that as anything against modernism. In our early magazines we were very much for these Catalan Gothic buildings that were very sober, with plain walls, and they had moldings where the sun cast a shadow. The fact is, you give up the possibility of having a building that casts shadows and one part of the building casts a shadow on another part of the building.

Breaking it like that was for me absolute death. You can refer back to my old lectures given over the years; since I didn't do so much work, I could do more talking. I always felt that modern architecture, especially when it came into the real modern city, would have to have a vocabulary. And a lot of the things that had been thrown out would have to be carefully picked up again.

CAMPBELL: *One of the things that everyone knows about you is your relationship with Le Corbusier. What was he like, and what was your relationship like?*

SERT: After we read his books, we saw in a local paper that he had come to lecture at a very expensive club in Madrid. It was actually a women's club, which was rather extraordinary in Spain at the time. About 1926 or '27 I boldly wrote to him and asked if he could come and give us a lecture in Barcelona. He asked for a fee, and it wasn't very much, so we went with a hat around the place and got the money, and brought him to Barcelona. When he came to Barcelona, he always complained. He asked, "When is the lecture?" When I said, "Ten in the evening," he said, "Who had the idea of having a lecture at ten in the evening?" I said, "I'm very sorry, but in Barcelona we live like that." And so it happened.

Then he became interested in the local Gothic, and he had great admiration for that particular kind of architecture and for the city itself and the life in the city.

Then he discovered Gaudí. For Le Corbusier it was a great discovery, and he stayed there a few days with us. We took him around, and as we knew the people in the government we got him in a plane and he could see Barcelona from above. We showed him some projects we already had, and—as we were already influenced by his books—he rather liked them. At the end of this visit we took him to a nightclub where he used to do little sketches of the flamenco dancers; he always enjoyed his nightlife in Barcelona, in the harbor district.

And then he said, "Why don't you, when you finish your studies, come to Paris and work with me in the studio?" He didn't pay anybody except the man who took care of the accounting and the secretary who took telephone calls. But the first thing I did when I got there was the second project of the League of Nations, and the Mundaneum project that was never built. This project was in Geneva, near the Swiss Jura mountains; it's in his complete works. It was a rather ambitious project; it was supposed to be a center of world information. He had a museum there that I think is a clever design. I preferred it even to his later designs for a museum. It was based on spirals, with the spiral going up in ramps and becoming a step-down pyramid, which is much the same thing at the Guggenheim, but reversed. So that has a sharp top and a wide bottom, with the idea that you take elevators to get to the top. And the culture of man begins from whatever it is, the Stone Age, with very few improvements and little to show. But as it goes developing in time, growing, it needs more space.

CAMPBELL: *What was he like? What was he like to work with?*

SERT: It was very nice to work with him. We got along well together from the beginning, and he had great sympathy for Catalonia. He told me he descended from the Albigensian heretics in the south of France who were pushed toward the cul-de-sac of the Alps where La Chaux-de-Fonds is located. He says his family came originally from southwest France—first cousins of the Catalonian people right across the border. So we sympathized from the beginning. I was interested in painting, and he showed me his paintings. That's a friendship that started in Barcelona and lasted forty-something years, until his death. I saw him about three months before he died in Paris, when there was a big UIA [International Union of Architects] gathering. A lot of the Le Corbusier people were there, so we had dinner and a celebration. Shortly after, I said goodbye to him in his apartment; he had invited me to lunch. A few weeks after, I saw in the newspaper that he was dead.

We had done a project together in Bogotá in 1948–51. Later, I knew that he wanted to build something in this country, and that's when this opportunity came to me at the Carpenter Center. One day [Harvard University] President [Nathan Marsh] Pusey and Dean McGeorge Bundy called me and said, "Would you advise us about an architect?" And it was for this building. The Carpenter family had given money, and I had been working with the people who were doing the program for a building on the visual arts.

And I said why not try Le Corbusier? It was just a thought. I didn't have any idea if he would accept it or not.

It was, compared to his dreams, really something reduced to a minimum. I had to convince him in Paris that although this was a small building of about sixty thousand or sixty-four thousand square feet, it was going to be very important because it was an international gathering center for young people, and Harvard it is and always will be. So finally he agreed to do it.

CAMPBELL: *I talked to I. M. Pei a couple of years ago. And I was surprised when he volunteered that he had a favorite twentieth-century building. I wondered if you had favorite buildings, buildings that you particularly admired other than your own.*

SERT: Well, I go beyond the twentieth century. I was always interested not only in modern art but in buildings in general. I had great admiration for Palladio's work. As soon as I was finished with school, I took a car from Barcelona with a couple of friends and went discovering these villas in the Veneto. Of course many things shocked me the first time I saw them, but I came by degrees to appreciate them. Venice is something that you have to be much older to appreciate.

CAMPBELL: *Why did it shock you?*

SERT: The first impression I had, I was more for architecture in Florence than for Venice. It was sad looking, and it was a gray day, and we saw they were loading the gondolas with garbage or something. At that time we were set on doing architecture seriously, with great reverence. And some of the small playful things in Venice, with

all these Oriental influences, were a little new to me. But I got to appreciate it very much, and now when I go to Venice, I really enjoy it.

But apart from Palladio, I always had as my ideal other things, like Brunelleschi's architecture. The Duomo Santa Maria and things like that to me are absolute tops, and as I've seen more, I have great admiration for many of the eastern things, and not only the architecture in India but also Persia. For me, Architecture is Architecture with a capital A. Of the more modern things, of course I was very impressed with Le Corbusier's work; I have great admiration for some of his buildings in Chandigarh, and the Unité d'Habitation in Marseilles is a great building. There were some early Dutch things—some of the work of Gerrit Rietveld and Mart Stam— I have great admiration for. And I like some, but not all, of the Brazilian work. I liked it at one time, but I think it has gone down considerably. Some of the Japanese things have great quality. Some of Aalto's things, although he is a northerner and I'm not from the north. Certain differences . . . the places where orange trees can grow versus places where pine trees grow. It's a different thing.

CAMPBELL: *Very different.*

SERT: Once they asked me the difficult question: what three cities were more extraordinary or that I admired most, and I said Venice for one— it's not a city, it's a miracle, it's a sort of happening. Paris for another, because although I don't like Parisian architecture, Parisian city planning is like some kind of a miracle come together.

The urban spaces in Paris are difficult to compare to anything else—the scale of things. The third one I chose was San Francisco, because San Francisco for me was a promise. The site to start with, the buildings up the hills, the small scale, the human scale.

CAMPBELL: *The way they set the grid right down on the hill without modifying it.*

SERT: Yes, exactly. Without any nonsense about the contours and so on. And then the courage to build those bridges, which for me were like cathedrals. They had the best of the cathedrals; they had the structure without the rest, as if the whole thing had collapsed.

CAMPBELL: *If you're interested, Pei's favorite building was the Salk Center in La Jolla, California, by Louis Kahn.*

SERT: I have great sympathy and feeling for Louis Kahn, and I like some of his things. I haven't seen the center. You have to see things. With space you can't take photographs.

CAMPBELL: *Kahn photographs very badly.*

SERT: You have to experience moving through the spaces.

CAMPBELL: *He photographs worse than most, I think. Your buildings also, in my opinion, photograph badly, especially in black and white.*

SERT: Because they don't give the feeling.

CAMPBELL: *You don't get a sense of it. What do you think of the postmodernists who are deliberately applying scrapbook art—you know, the past—onto architecture, and also the most exaggerated modern-*

ists, such as the Pei firm's John Hancock building, where certain elements of modernism are carried through to an extreme?

SERT: I think we are suffering from something today—it's extremes. We lost something that was very beautiful in environments, in life in general; there was a certain balance. For me "balance" is a word I've thought about carefully. It's a matter of scale, a matter of putting certain things near other things that would have a relationship. That has been lost—a matter of measure. In the cities the great loss in applying modern technology—whatever admirable things the skyscraper had—is that it hasn't fit into the infrastructure. America has discovered great climaxes, great things, but the city is a puzzle that nobody can put together yet. I think the task for the future—if it really can ever be done—is to use technology, but technology with the understanding that it's made for people and that people have to live happily.

In our times we have a great admiration for the nineteenth century. I admire it more now as I see some of the things that were done then. They still had urban spaces. And for me the twentieth century may go down in history as essentially destroying urban space—urban space of quality, I mean. When you compare it to any other period, the reputation of architects is bad, frankly. The Cour de Louvre, added to the Tuileries, added to the Champs Elysées and the Arc de Triomphe and the Place de la Concorde. Those are great urban spaces. But I'm talking perhaps of the larger scale—you go to Rome and you find them all around: Piazza del Popolo, the Piazza Navona, et cetera. And I don't think we have in our time, with all our advanced technology, ever done anything that can compare even remotely in terms of urban spaces to their spaces. I know that we've invented many things—we have extraordinary expressways and we have many things—but these things have never come together. The expressways and the skyscrapers aren't related.

CAMPBELL: *I think it was Jean-Paul Sartre who said somewhere that what characterized America was discontinuity. He liked it, I think.*

SERT: In our cities there's nothing that seems to come together, everything seems to come apart. It's a process of careful integration in a building itself, and disintegration of the total environment.

CAMPBELL: *Do you have any particular regrets, things that you might have done differently?*

SERT: Oh yes, I do. [LAUGHTER]

One of the exciting things about architecture is that you are never entirely happy with a building. I don't know the fellow who designed the Taj Mahal. I suppose he was the closest to being satisfied. But I feel that our buildings are in many ways so experimental today, you can't always blame the clients. Our firm, if we make a mistake and we see when it's too late, then what keeps us going is that we think in the next one we are going to correct that mistake or make it better.

CAMPBELL: *I was always struck in the office by your lack of interest in your previous works and your tendency to downplay them.*

SERT: What happens is that we like to do it

better, and I wish I was given the opportunity to do this other thing.

CAMPBELL: *Do you have works that you've been involved in that you particularly like?*

SERT: I still particularly like the Harvard married students' complex, Peabody Terrace. Some things I wouldn't do in the same material, and some things don't resist the weather as one would like. But as a whole, I like the complex. The relationship of the towers to the spaces . . . and when you turn and go along the river, you see change. For me, that has life to it. I like some things in the Harvard Science Center. That was a challenge, to put different buildings together. I consider that it is several buildings, and what would happen if in an urban complex I had to put streets in between or separate them?

One of the things that I never was moved by in Washington is that they have this big mall and all these buildings. They all look like models, when you finish third-year studio and present them for the jury. And you put the models close together, and every model has been done by a different man, without any concern for the model next to it—without any concern that they had been put together. But there they knew they had to put them together, so why didn't they do something about putting them together? This is again this urban concept of things. I don't think these things are done by one man alone but with a group of people, who could do bigger ensembles that would fit together. When we did this Roosevelt Island work and Yonkers work, we tried our best to do that.

CAMPBELL: *Besides Peabody Terrace, are there others that you would single out?*

SERT: The Miró Museum in Barcelona was a pleasure to design. And parts of the Fondation Maeght, although there I didn't do everything I would have liked to do. I like that kind of approach to the display of works of art in smaller buildings, and to take the village pattern and the small square instead of monumental buildings. Of course we didn't have the money to do them; that's also true. So the temptation wasn't there.

What has been called postmodern, I don't think really is postmodern; it's more premodern than postmodern. But I'm not a purist, I wouldn't have a bad conscience about putting some things in that I believe would make things more lively, more enjoyable. In the end there's a certain enjoyment that you get out of architecture. But I believe that what has been done to date is very limited. I'm surprised that they've taken this turn of going to things that are what the world already had. When you get to decoration, the world has done wonderful things—some of the Gaudí things, the Aalto things have extraordinary quality in decoration. As decoration, it belonged to that period, and now they've gone back to, let's say, 1925. Already '25 was a period that we revolted against.

CAMPBELL: *It's very Oedipal.*

SERT: But having, as you have today, good reproductions of photographs, color slides, films, and the whole history of art, why don't they plunge further back? There are so many things to readopt and reuse in architecture. You can find it in Egypt, certain tricks with effects in light and so on, all manner of things that we don't do today, you can find in other periods.

CAMPBELL: *Some of them do go back, of course. There's this great interest in Hadrian's Villa.*

SERT: I have a great attraction for Hadrian's Villa. I always had discussions with my dear friend Joseph Zalewski, who was more of a purist in modern architecture maybe than I am, because I was taught in the Beaux-Arts school.

I believe certain things like that can be recuperated—they're in nature, everywhere. They're part of the design of the whole world, of our whole environment. I think we have to go further into the possibilities of the future. There are tremendous things that I would do if I was a younger man: I would start exploring the possibilities of things like solar heating that lend themselves to new approaches to design, to designing new forms and to creating all manner of things. In my buildings in the Miró Foundation, I was influenced . . . by the many things I saw in North Africa that impressed me very much. I saw some things in Venice that impressed me, and maybe there is an influence of some of these. But when I did the embassy in Baghdad, there are arches there, there are vaults, there are all manner of things that were not the straight line.

CAMPBELL: *When I asked if you had any regrets, you quickly skirted around that and went on to something else. I wondered if you had any, about projects that were unbuilt. The Presidential Palace in Cuba, that struck me . . .*

SERT: The Presidential Palace in Cuba was a building that interested me because it was a system of structure—the parasol, by the way, was designed with Felix Candela—that I appreciate very much.

CAMPBELL: *And you have a similar thing going on now.*

SERT: Not actually. We are not doing anything with the parasol now. But the idea of unifying these different buildings and courtyards with the parasol that was casting shadows, protecting from the sun, and so on . . . I thought that had some possibility.

CAMPBELL: *I thought it was very interesting; I would have loved to have seen it built. Another one was the Carmel Convent, which was never completed.*

SERT: Never properly built. We are still having difficulties with that.

CAMPBELL: *It is my favorite among your designs, as far as I can tell from models and photos.*

SERT: Carmel is quite nice. I still hope that one day we could properly finish it. Some of the religious buildings, as Gaudí says, may take four hundred years.

CAMPBELL: *There was something special about it; it had an anthropomorphic quality that I'm sure you know, of a gathering within the wall and coming down the mountain. It's a very moving expression, as well as being an interesting program.*

SERT: Well, it was a very desirable commission.

CAMPBELL: *You never built a church.*

SERT: I never built the church that I had designed for the Boston Government Center. It was a building that perhaps had some qualities.

CAMPBELL: *How do you feel about your years of teaching and administration, committee work, that aspect of your career?*

SERT: Well, I always hated administration and committee work.

CAMPBELL: *Committee work isn't a very nice way of putting it, but you know what I mean. That's been a major part of your career.*

SERT: It's a major part of my career . . . I have the convictions, but I am not—as I told the Harvard people when I came here—especially gifted for administration. I tried to do my best where I could. Committee work, it depends on what committees. If it's a committee that is a sort of teamwork where it really comes to something, that's one thing. Committee work when you have to discuss the rules of something, that's the part I don't really enjoy. I go through it because I think it's necessary, and I enjoyed my years at Harvard very much. I think we had many good moments there and remarkable people in the faculty. People that one could agree or disagree with, but certainly not ordinary people. It was a great experiment and a great lesson, and I think I learned as much from the students as they did from me. In the master class I taught for many years, we tried many things that had a certain value. And I have a good recollection of both the years in CIAM, which was committee meetings and discussions. CIAM lasted for twenty-six years; I must have been with it for twenty-four.

Figure 10.2 Mirko Basaldella and Josep Lluís Sert, 1965

CAMPBELL: *If you were teaching now and you had an incredibly promising student, someone as you might have been when you were twenty, what would you say to that student? What advice would you give?*

SERT: If I was teaching in a school, I would try to do certain inventions. It would bring the people much closer immediately to the actual fact of what architecture really is, in my mind. Basically the shaping of spaces, the enjoyment of people and better living, giving them better living conditions. And I would try to bring them into that picture at an early stage. I think a lot of things now are going off on a tangent.

CAMPBELL: *A tangent in what direction?*

SERT: Well, they are discussing many things now that are in my mind not that important, seeing what's happening in the cities. A lot of long discussions that pivot around such and such a job. Then you say, maybe those are good, et cetera. And then hundreds of buildings are being built all around that are real horrors—nothing ties them together, things don't work, traffic conditions haven't been solved, they're getting worse.

CAMPBELL: *That's what these people have withdrawn from. Richard Meier, "this building is a work of art," that kind of thing.*

SERT: They become more precious. Among the people whose work I like is Richard Meier. I always did like his work since I was struck by his first houses. They have a resemblance with Le Corbusier's early houses, but are well understood and I think he is a good man.

CAMPBELL: *He's a brilliant man. But he doesn't have the interests that you have in context, how things might go together in a larger way.*

SERT: And I'm distressed when I see the architecture magazines, how they illustrate one house after the other, and you say, who the hell can pay for them?

CAMPBELL: *Palladio's clients.*

SERT: Palladio's clients—they're still there, the people who could afford these extraordinary houses. There was one in the *New York Times,* a house on Long Island, again an enormous house.

CAMPBELL: *I didn't see it.*

SERT: With a kind of applied brise-soleil, it has its qualities, undoubtedly. There are many talented young people today, and I think that if they got the chance of pulling things together, not just building isolated little houses, something might happen.

COMMENTARY ON SELECTED PROJECTS BY SERT

Curated by Inés Zalduendo and Mary Daniels

HUSON JACKSON

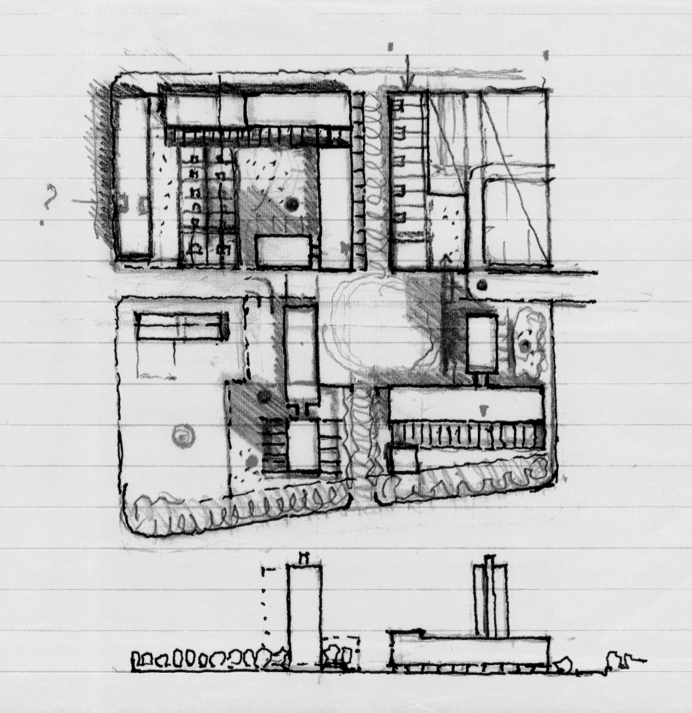

Figure 1a Interior toward patio, 1933. Photograph by Louis Reens.

Figure 1b Interior view of living area, 1933

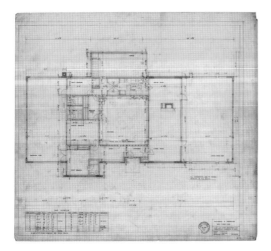

Figure 1c Floor plan, dated 1957. Pencil and ink on vellum.

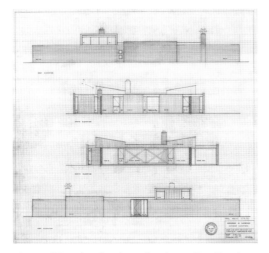

Figure 1d Exterior elevations, dated 1957. Pencil and ink on vellum.

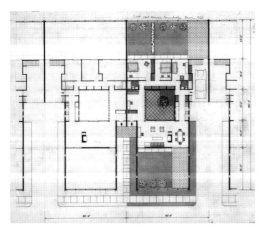

Figure 1e Floor plan of proposed row house scheme. Ink and Zipatone on vellum.

SERT HOUSE
CAMBRIDGE, MASS., 1956–1958

Figures 1a–1f

This is a most interesting example of Sert's dedication to urban design and the larger environment. It's hard to find a problem more restricted and personal than the design of one's own house. Yet when Sert set about to design his house in Cambridge, he looked on it not just as a private space for himself and Moncha, which it was to be, but as a possible prototype of a housing neighborhood. The freestanding house organized around a courtyard, reduced somewhat in scale, could be attached to its neighbors to become a modest and attractive row house.

This concept was actually put to the test. Jaume Freixa, a former associate of the firm now practicing in Barcelona, has built a housing neighborhood for a university community on this prototype.

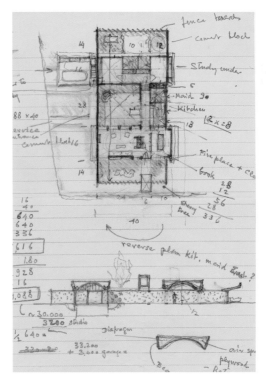

Figure 1f Josep Lluís Sert, preliminary sketch. Color pencil on paper.

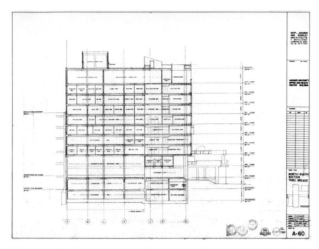

Figure 2a North-south section through arcade, dated 1960. Pencil on tracing cloth.

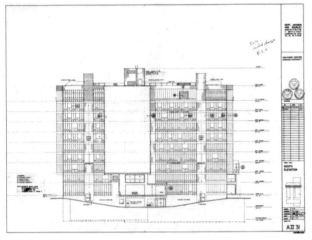

Figure 2b South elevation of main office block, dated 1960. Pencil on tracing cloth.

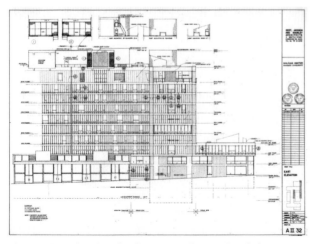

Figure 2c East elevation, dated 1960. Pencil on tracing cloth.

HOLYOKE CENTER
CAMBRIDGE, MASS., 1958–1965

Figures 2a–2g

When Sert was approached by Harvard to design new health care facilities for the university community to replace an existing clinic occupying part of a central block in the Harvard Square area, he decided to look not only at the assigned project but at the potential of this very valuable piece of land. It was occupied by a variety of buildings, some from the nineteenth century. They housed a mixture of commercial and university uses, including the headquarters of the Cambridge Trust Company. The entire block was in Harvard ownership.

Although the site was strategically located to serve university purposes, it was also an integral part of the urban fabric of the Harvard Square area. The bank, shops, and restaurants were important to the street life of the area and to the tax base of the city as well. It was decided that redevelopment of the site would retain the bank headquarters and commercial uses at street level and that planning for the new construction would be for the full floor area then allowed by code, a ratio of four times the site area, even though the new health facility and other identified uses did not call for that much space. It was Sert's conviction that a growing university would soon find uses for all this well-located space, and of course this happened. Indeed, we were subsequently invited to study how the building might be enlarged.

The building site is aligned with a pedestrian path and gate leading from Harvard Yard, and this became the alignment of a pedestrian arcade through the building, which provides for increased retail activity at ground level. The floors above are devoted, in addition to the clinic and infirmary, to a mixture of academic and administrative uses. To concentrate activity in the arcade, access to the upper floors and the health center is from this arcade.

Figure 2d Massachusetts Avenue entrance.
Photograph by Phokion Karas.

Figure 2e Holyoke Center façade detail.
Photograph by Phokion Karas.

Figure 2f Holyoke Center arcade.
Photograph by Phokion Karas.

Figure 2g Massachusetts Avenue façade. Photograph by Phokion Karas.

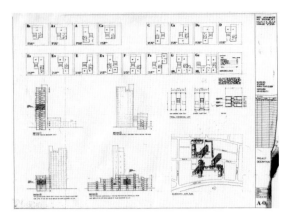

Figure 3a Project description, unit types, dated 1963. Pencil on tracing cloth.

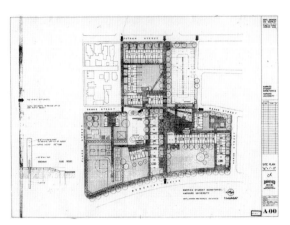

Figure 3b Site plan, Married Students Dormitories, dated 1964. Pencil on tracing cloth.

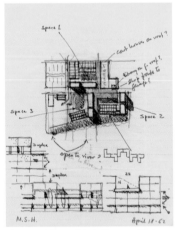

Figure 3d Josep Lluís Sert, preliminary sketch, dated April 18, 1962. Ink and color pencil on yellow paper.

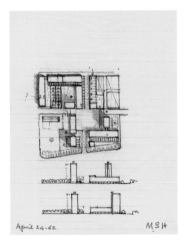

Figure 3e Josep Lluís Sert, preliminary sketch, dated April 24, 1962. Ink and color pencil on yellow paper.

PEABODY TERRACE
CAMBRIDGE, MASS., 1962–1964

Figures 3a–3g

When our office was formed in 1958 our efforts were not in immediate demand, and we used some of this slack time to study ways in which Harvard, then about to launch a fund drive and expansion, might add to its physical plant. Our particular emphasis in this study was on housing for students and young faculty. This may have alerted the university to our interest in dwelling design, and when they decided several years later to move aggressively to meet the housing needs of its married students, our interest was remembered.

In the days before river frontage was valued for recreation and residential use, the banks of the Charles had developed largely in industrial uses. The university possessed a substantial piece of riverfront property on which stood an unused factory. We were asked to plan for development of the site as housing for married students. The university was aware that it had few accommodations available for such students at that postwar time, when the enrollment of married students was growing rapidly.

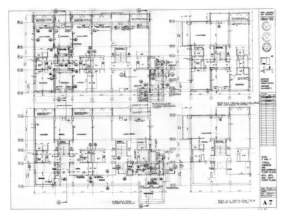

Figure 3c Building X and Y, typical corridor and noncorridor floor plans, dated 1963. Pencil on tracing cloth.

Figure 3f Aerial view of Peabody Terrace, toward river. Photograph by Lawrence Lowry.

Figure 3g View from across the Charles River. Photograph by Lawrence Lowry.

Our studies quickly indicated that if we were to provide surface parking in the ratio required by the city of Cambridge (seven parking spaces for each ten dwelling units, as I recall), the number of apartments we could provide would be needlessly limited and the potential of this valuable site not fully realized. Harvard agreed with our recommendation for structured parking, and our studies indicated that we could suitably accommodate some five hundred units on this six-acre site in a combination of high-rise and walk-up buildings.

The community, always alert to the university's expansion, was concerned that access to the parkland along the river from their houses on Putnam Avenue and beyond be preserved, and that Harvard's housing not appear as a wall between the neighborhood and the river. Our response was to provide a broad pedestrian walkway from Putnam Avenue to Memorial Drive and the river, which was open to all. We placed walk-up buildings along Putnam Avenue to match the scale of the neighboring houses. The high-rise structures necessary for efficient use of the site were placed toward the river, where their presence and their shadows would present the least encumbrance to the neighborhood. Still, I am told, the neighbors hate the project, perhaps more as a symbol of the university's presence than for any more specific grievance.

Figures 4a and 4b Views of model (representation) for Worcester Business District

WORCESTER CENTER REDEVELOPMENT
WORCESTER, MASS., 1965

Figures 4a–4d

Worcester, like many American cities in the 1960s, was experiencing a decline in its central business district brought on by the development of easily accessible retail centers in the outlying communities. To counter this trend, the Worcester Redevelopment Authority invited our firm to prepare a master plan for the redevelopment of a substantial area located in the center of the downtown, adjacent to the city common, town hall, and major shopping street.

Since the mobility provided by the automobile was a major source of the downtown's decline, it was recognized from the start that a successful project to reanimate the traditional city center would have to cater to the motorcar. This determined a salient feature of our master plan, an encircling wall of structured parking to accommodate several thousand cars. Within the area encircled were department stores, office buildings, and a two-story pedestrian street of smaller shops sheltered by a transparent vault. This covered street was deliberately oriented to make easy pedestrian passage to and from the major shopping street.

The master plan was used by the city to invite proposals from a number of development teams. The successful team constructed the project following many of the principles of our master plan, including the emphasized parking. I read in the paper not long ago that the project has suffered financially from the competition of continued suburban shopping center construction, and the site may be subject, in part at least, to another redevelopment, this time as a residential community.

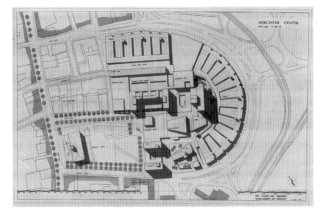

Figure 4c Roof plan, Worcester Business District.
Ink and Zipatone on vellum.

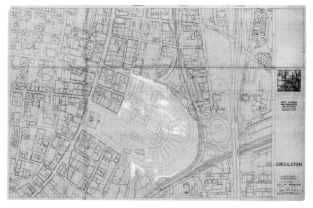

Figure 4d Site plan, Worcester Business District.
Ink and pencil on vellum.

Figure 5a View of model (representation) of South Station

SOUTH STATION REDEVELOPMENT
BOSTON, 1966

Figures 5a–5f

The Boston Redevelopment Authority invited competitive proposals by development teams for the modernization of Boston's South Station. We were asked by the Massachusetts Port Authority to prepare their submittal.

Our project involved the removal of the existing head house, a building dating from 1903, I believe, and its replacement with a multiuse structure accommodating transportation functions at grade and an office building above. A hotel was also provided. An elongated structure was proposed above the track area to house a central bus station and substantial parking. The Port Authority was selected as the developer for this project, but was subsequently disqualified when a court ruling declared that its funding could be used only for public purpose projects, not for the development of office or hotel properties. Subsequently the head house has been declared of historic interest and worthy of preservation.

Figure 5c Perspective of South Station Terminal. Pencil on vellum.

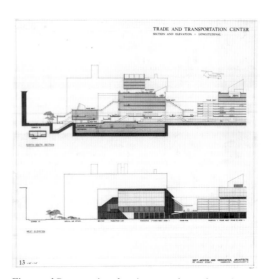

Figure 5d Presentation drawings, north-south section and west elevation, South Station Terminal. Ink, pencil, and Zipatone on vellum.

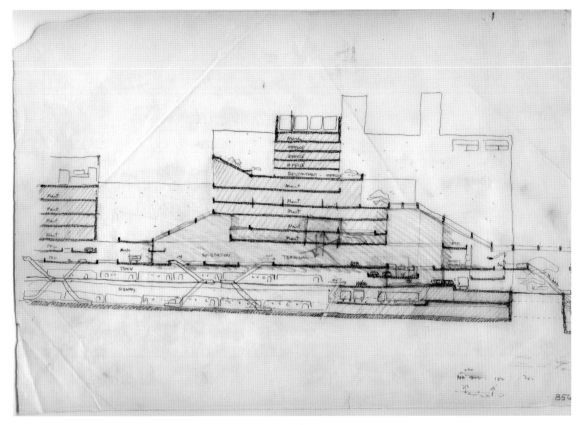

Figure 5b Josep Lluís Sert, schematic section. Ink and color pencil on trace.

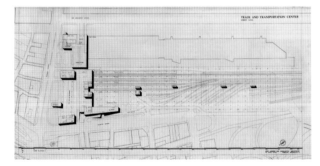

Figure 5e Presentation drawings, South Station Trade and Transportation Center, street-level plan. Ink, pencil, and Zipatone on vellum.

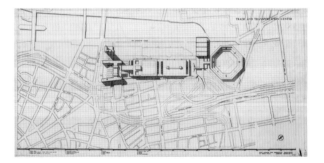

Figure 5f Presentation drawings, South Station Trade and Transportation Center, site plan. Ink, pencil, and Zipatone on vellum.

Figure 6a Josep Lluís Sert, preliminary sketch, Boston University campus. Pencil on yellow-lined paper.

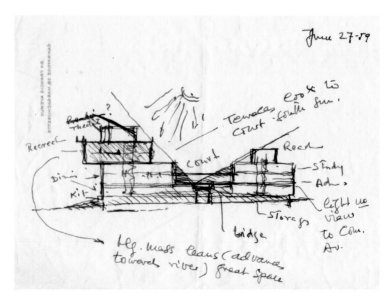

Figure 6b Josep Lluís Sert, preliminary sketch, Boston University schematic section, dated June 1959. Ink on trace.

BOSTON UNIVERSITY CENTRAL CAMPUS
BOSTON, 1959–1966

Figures 6a–6d

Our relationship with Boston University began when the university asked us to associate with another firm previously selected for the design of a university union. BU was at the start of a substantial postwar expansion. In studying the union design, we asked to see the existing campus plan to guide our efforts and found that there had been no campus planning of any significance since the original development plan of the 1920s.

Initially the university was planned as a row of buildings oriented toward Commonwealth Avenue with a centrally located chapel. Behind the chapel in the original plan was to be erected a Gothic tower, a replica of the tower of the cathedral of Boston, England. Since that original plan was made, Storrow Drive had been built along the Charles River basin. Now far more people, in their daily movements, passed the university on the north side than on the Commonwealth Avenue side, and the university's major image at that time was the backsides of the buildings facing the avenue.

We felt that a study of how the campus might grow, although not requested as part of our design of the university union, was essential, and we undertook to make it. The university received this plan for the development of its land along the river basin most enthusiastically and was happy to have a new public presence.

Recognizing the scarcity of urban land and the need to use it efficiently, our plan called for a certain density of development. Instead of a replica of the Boston Cathedral tower, our plan included a high-rise tower to house the law and education schools, flanked on one side by the law school library and moot court and by the central library on the other. The university asked us to associate with other firms previously selected for the design of each of these projects.

Figure 6c Exterior view of Mugar Library. Photograph by Phokion Karas.

Figure 6d View of Boston University from across the Charles River. Photograph by Phokion Karas.

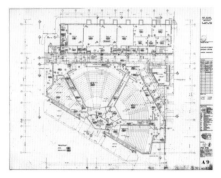

Figure 7a First-floor plan west, dated 1970. Ink and pencil on vellum.

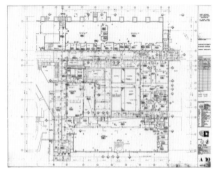

Figure 7b First-floor plan east, dated 1970. Ink and pencil on vellum.

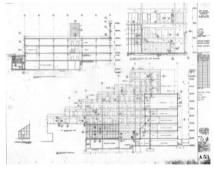

Figure 7c East elevation office wing, dated 1970. Ink and pencil on vellum.

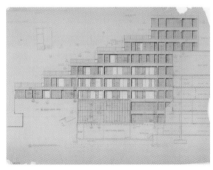

Figure 7d Elevation studies. Color pencil on diazotype copy.

HARVARD UNDERGRADUATE SCIENCE CENTER
CAMBRIDGE, MASS., 1968–1973

Figures 7a–7i

The teaching of the physical sciences at the undergraduate level took place in various locations about the campus, usually associated with research and graduate studies. The university received a substantial gift from an individual interested in stimulating more interest in the sciences among undergraduates. The funds were intended to provide a single setting for the teaching of introductory courses in a variety of disciplines. It should be a place where faculty and students could mingle, where students would be attracted to linger and become involved. In this environment, it was the sponsor's hope, bright students would become "hooked" on science as a career choice.

The building consists of a number of distinct elements serving a variety of functions. The major east-west wing contains the laboratories and is designed with large column-free spaces providing flexibility for future alterations, which science inevitably brings. The mathematics wing has more conventional classrooms and offices. A large science library occupies one wing, and four sizable lecture theaters are arranged in a fan pattern about a common preparation area.

The disposition of these elements follows the same principles as our office frequently used in urban design work. Circulation paths are given special emphasis. The main pedestrian ways into and through the building are two stories high with special treatment where they meet. Corridors on the upper floors of the lab block are glazed to reveal the activity inside and animate the façade. The building wings enclose an accessible courtyard. Facing this courtyard is a lunchroom where informal contact of students and instructors can take place.

The building has recently been enlarged with additions designed by the firm of Leers Weinzapfel Associates.

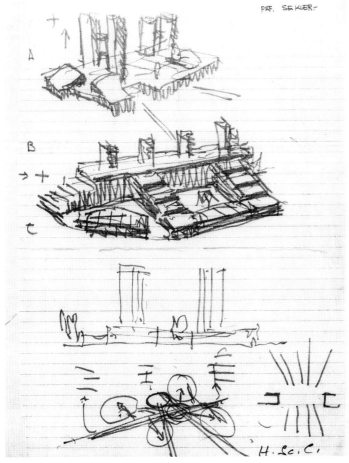

Figure 7g Entrance from Harvard Yard.
Photograph by Steve Rosenthal.

Figure 7e Josep Lluís Sert, preliminary sketch, c. 1968.
Xerographic reproduction.

Figure 7h Entrance from Oxford Street.
Photograph by Steve Rosenthal.

Figure 7f View of model (representation) for Science Center.

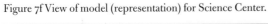

Figure 7i View of courtyard.
Photograph by Steve Rosenthal.

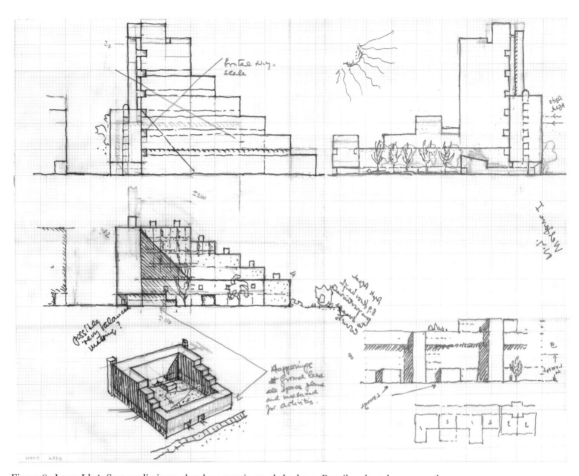

Figure 8a Josep Lluís Sert, preliminary sketches: massing and shadows. Pencil and marker on graph paper.

Figure 8b Aerial view of Roosevelt Island

Figure 8c View of model (representation) for Roosevelt Island

Figure 8d Presentation drawing, exterior view along the main street. Pencil on trace.

Figure 8e Presentation drawing, exterior view along the main street. Pencil on trace.

ROOSEVELT ISLAND
NEW YORK, 1970–1976

Figures 8a–8f

Before he became director of the New York State Urban Development Corporation, Ed Logue had been director of the Boston Redevelopment Authority, and as a consequence he called on members of the Boston/Cambridge professional community for the work of the UDC. We were happy to respond to this call.

A major undertaking of the UDC was the redevelopment of Roosevelt Island as an integrated residential community. In 1970 this large island in the East River, then known as Welfare Island, was largely unused. Previously it had served as a location for hospitals, jails, and asylums. The UDC had commissioned Philip Johnson to design a master plan for its development. This plan, in addition to housing, called for retail shops, schools, parks, and recreation facilities. A parking structure was placed at the motor access to the island, and the central street was intended primarily for public transport and servicing. Access to the community is also provided by subway and by cable car.

We were invited to undertake the development of approximately a thousand units of moderate rental-subsidized housing. Adjacent parcels were assigned to other architects for the design of dwellings to be rented or sold at market rates. Our design adhered to the general principles of the Johnson master plan. High-rise buildings stepped down from the central road to the river; the blocks along this central spine were kept more modest in height to preserve light at street level; and building blocks were introduced along the river frontage to form closed courtyards and to mask the power station on the opposite riverbank.

In this project we created a preponderance of floor-through units, units with exposure on opposite sides, using a "skip stop" access system with corridors on every third floor. This was a design type we had previously explored at Peabody Terrace. An arcaded sidewalk at street level gave access to the retail shops. A two-story wing projecting toward the open parkland accommodates elementary school classrooms. I understand that the New York City school authorities have abandoned the school facilities disbursed among the habitations and returned to the single traditional schoolhouse.

The UDC later asked us to design one of the market-rate apartment projects on the west side of the island facing Manhattan. This project follows many of the same principles as the subsidized housing project, but with larger units and corridors serving each floor rather than the skip stop.

Figure 8f Exterior view of Roosevelt Island. Photograph by Steve Rosenthal.

Contributors

MARDGES BACON is Matthews Distinguished University Professor and professor of architecture at Northeastern University. She is the author of *Le Corbusier in America: Travels in the Land of the Timid* (2001) and *Ernest Flagg: Beaux-Arts Architect and Urban Reformer* (1986). In conjunction with the Temple Hoyne Buell Center for the Study of American Architecture at Columbia University, she served as editor of *"Symbolic Essence" and Other Writings on Modern Architecture, Art, and American Culture by William H. Jordy* (2005). Bacon has been the recipient of a Guggenheim Fellowship and grants from the Graham Foundation. She has served as an associate at the Center for Advanced Study in the Visual Arts (CASVA), National Gallery of Art, Washington, D.C., and a director of the Society of Architectural Historians. She is currently a member of the editorial board of *Massilia*, the international journal of Le Corbusier studies.

ROBERT CAMPBELL has been architecture critic of the *Boston Globe* since 1973. His work has received awards, including a design fellowship from the National Endowment for the Arts (1976), the medal for criticism of the American Institute of Architects (1980), and the Pulitzer Prize for Distinguished Criticism (1996). Campbell helped found, and is now an advisor to, the Mayors Institute for City Design. He is a fellow of the American Institute of Architects and the American Academy of Arts and Sciences.

TIMOTHY HYDE is an architect and an assistant professor of architecture at the Harvard University Graduate School of Design. His recent writings include a genealogy of mat building, published in *Le Corbusier's Venice Hospital and the Mat Building Revival* (2002), and an essay on Sir John Soane and eighteenth-century libel law, published in *Perspecta* 37. He has practiced architecture in New York, Cambridge, and Ho Chi Minh City, and has taught at Northeastern University and at the GSD.

HUSON JACKSON (1913–2006) was a founding partner of Sert, Jackson & Gourley. He worked for Charles Eames, established private practice in Boston and New York, and taught at several universities, including Columbia, Pratt Institute, and Harvard, where he was appointed professor of architecture in 1958. He was author of *A Guide to New York Architecture, 1650–1952* (1952).

CAMMIE McATEE is an independent scholar based in Montreal. She was the assistant curator and research coordinator for the exhibition "Mies in America" (Canadian Centre for Architecture/ Whitney Museum of American Art, 2001) and contributed an essay on Mies van der Rohe's first trip to America to the accompanying publication. She has also published articles in *Harvard Design Magazine, Bauwelt, Casabella, Constructs,* and *Genesis* (CNRS).

RICHARD MARSHALL is director of urban design with Woods Bagot, based in Sydney. He has worked as an urban designer and architect in Australia, the United States, Japan, Singapore, Malaysia, Indonesia, China, Vietnam, and Thailand. He was previously associate professor of urban design and director of urban design degree programs at the GSD. Marshall is a member of the Royal Australian Institute of Architects. He has lectured widely and is the author or coauthor of *Emerging Urbanity: Global Urban Projects in the Asia Pacific Rim* (2003), *Waterfronts in Post-Industrial Cities* (2001), and *Urban Design in the American City* (2003).

JORDANA MENDELSON is associate professor of European modern art and history of photography at the University of Illinois, Urbana-Champaign. She is the author of numerous articles on early twentieth-century Spanish art, including "Architecture, Photography and (Gendered) Modernities in 1930s Barcelona," in the journal *Modernism/Modernity* (January 2003), and "Of Politics, Postcards, and Pornography: Salvador Dalí's *Le Mythe tragique de l'Angélus de Millet*," in the volume *Surrealism, Politics, and Culture* (2003). Her book *Documenting Spain: Artists, Exhibition Culture, and the Modern Nation, 1929–1939* was published in 2005.

ERIC MUMFORD is a historian of modern architecture and urbanism. He is associate professor of architecture at Washington University in St. Louis. His publications include *The CIAM Discourse on Urbanism, 1928–1960* (2000) and the edited volume *Modern Architecture in St. Louis: Washington University and Postwar American Architecture, 1948–1973* (2004), as well as numerous articles on various aspects of twentieth-century architecture and urbanism. His next book, *Defining Urban Design: CIAM Architects and the Formation of a Discipline, 1937–1969,* will appear in 2009. A licensed architect, he was visiting associate professor in the department of art and architecture at Harvard University in spring 2004.

FRANCESCO PASSANTI has taught history of architecture at MIT and has lectured at the GSD and elsewhere. His essay on Le Corbusier appears in the exhibition catalogue *Le Corbusier before Le Corbusier* (2002).

JILL PEARLMAN teaches the history of architecture and urbanism at Bowdoin College and is the author, most recently, of *Inventing American Modernism: Joseph Hudnut, Walter Gropius, and the Bauhaus Legacy at Harvard* (2007).

HASHIM SARKIS is the Aga Khan Professor of Landscape Architecture and Urbanism in Muslim Societies at the GSD. Sarkis is a practicing architect and urban designer based in Cambridge and Beirut. He is the author of *Circa 1958: Lebanon in the Pictures and Plans of Constantinos Doxiadis,* and editor of *Projecting Beirut* (1998; coedited with Peter G. Rowe) and *Le Corbusier's Venice Hospital and the Mat Building Revival.*

EDUARD F. SEKLER is the Osgood Hooker Professor of Visual Art, Emeritus, and professor of architecture, emeritus, at Harvard University. Sekler was the founding director of the Carpenter Center for Visual Arts. He is a member of the advisory commission of the Austrian Historic Monuments Office and was a UNESCO consultant and cofounder of the Kathmandu Valley Preservation Trust, which he chaired from 1990 to 1996. He has taught at the Vienna Technical University, at Washington University in St. Louis, and at the University of Florida at Gainesville as the first incumbent of the Beinecke-Reeves Distinguished Chair in Architectural Preservation. He has published widely; his architectural work includes several housing schemes and the restoration of historic buildings in Austria. As a historic conservation consultant, he has worked in Bhutan, India, Nepal, and Thailand. He has been awarded AIA Institute Honors, the Jean Tschumi Prize by the International Union of Architects, and an honorary doctorate by the ETH Zurich.

NEYRAN TURAN is a doctoral candidate at the GSD. She has taught graduate courses and advanced-level design studios, and has acted as guest critic at various institutions. Her work has been published in journals including *Thresholds* and *Domus m*. Turan serves as the publications coordinator for the Aga Khan Program at the GSD, and as editor-in-chief for the journal *New Geographies*.

Index

Illustration Credits